"*Speaking Your Truth* provides extraordinary internal lives of with every day. This book provides a compelling look into the heart of what it means to be human and opens up a new level of compassion for and interest in those around us. Not only do we recognize ourselves in these stories, but we learn to acknowledge the insightful and inspirational power of life living in every human being."

Jesi-Grace Dobosz, clairvoyant healer and
owner of Energetic Creations Life Coaching

"Each story in this collection is a gem sparkling with truth and authenticity. Together, they comprise a kaleidoscope of inspiration that opens the heart and touches the spirit."

Ashley Davis Bush, author of
Shortcuts to Inner Peace and *Transcending Loss*

"Real women sharing real issues offering REAL solutions that are both powerful and practical. A touching and inspiring must-read for any woman on the path to personal empowerment!"

Debra Gano, CEO of BYOU "Be Your Own You,"
award-winning author of the *Heartlight Girls* series,
and women's/girls' self-esteem expert

"Reading *Speaking Your Truth* feels like each story is one told by a close friend. The book depicts the fragility of life and how our inner strength, faith and courage enable us to overcome all obstacles and help others do the same. Truly inspirational!"

Becky Glück is a daughter,
a sister, a friend and an import manager

"A brave and enlightening work that should be required reading for everyone. Each contributor has an important story to tell and does so with courage, honesty, and hope."

Alice J. Wisler, author of *Rain Song,*
How Sweet It Is, Hatteras Girl, A Wedding Invitation,
and instructor at Writing the Heartache Workshops

"Powerful, motivating, and inspirational. *Speaking Your Truth* Volume II is a must read!"

Judith M. Charles, licensed counselor, critical incident specialist

"We are saturated with empowering and inspirational stories of and about women, but *Speaking Your Truth* stands above the crowd. Rather than fluff, it exposes struggles common to us all. In exchange for platitudes, it is infused with honesty. And instead of easy answers, it heralds courage."

Anne K. Gross, Ph.D., clinical psychologist and author of *The Polio Journals: Lessons from My Mother*

"These stories and the women who wrote them are a powerful testimony of the strength of the human spirit and an incredible source of courage, hope and love. These stories are also a constant reminder of the importance of being true to ourselves regardless of what life throws at you. This is a book I'll read over and over."

Anabelle Calderon, CRSP transition consultant

"*Speaking Your Truth* presents a powerful, honest, and raw insight into real lives. The stories remind us of the power of faith and hope. I found myself applauding the courage of the authors and celebrating their personal discoveries."

Reverend Carolyn A. Abrams, United Methodist minister and community activist

"*Speaking Your Truth* Volume II is packed full of life experiences that resulted in profound wisdom that will expand the heart of each reader. Everything from grief to the mountain top experiences on this journey offer profound opportunities for learning and growth. This book contains insights from some AMAZING women who have walked through the storms and mountain tops of life emerging with stories that reveal essential simple truths that hold within themselves the ability to transform your perspective of life. Rediscover your own voice, learn how to roar like a lion and light up your world. The words contained in these pages are truly an inspiration!"

Lauren E. Miller, stress relief expert/best selling author/ international speaker, www.laurenemiller.com

"We learn through stories. In this amazing and candid book, there is a story written just for you. It might actually change your life. And, I know, it will surely be a wonderful learning experience. Be sure to read it!"

Elinor Miller Greenberg, Ed.D., co-author of
A Time of Our Own: In Celebration of Women Over Sixty;
founder and sponsor of the quarterly
Colorado Feminist Luncheon

"The women of Denver have done it again! *Speaking Your Truth* Volume II continues to whisper inspiration into our hearts and shout triumph into our ears."

Angel Tuccy, radio host and bestselling
author of *Lists That Saved My Life*

"As an author in the first volume of *Speaking Your Truth*, I am aware of the emotions and commitment these ladies have made to submit a work to this collection. Again, as I have read the small snapshots that these stories provide, I see myself among the pages. I nod in agreement at the lessons I've learned and empathize with the ones I haven't had to (or haven't yet had to). I cried with the ones that hit home, some more than others. I've gathered insight from different points of view and learned from perspectives different than my own. The true beauty within this collection is that our variety and uniqueness come through at the same time our humanness and our identification with being women bond us together. I'm so happy to have been able to hear these voices, these lovely stories, each woman's truth, as told as only she can tell it. Thank you, thank you for sharing!"

Kris "PlumbingGirl" Jordan, Garvin's Sewer Service

"My young adult daughters were the grateful recipients of Volume I and I know they'll love this one also. The stories are real from women anyone can identify with – intensely personal struggles, celebrations, learning and redemption. *Speaking Your Truth* is inspiring and will help anyone navigate a richer, more rewarding journey through life."

Robert White, executive coach and author,
Living an Extraordinary Life

"I am continually amazed at the inspiring stories that are told in *Speaking Your Truth*. As I read story after story, I feel connected to women I've never even met, just through their words. Their courage to speaking their truth has given me the courage to reflect upon my own."

Kelly M. Calton, owner of Confluence Family Office

"The lessons in *Speaking Your Truth* are many and profound. Stories of triumph over childhood abuse, illness, poverty and failure are mixed with reminders that we are braver, stronger and smarter than we know and that neither money, appearance nor our own pasts can define who we are or who we can become. The gentle beauty in this book lies in the heartbreaking, joyous and ultimately candid stories of everyday women and their ability to survive and, indeed, to blossom."

Diana DeLonzor, author of
Never Be Late Again: 7 Cures for the Punctually Challenged

"The voice of the universe speaks to us through these courageous women who share their personal, heartfelt stories of truth, wisdom and courage. I was deeply moved. This book speaks to our souls and will stir you to feel more passion, depth and meaning in your own beautiful life. Read and share this book! It is a treasure."

Diana Drake Long, author, speaker, coach
www.DianaLong.com

Speaking Your Truth

Courageous Stories from Inspiring Women

Volume II

Compiled by
Lisa Shultz & Andrea Costantine
Illustrated by Janice Earhart

www.speakingyourtruthbook.com

Illustrator: Janice Earhart, iZoar
Book Cover: Nick Zelinger, NZ Graphics
Editing: Elizabeth Wolf
Layout/Design: Andrea Costantine
Author Photograph: David Weihnacht,
David Marc Photography

Printed in the United States of America

First Edition
ISBN 978-0-615-50379-0

*To my daughters and to the women readers looking
for hope and inspiration.
- Lisa Shultz*

*To all the people who have believed in me, even when I
haven't. Especially Rob, Kim, Nicole and my parents.
- Andrea Costantine*

SPEAKING YOUR TRUTH

Speaking Your Truth
Is not always easy
Accepting yourself
A challenge at best

Search for answers
While seeking your purpose
Things become clearer
Each step of the way

Hardships overcome
Brings grace to some
Inspiring others
While healing yourself

Courageous stories
Shared with the world
Told with compassion
By amazing women

Speaking Your Truth
Is not always easy
Accepting yourself
A challenge at best

- Carol Calkins, PhD
excerpt from *Bring Poetry into Your Life*

Contents

PART FOUR
SURVIVING TO THRIVING

PART FIVE
FAMILY MATTERS

PART SIX
FINDING YOUR PATH

FOREWORD

I am honored to write the foreword to the second volume of *Speaking Your Truth*. Just the statement, "speaking your truth" is a powerful mantra that the women of this book have embraced, as you will see from their inspiring stories beautifully written in this book.

Each of us was created like no other person. We are unique; one of a kind; not a clone; the original masterpiece; and only we can fulfill our own story. Eleanor Roosevelt said, *"Women are like tea bags. They don't know how strong they are until they get into hot water."* That is what *Speaking Your Truth* is all about: women, who have endured the hot water and surfaced to be stronger and more courageous, not fearful, and most important, have found their voice.

Helen Keller wrote, *"I am only one; but still I am one. I cannot do everything, but still I can do something; I will not refuse to do something I can do."* The women of *Speaking Your Truth* have demonstrated that they do not have to be everything, but instead they only need to be themselves. They have demonstrated that an unstoppable power lives in each woman, and it sometimes takes a significant emotional event for that power to be released, but when it is, look out, world! I greatly admire the women in this book and am humbled by their courage to speak their truth and share that truth with others.

We do not have to be someone that we are not, or wish that we can rewrite our pages, but instead, we can be proud of all that has been and is being written. Think of your story – it is filled with challenges and opportunities, failures and achievements, joys and sorrows, love and death, romance and lost loves. Someone is waiting to hear your story; your story could save her life. Tell your story and observe what a difference you make. Sociologists believe the most introverted of people will influence 10,000 others in an average lifetime. Who are you influencing with your story?

The second volume of *Speaking Your Truth* can be best summarized by a quote from Nora Ephron, *"Above all, be the heroine of your life, not the victim."* The women in this book are all the heroines of their lives, not the victims. Become the heroine of your own life and *Speak Your Own Truth.*

Michelle Post, Ph.D.
President, Reach Your Potential, LLC

INTRODUCTION

It's been over ten years since I was truly in the muck in my story. I felt so incredibly alone during that time. There were moments where I felt singled out in a way, like I was the only person on earth experiencing heartache, sadness and grief.

I would occasionally stumble upon a book or a story that resonated with my own life experiences, and seeing how another person had survived and thrived again gave me a glimmer of hope to carry on. It was in those brief flashes of connection to a complete stranger that I too began to heal.

As humans, we often need that vital connection. It can give us strength or hope that one day we will feel better, we will find joy again and rejoice in our own life. It is my hope that one of the stories in this book will be a guiding light to someone in need. Maybe that person is you, your sister, your mother, or even a friend or co-worker.

When the idea for a book of collaborative stories first came to me in early 2009, I had no idea the magnitude and the impact the stories would have on, not only my life, but on everyone else's life who was also involved — from Andrea, who joined the project in late 2009, to the 47 contributing authors in Volume I, along with the many readers and supporters of the book. Even before we wrapped up production on the first volume people were asking us if we would do another, and we were already considering it. By the time the book launched in the fall of 2010 we had already decided – yes, indeed, we would create a second volume.

We have personally found the stories in Volume II to be heartfelt, inspiring, and empowering and we are excited to share these remarkable tales and the women behind them.

There are two quotes that we believe represent the work we are doing with *Speaking Your Truth*. The first is by Maya Angelou and states, "There is no greater agony than bearing an untold story inside of you." What we have found is that speaking your truth is a healing process for both the writer and the reader. When a person gets to share a story that makes up who they are, and what their life has represented, something happens inside of them. New awareness is found, opportunities are sought, and connections are made. When Andrea wrote her story for Volume I, it was the first time she ever verbalized many of the details she remembered about her father's passing. When I wrote my story of my previous marriage, I had to go back and relive the pain and experience to let the reader see the true story of where I had come from. Like Angelou says in the quote above, there is an agony that comes with keeping a story stuffed up inside of you. *Speaking Your Truth* is that outlet to be able to share those personal stories, so people no longer have to carry that burden around with them.

The second quote is one of my favorites and perhaps you might recognize it. This is just the tail end of what Marianne Williamson so brilliantly wrote, "As we let our own light shine, we unconsciously give other people permission to do the same. As we are liberated from our own fear, our presence automatically liberates others." This is what we have seen from the inspiring and courageous stories that make up *Speaking Your Truth.*

It is our hope, and our deepest wish that you will shine your own light and be liberated from any fear, loneliness, or sadness that may creep into your life.

Lisa Shultz

Self Discovery

THE JOY IN DISCOMFORT

Melinda Anderson

I can't do this. It's too much to ask of me. I sat on the sofa staring in disbelief at what I had just written in my journal. The intuited message was asking me to do the unthinkable. I felt frozen with fear. I promised myself I would follow my higher guidance, but please…not this. This was too big. Yet even as part of me begged for a way out, another part somehow knew that I could—and I would—do the scariest thing imaginable for me. After a lifetime of hiding under a wig, it was time to expose my bald head to the world.

At that point in my life, I could barely choke the words "bald" and "wig" out of my mouth. I was born without hair and doctors have never found a cure for this genetic condition. From an early age I was indoctrinated with the shame my mother carried around her own baldness. There was something wrong with us, something missing, and it was unacceptable to be bald.

My guidance instructed me to reveal my baldness through an inspirational speech to my Toastmaster group, culminating with the removal of my wig. The notion was horrifying.

It had been several months and I still found myself avoiding writing the speech. I knew it was inevitable because of my deep-seated commitment to following my inner guidance; however, it seemed an insurmountable task. Eventually, a speech I had previously given at Toastmasters popped into my head: "Fear—The Only Way Out Is Through." Hmmm…could that apply here? A voice inside me finally asked, *How badly do you want freedom from your personal prison and the bars around your heart?* From the depth of my being I knew I wanted that freedom more than anything. I let out a heavy sigh. I knew what I needed to do.

When I was a little girl, I would lie in bed every night and pray, *God, please give me hair so I can be like everyone else.* Each morning I would wake up disappointed. I truly believed a miracle would happen and I would wake up with a foot of hair. After years of praying and asking, one day I just stopped. I felt hopeless so I finally gave up and knew I would always be bald.

My parents were loving and supportive and did their best to help me feel comfortable with my bald head. They scrimped and saved to take me to doctors and to buy wigs for me. Beginning in the first grade, I started wearing a wig to help me fit in with the other kids. I've come to realize when I started hiding my "flaw," the little girl inside of me that was born with wings and wanted to fly, also started hiding. I felt defective and nothing could ever make me perfect and whole. I always had to keep myself carefully guarded to make sure my wig stayed on. I was never able to let go and just be a kid. In school, I never knew the freedom of doing flips on the jungle gym, jumping on the trampoline, or playing sports. There was always a feeling of being different and left out.

Throughout my adult life, fear haunted me when I got physically close to men. I kept myself closely guarded and would noticeably cringe and pull away when their hands moved close to my head or neck. *What if they discover my wig?* There was always the dreaded moment when I had to tell them that I was bald and fear their rejection. I felt enormously relieved when my former husband and I were married because I knew he accepted me. At the time I believed I would never have to reveal my secret of baldness to another man.

Over time, I developed a strong sense of unworthiness and being unlovable. My working life was dominated by a tremendous desire to achieve and be successful. My self-esteem and identity were wrapped up in approval from others. I always sought promotions and needed to be the best at whatever I was doing because then people would love and approve of me. Then I would be worthy.

I lived most of my life in fear of humiliation. None of the terrible things I had imagined as a child ever happened. I was never teased or ridiculed growing up. The only thing causing me pain and heartache was my judgment about myself. I certainly didn't think that someone in a wheelchair, missing a body part, or whose face was scarred was unworthy or less than. Because of my own experience without hair, I felt enormous compassion for others. I just couldn't find it for myself.

Despite feeling unlovable, I had a lifetime of wonderful relationships with people who loved and accepted me unconditionally. I remember how much it hurt my former husband when I told him I thought I looked like an alien without my wig. He honestly thought I was beautiful, inside and out. I didn't like to look at myself in the mirror without hair because it scared me. I thought I looked like a freak.

Eventually I sat curled up in my recliner writing my speech for Toastmasters. I don't know where the strength came from to begin. The tears were generous as I opened long buried and carefully protected doors inside of me. My most private and guarded secret would be revealed. It was a vulnerability that I had never experienced. It felt like someone was cutting me wide open. I couldn't even read my speech out loud to myself without crying, let alone to a room full of people.

I sought advice from a professional speaker regarding struggles telling my story. He told me that I had to practice my talk until I could move through the emotion. Staring at a mirror for hours, I rehearsed my story over and over, choking out the words and lost in my sorrow. Next came repeated practicing in front of an audience of one, my boyfriend. It was even harder to speak these words in front of a beloved. Eventually, I found myself crying less and less. I felt amazed at what was happening as I started to feel more empowered around my words.

Another round of fear came with the idea of taking my wig off in public. My boyfriend suggested we make a practice run. We went to the local rec center to play in the pool, one more area of fun that I had avoided because I wore a wig. The concrete floor was cold and wet beneath my feet and I couldn't have felt more exposed as I stepped through the doorway of the women's locker room. His warm hand felt safe as it wrapped around mine. He told me later he was really scared for me but couldn't show it. We walked towards the pool with me dressed in my bathing suit, no make up, and for the first time in public—no hair. I felt both scared and secretly exhilarated. *Oh my gosh, it's really happening.* I sheepishly looked around to see who might be staring at me and was surprised to notice only passing glances. Even the kids on the water slide were ignoring my bald head. As I climbed the stairs on the slide, I let free the joyful child inside of me. I screamed as I sped down the slide and splashed into the water. No worries, no being constantly on guard. It was a freedom I had never experience before. We laughed and played for hours. My light was shining brightly and nothing could have broken my newly freed spirit that day. I had made this moment of unveiling so big, but now I saw that it was only big in my mind. The world didn't change that day, I did.

Consumed by fear, the day of my speech came too quickly. I felt grateful to be supported by several friends who were praying for me. As I stood in front of the room and began speaking, something magical happened. I was lifted up by a power that I couldn't explain. I had a sense of peace and empowerment that I had never known while presenting. At the end of my speech I took my wig off, received a standing ovation, *and* I won the best speaker award. I sat down, put my wig back on, and let out a huge sigh of relief. Thank goodness that was over.

A few weeks later I cringed at the words that appeared on my journal pages: *It's time to take it off and leave it off.* Did I really think I had learned my life lesson of self-love and acceptance with that one brief, empowering moment?

My procrastination was shorter this time, a mere week instead of months. The distressing guidance sent me spiraling into emotional and physical detox. But by the end of the week I felt better and had found new strength and courage for what I needed to do. The next morning I got up and birthed the new me—wigless.

My first day of showing up bald was completely unnerving. I resorted to wearing scarves for a couple of months. I never did like them because they slid around and my head was *still* covered. My inner child was always screaming at me to get them off. I would tell her, *Baby steps, dear one, I am trying to feel safe here.* Each day, countless people approached me asking if I had cancer. Opportunities presented themselves everywhere for me to talk about my baldness. From the cashier at the gas station to people literally stopping their car in the street, everyone wanted to talk to me. I resented the assumption that I had cancer and I was tired of my bald head being a constant topic of conversation. It took several months for me to realize that talking about it was instrumental in my healing process.

For someone who never liked to be the center of attention, I felt like I was living with a huge spotlight on me every time I left my house. I wanted to stay under the covers and hide because I just didn't want to face the world in this way, bald, knowing it wasn't temporary and I would have to show up this way for the rest of my life. Every morning I found myself needing to recommit to my dreams and my journey of ultimately freeing my spirit. I gave myself permission to feel what I was feeling instead of blocking it, cry if I wanted to, and then I would get over it and move on.

As the months went by and I was feeling greater confidence, I noticed fewer and fewer people approached me. I had the huge realization that the world was simply reflecting back to me the type of energy I was projecting. Once again, the world around me hadn't changed, I did.

Occasionally, people still ask me if I have cancer. It is typically a compassionate soul who is relating to their own journey with cancer, offering support and encouragement. I can now easily embrace their questions and conversations. Now what I mostly hear are inspirational comments like "way to go," "good for you," or "I admire your courage." My favorite is "you are beautiful."

It's been three years since I first took my wig off. Taking that first step was like flying off of a mountain. It instigated amazing, positive change in my life. I'd spent the majority of my life wanting to have hair and feel normal. Now, I feel empowered and have embraced my unique appearance. I've learned my physical body is not the truth of who I am and my true beauty radiates from the inside. My baldness has been one of my greatest teachers for learning to love and accept myself. I aspire each day to step more fully into my God-self. Learning to be comfortable, allowing myself to feel and move through being uncomfortable, is key. The greatest joys I know today have come from the times I embraced my fear.

Melinda Anderson is committed to inspiring, teaching, and assisting others in living a deliberate life and knowing their own heart. She aspires to "be the change she wishes to see in the world." She teaches meditation and life skills and works with multiple energy healing modalities. Her greatest passion is personal transformation—for herself and others. Melinda resides in beautiful Denver, Colorado, and is the owner of Angelheart Healing. To learn more, please visit www.angelhearthealing. com. She can be reached at melindanderson@mac.com.

HIDING ALL OF ME

Andrea Weyand

I tried to hide. But when you're a woman who is 6'2", when you stand up, you stand out.

It's amazing how something you can't control can control you. For as long as I can remember, I knew that I had to shrink.

I was five when I had my first, I-am-too-tall-and-there's-something-wrong-with-me moment. It was school Picture Day, and we had to line up from shortest to tallest. It was the end of the line for me—the very end of the line. I was the last person. Up until this moment, I hadn't manipulated anyone. Only once had I even tried that I can remember. My mom had told me I had to clean my room, and I wandered into a vast wasteland of dolls, books, clothes, blankets, and probably a cat that was hiding as best it could. I turned out of the room, looked at my mom and said, "You're so pretty." She thanked me, smiled, and sent me back to my room. I tried; I failed; crafty wasn't me.

But I was a few weeks older now, and in kindergarten-time, that's a lot of aging. So I tried again. There was no way that I was going to stand in the back of the line, pulling up the rear, bending from side to side to peek around to see how Picture Day was going for all the cute, normal, shorter kids. So I stepped out of the line that our teacher had put us in, and I told the twin boys ahead of me that they were taller than I was.

"I am shorter than you. You need to move behind me," I told them.

They looked at me skeptically. The teacher had put us here, they told me.

"She is wrong. Can't you see that you are taller than me?" I could tell they couldn't see that. How could they? I stood easily two inches taller. Darn black patent leather shoes, so shiny, with their half-inch soles boosting me even higher. I did what any self-respecting, too-tall kindergartner would do. I slouched. They looked at me again. We switched places in line. I was toward the

25

end, but I wasn't at the end.

And that's when I first realized that there was something seriously wrong with me. I was five, and I was too tall. And there were no support groups for me.

Even when I was a kid, adults could not stop themselves from saying, "You are so tall. You could be a model." Really? I could model? Unattractive boy-like girls could model? To make it easy to tend to our hair, my mom had cut it short on me and my sister...boy hair short. So I was tall and I had short hair.

One day when I was about eight, my brother and I were playing on swings at the park. We'd swing and swing and swing and jump. Another kid ran up to take my swing after I leapt off of it. His mom stopped him saying, "Not that swing. That's that boy's swing." She could have sugar coated this by saying the swing at least belonged to "that LITTLE boy," but she didn't. Because not only did I look like a boy, I looked like a BIG boy. Another woman grabbed me by the hood of my yellow slicker one rainy day, while my family was in a store. "Come on," she said to me. She looked down and apologized profusely. "I'm sorry. I thought you were my son."

There was no end in sight. I was tall and now I looked like a boy. And I had ugly clothes. Why couldn't I have a raincoat with little whales or umbrellas on it? Little girls had those.

I could model boys' rain gear and galoshes.

Throughout my childhood, I knew that being tall was equivalent to being odd. It was weird. I was weird.

The only way out of this was to slouch. If someone shorter was standing next to me (translation: if *anyone* was standing next to me), I bent my knee, turned my ankle, jutted out my hip, and did everything I could to lose an inch. It wasn't a permanent solution, but for the time being it worked.

When my mom noticed this trend, she couldn't mind her own business. "Don't slouch." "Sit up straight." "Stand tall." What was the matter with her? If she wanted to be tall, that was her business, but must she ruin my life along the way?

So I stood up straight and tall.

There had to be another way out of this.

In high school I had to work at being shorter harder than I had before. I was 5'11" in ninth grade, and I didn't play basketball, though I was recruited hard. I wasn't graced with coordination, and running up and down a basketball court dribbling a ball, seemed like it took a lot more eye-hand-foot coordination than I thought I could deliver.

I did, however, stand out by being in the marching band. Me, my clarinet, my exaggerated frame, and a green hat. Our band uniform consisted of bad black Army surplus shoes, pants held up by suspenders, a heavy coat, and a big, green, furry hat that resembled a beehive and stood a foot off our heads. At every football game when I wrapped the chin strap under my neck, I prayed, "Dear God, make this stop."

As the kids stood on the sidelines and watched us move to our seats and then eventually to the football field, I moved like a galoot. You can't hide a nearly 6-foot frame under a beehive hat.

There had to be another way. I needed something else to get me out of this. Ah…if I lost weight. If I lost weight things would be better. I saw the small girls at school, the cheerleaders, the girls with the best clothes and the boys who met them at their lockers and called them after school. I could be like them if I lost weight. If I were skinny, I would shrink.

So I tried to diet. I bought clothes from the "Women's" section of the department stores. I am tall, thus, I am fat. It's amazing how the mind works.

But the diets didn't work. I was still tall and, now, sometimes hungry.

Perhaps I could hide my height with fashion. I bought some new clothes. It was the 1980s, so my new purple pants and purple and white striped shirt were just what I needed to make me look and feel pretty, and if I may say so, "model-like." After all, I heard regularly that I could be a model.

I put on my purple pants and my purple and white striped shirt and I went to school. I knew the compliments would pour in. There would be no way to stop them. "You look nice." "Great pants." "Cool top." These were just a bus ride away. No one said anything at the bus stop itself, probably because I was wearing a coat.

I made it through homeroom and first period with no compliments. Everyone was most likely jealous. But I felt good about what I was wearing, and I walked down the hall fully erect and not even caring that I could see over all of the heads ahead of me. "Look at me," I thought. "I'm pretty. I have purple pants."

And then walked into a garbage can. I'm sure the garbage can was always in the hall in this spot, but from so high up, I never had a chance to see it. My purple pants caught on something and ripped horizontally across my thigh. "There's no way to patch these," my mom told me. It was over. Fashion wasn't going to make me shorter.

I made it through high school, hiding as I could, building up anxieties inside that I know no short person ever felt. I avoided standing in crowds because I hovered. I didn't like to speak in front of others because I was a clod, and there was nothing I could say that would change this fact.

Then I went to college—by this time I was 6'2"—packing my boxes and bags, and whatever baggage I needed to bring with me. I was learning to live with people asking me how tall I was, calling me odd names like "Too Tall," "Stilts," or "The Tall Girl." I found clothes with sleeves that reached past my wrists and learned that I could wear a skirt and it wasn't always important if it was exactly the right length.

Then I gained the notorious "Freshman 15." I had gained the weight I tried so hard to lose before it existed. "Shrink," I told myself. "Slouch," I said before I had to speak to others. "Hide." I was frustrated again. I was too tall and now I was fat.

By my junior year of college, I was exercising regularly and had lost the weight I had gained, but the memory lingered. Old voices crept back in reminding me that there was something wrong with me. I was weird; I was tall; I didn't play basketball.

I worked at a small grocery store on weekends and holidays, and a regular customer whom I hadn't seen in a while came in. When she saw me she said, "You have lost weight." I smiled and nodded. "That's good," she said. "A lot of women can carry the extra weight, but it didn't look good on you."

Ah...a compliment followed by an insult. Or, more accurately, an insult couched in something resembling a compliment. It was because I was tall. A shorter woman could have carried the weight. That's all I heard. Hide behind the deli slicer.

Overall, I had normal college years, going to parties and feeling awkward, going to class and feeling like a goof. As I watched others—really watched others and paid attention—it seemed like everyone felt that way at times. They were too short, too fat, too skinny, too smart, too dumb. Everyone had something. I started to relax. Being tall wasn't as bad as it seemed. Interestingly enough, the guys in high school whom I used to tower over, had grown. College boys were tall, too. It was a refreshing change of course.

Then one day I was full-on adult. My life was up to me. I could hide or I could embrace what was mine. And my height was mine to embrace. I was obviously too tall to hide.

I had a job that I enjoyed. I met interesting people and, when I let them, people saw a lot more in me than how tall I was. Men took an interest in me. At one time I would have thought they liked me as a novelty, but it turns out, I had a lot more to offer than long legs. That's not to say that being tall didn't lend itself to odd pickup lines. I have heard them all including, "Do people call you 'Amazon'?" "I want those long legs wrapped around my neck," and "Here's my card; fax me some tall jokes." Though the first two lines are brazen and somehow insulting, the last one keeps me thinking. I wonder where I would find tall jokes, and would they all end with someone hitting his head?

I was 29 when I finally stopped trying not to be tall altogether and realized it was just a part of who I am. I started teaching a class at a university, knocking my inability to stand in front of a crowd and talk right out of my system. I no longer let slouching cross my mind, and today I have to stop the urge to pull a fellow tall girl up by her shoulders and whisper, "Stand up straight!" when I see her trying to shrink. And I wear heels. Two inches, three inches, it doesn't matter to me. I feel pretty in heels. When I walk in a room, people see me and they remember me. No one ever says, "Oh, I didn't see you there." You saw me. I was tall, and I was wearing heels. And a purple skirt.

Andrea Galloy Weyand specializes in working with businesses and nonprofits to ensure that employees communicate professionally. She teaches workshops in business communication, writing, public speaking, and more. She has nearly 15 years of experience working with nonprofits to improve their communication efforts, and taught communication and writing for 10 years at a university in Georgia.

BREAKING OUT OF SHYNESS

Lisa Shultz

Many people who know me today see me as prolific in both writing and speaking. They see me active on social media, they see many books I have written or been a part of, and they see me speaking on a regular basis. These newer friends and acquaintances might assume that I have always been speaking publicly. The truth is, the contrast between my past and the present is night and day in regards to my comfort in talking and being vocal.

As a young girl, I was quiet and often painfully shy. The youngest of four children, my three older siblings were much older than I so I had little interaction with them as a child. They were already off doing "older kid" things, and I was left to my own devices. They had already moved out of the house by the time I was in elementary school. Also, my dad worked a lot and I would go long periods of time without seeing him.

When I was 10, my parents separated and I lived mostly with my mother. She went to work shortly thereafter. We lived in a neighborhood where neighbors were not close by and none near us had children. My mom had to drive me to other kids' houses to play. Consequently, I spent a lot of time alone, and the house was often empty. It felt normal to me and I rarely complained or felt bored, as many other kids might have.

In my youth, I spent a lot of time outside shaping and trimming the bushes and trees in the large yard we had. I flew a kite and took bike rides for hours by myself. I read a lot and listened to music. I did get together frequently with my girlfriends, and my mom and I did stuff together a lot, but much of my non-school time was alone. As a result, I was very comfortable with solitude and not talking much. This comfort with not speaking much was labeled as "shy," which was considered a big negative. I wasn't happy about that because I didn't think there was anything wrong with being quiet.

It was confusing to know that others felt my quietness was negative, when I felt comfortable with it. Ironically, the more people labeled me as shy and drew attention to it, the more I wanted to keep quiet. I would observe others and was highly involved in my own way. I just didn't verbalize much publicly.

In high school, I never spoke a word in class unless I was asked to by the teacher. I did everything possible to avoid talking in front of classmates, and I never raised my hand to answer a question even if I knew the answer. My shyness was always a big topic of concern at parent-teacher conferences. I didn't have much confidence in my social skills, but I got good grades and was on the swim team. Personality tests of all sorts ranked me high on the introvert scale and further confirmed that I was indeed a shy person. I wanted to change but felt trapped by my shy label. It seemed that every situation I was in, I was reminded of this label. As I grew older, I realized it was something that I did indeed wanted to change.

I realized that as a result of not speaking much around school, I was rarely noticed by guys. I was often left out of invitations to parties and social activities of my peers. That part pained me. The hardest part about being shy as a teenager was the lack of dating. All of my friends and other kids at school were starting to date, have boyfriends, and even have their first kisses. I was sad and frustrated. I didn't have the courage to talk to boys I was interested in and it made me feel left out. It was the first time my shyness really started to bother me.

Prior to high school I never even considered that my introverted personality had an affect on my life in general. Throughout my high school days, I didn't attend any dances nor did I go to prom. That night of my senior year when prom was happening, and all the girls were in their pretty dresses, with corsages, and dancing the night away, I was at home wondering what it would feel like to have a boy pick me up and to go on a date.

I felt like a nerd, a lonely, teenage girl without a word to say. Despite those devastating feelings I still couldn't muster up the courage to find my voice and to start speaking out loud to others. Needless to say, I was definitely not in the popular crowd. Fortunately, I did have a good group of high school girl friends, and we hung out and had a good time. My time with friends made my shyness more bearable, but I really wanted to have a boyfriend and feel more socially adept.

I busied myself with studying to distract myself from the lonely feelings. I also started to prep myself for college. I dreamt of going to college and starting over. I began to realize I could reinvent myself in a place where no one knew me. I was determined to change.

I chose a college that was located in another state. It was far enough away that people wouldn't know who I was and I could start fresh with my new college classmates. I could finally drop the shy label and come out of my box. That fall I walked on campus with determination to change!

And I did talk! I talked to guys and I talked to teachers and I talked to everyone. Yes, it felt a bit strange for me to do so after so many years of being quiet, but I just did it. And it worked. In college I never again heard the word "shy" used to describe me. I had simply made up my mind, found my courage, and began speaking every chance I got.

When I reflected on how I could make such a big change, I knew that it was because I refused to accept the label of "shy" any longer. It was accurate in high school, but I hated it and was determined not to take it with me to college. Making the conscious choice to detach from the title helped me leave it behind.

Sometimes it felt surreal. I felt like I was observing myself from out of my body. I thought, *That can't be me!* But I just kept talking. The coolest part was that guys started to ask me out! I was in a sorority and went to a lot of parties and dances on campus. This gave me more confidence and made college a lot more fun. As I continued to break out of my shy mold, I saw that life could be exciting and adventurous, and even though I would occasionally return to my shy roots, I found an extroverted part of me as well.

At the same time, I became aware of how I was dressing and carrying myself. I wore clothes that were more flattering and stylish and was vigilant to stand up straight to show confidence. I wore a bit more makeup and took more care of the whole package of my appearance before I walked out the door in the morning.

In college I took the step of getting comfortable talking to people one on one or to a few people together. I joined some clubs and organizations so that I could grow my comfort zone of interaction with groups. The groups were small at first, and I was never the leader, but I attempted to converse and follow along.

Despite my improved social abilities, I still wasn't considered the life of the party and I still preferred one on one conversation or with just a few people together.

One book that helped break me out of my shell was *How to Win Friends and Influence People* by Dale Carnegie. I read the book and listened to it on audio, and then I would go practice with people. I didn't tell anyone I was practicing, I would just do it. I would engage in chit-chat with store clerks and wait staff at restaurants. I would give compliments or wish them a nice day. I would ask people questions about themselves. I would be inquisitive. I looked at each day as an opportunity to practice and gradually get more comfortable talking.

After I finished college, I began my career as a physical therapist. Most of my interaction was one on one with patients, so I did fine with that. After work the other PTs I worked with would go out and have fun on payday. It was another chance to socialize in bigger groups and continue my journey of breaking out of my shy label. I still had no drive towards larger groups or leadership roles. I was content with being an employee and following the leader.

Through the years I married and divorced. The marriage took a toll on my self-esteem, but after some time to reflect and heal I soon found my voice again. I found myself being a landlord of an apartment building that had over a hundred units in it. I did not choose that role, it was handed to me in the divorce settlement. I found myself making decisions on a large scale with absolutely no one to ask for help. I was a solo business woman predominantly working in my home office alone. This was my ex-husband's business, not mine, and I felt like it was a struggle for me to do something that I had no passion for. I knew I needed to sell it to be able to enjoy my life. I did eventually do just that, but as a result of being a landlord for several years, I realized that I could lead others and be a decision maker in business.

After the apartment building was sold, I explored several home-based businesses. I found myself in a networking environment for the first time. I pulled out my handy-dandy Dale Carnegie book and began to practice his techniques again. I also began reading tons of networking books. I studied networking like it was a college course. As a result, I found myself getting better at it and feeling more talkative again.

A business partner of mine, Julie Berra, and I began giving luncheon presentations to small groups. For the first time in my life, I was speaking in front of a dozen captive eyes. After three years of that, I got much more comfortable speaking. When Julie began to have children and stopped doing those events with me, I had enough confidence to do my own events.

I then founded the networking organization Women, Wine, and Wellness in January of 2008. I spoke in front of these groups for years. When the first *Speaking Your Truth* book came out in 2010, my new business partner Andrea Costantine and I went on a radio show speaking bonanza and live event promotions for our book. We added teleseminars and workshops into the mix as well. Speaking on the air or in public was becoming a regular routine for me.

Becoming a leader just evolved as I spoke more and more and studied the art of networking. I would never have imagined myself on a stage before ever-growing audiences. I began to have fun and look forward to and seek out such events. I definitely raised my hand and participated in workshops and seminars and would take a microphone with excitement. My knees or my voice might have quivered a bit, and I had to wear clothes to hide evidence of perspiration, but I didn't let those things stop me from talking publicly. It's amazing to think back to that teenage girl who wouldn't raise her hand in class, and who was regarded with speculation and concern.

Due to my introvert roots, I still enjoy quiet time after I am in public or have just spoken. To recharge, I like to be alone. Even in everyday life, I love my alone time. If I have had a busy day running around town for appointments, I can't wait to come home to refresh. I love people but I also love to be with just me (and my pets). I love motherhood too and relationships, but with each of those, I am at my best with some balance of time for just me. Perhaps it's just my nature.

I have now exercised the muscle of speaking to larger and larger groups to the point that I have had several events this year with an audience of hundreds. I still find my growth in speaking surreal but at the same time exhilarating. Stepping into a leadership role and finding comfort with talking in front of groups was a gradual process that began with a simple decision to make a change in my life. It's proof to me that what we focus on expands. As that young girl, it was all I could see in myself, a shy, quiet, introverted soul. Now, I see someone with confidence, courage, and fortitude.

I stepped out of that box consciously, and I am glad that I did. I now crave leadership roles and seek speaking engagements. I celebrated my 30-year high school class reunion in the summer of 2011. Each 10-year reunion that I attend, classmates remark on how much I have changed. These comments are not about my basic physical appearance because my hair and body weight stay relatively the same. Okay, I have put on a few pounds and color those grey hairs, but my energy and confidence in conversation certainly has transformed!

I feel that as each decade passes, I just keep improving and realizing more and more of my potential. Some people look back and wish they were still a teen or enjoying their youth. Not me, I wouldn't go back to that time because it wasn't nearly as fun as living with confidence today. I am looking forward to many more decades of growth and amazing experiences as a result of coming out of my shyness shell!

As Marianne Williamson says, "As we let our own light shine, we unconsciously give other people permission to do the same. As we are liberated from our own fear, our presence automatically liberates others."

Lisa Shultz enjoys an entrepreneurial life, which includes writing and speaking. Through sharing her story and the stories of the contributing authors in Speaking Your Truth, *she hopes to connect women together who might resonate with the messages they read and so realize they are not alone. An avid swimmer, Lisa is the mother of two delightful daughters. She has written or contributed to several other books. Find out more about Lisa at www.LisaShultz.com.*

LESSONS FROM THE SEAT
OF MY BIKE

Dawn Cochlan

As we go through life, we are offered many opportunities to learn lessons, usually appearing in the course of everyday situations and circumstances. I've learned some of my most valuable and significant life lessons on the seats of my bicycles. In fact, the very first lessons I can remember presented themselves on the seat of my little green Schwinn bike, when—as a young girl—I faced learning to ride it without training wheels. With the help of my dad, on a sunny, summer afternoon, we ventured out to our big driveway to accomplish this feat.

We lived on five acres with plenty of dirt roads. Luckily for me, sometime before this momentous day, my dad paved our driveway. It was the perfect place for a young girl to make her two-wheel debut—flat and smooth, long, and extra wide. The day the training wheels came off was the most magical one I can remember. As my dad let go and I rode straight ahead, I knew I could do anything. I was standing—well, sitting—and riding on my own two wheels!

For hours and days, I practiced riding my bicycle on our paved driveway, making big, wide turns and looping back to where I started. I knew I'd accomplished something amazing, but I also knew my biggest challenge was still in front of me—getting onto one of our dirt roads so I could visit my best friend.

The day arrived when my mom wasn't available to drive me to my friend's house. She told me I'd have to go on my bike if I really wanted to visit my girlfriend. My mom didn't know how frightened I was of that dirt road—afraid of falling on the dusty, gravely path and getting scraped up and dirty. She also didn't know that every day as I rode my bike in our driveway, I was trying to build up my courage so that I could actually do it—get on that road and ride.

On this particular day, I was faced with a choice—either stay home and continue to ride alone in our driveway or get on my bike, face my fear, and visit my friend. All of a sudden, something happened. I felt a fire in my belly and heard a voice in my head say, "Soar!" I got on my bike and took off down that dirt road. Not only did I venture off the paved driveway, but I made it onto the dirt road without falling! And I was doing it all by myself! All the way to my friend's house I giggled with joy. What a freeing feeling I experienced—the wind in my hair and the warm summer sun on my face—as I rode my bike that day. It was euphoric.

I look back on that memory now and think, "Wow! What courage I had at seven years old. How proud I was. What tenacity!" Turning fear into courage was thrilling, freeing, and exhilarating. On that special day, from the seat of my little green Schwinn, I knew I could accomplish anything if I set my mind on the end result.

After conquering the dirt road, my bike became my constant companion. With it, I could go anywhere and be anyone. I loved the way I felt whenever I rode my little green Schwinn. It was so liberating to know I was the only one who would steer my bike wherever I wanted to go. The wind in my hair and the warm summer sun on my face also connected me to the quiet strength of the earth. It was as if time stood still just for me. Riding my bike allowed me to think, and sometimes, I actually heard answers to my questions.

Our family spent entire summers at my grandmother's cabin on Hubbard Lake. My bike came along—strapped to the top of our Chevy station wagon. Once at the lake, I was able to ride in the north woods of Michigan. My little green Schwinn quickly became my vehicle to venture out to new territories in those north woods. I found trails, a teepee, and a fort made of fallen-down trees and old wood.

I spent many hours in this secret fort with my sister. We'd pack lunch and ride our bikes to this paradise that allowed us to escape all reality and create our own world. As the Cowboy and Indian of our own movie, my sister and I were able to forget the "way we were supposed to be"—imposed on us by our strict Catholic upbringing— and become whoever we wanted to be. Our trips to our secret, magical place in the woods allowed our spirits to soar. We became the joyful, wondrous, and playful children we were really intended to be. My bike was the way out of the house to a space and time that provided such a relief.

Back at home on our five acres, my little green Schwinn continued to be the key to unlocking and unbinding me from my daily routine. I rode a different path each time I ventured out, going to other magical and mystical places. If the ride became dull or boring, I'd princess-pretend I was back in the north woods of Michigan. On the seat of my bike I was able to transform my otherwise mundane and often oppressive day-to-day routine into anything I wanted.

By the time I turned 10 years old, however, I'd outgrown my little green Schwinn. Sadly for me, it was hung up in the garage of the Hubbard Lake cabin. For a couple of years, I didn't ride at all, until, on my 12th birthday, I received a 10-speed bike. What a cool bike it was! A frame of white with rainbow stripes replaced the green of years past. This bike became a real mode of transportation for me, at least for a while, since I was allowed to ride it to and from school each day.

One morning, on my way to school, I saw a friend up ahead walking on the sidewalk. I pulled up alongside her and continued to ride slowly and talk with her. I became so engrossed in our conversation that I forgot to look ahead and rode right into the back of a parked car! The impact forced me off my seat, and my body landed on the middle bar of the bike's frame. The pain was intense, and I began to cry. The tears that continued to stream down my face were both from the pain and the embarrassment of what I'd done. As I sobbed, my friend's mom came running out. She phoned my mom, who came and picked me up. The accident that day became a recurring theme in my life—I often allowed the periphery to blind me from seeing what was right in front of me.

Because of the damage done to my bike, I was unable to ride it anymore. The tire was bent and needed repair. My parents told me I wouldn't be allowed to ride again until I earned the money to pay for a new tire. At 12 years old, I had no concept of how to make money and accomplish such a goal, so we hung my bike on a hook in our garage. Along with my bike, my sense of freedom and all my imaginary worlds went on that hook as well.

Nothing could ever replace what I lost that day, but I did try my best to find other ways to feel free. Music became the next best thing to a bicycle. I immersed myself in my radio. My eight-track player became my new best friend. In time, I forgot all about my bike and the need to have it repaired. It hung on that hook for the next five years.

When I graduated high school, my grandmother and two uncles came to celebrate my accomplishment. One of my uncles noticed the white bike hanging on a hook and asked me if I still rode it. "Ride it? How could anyone use it in its current condition?" I asked. And if it were possible for someone to ride it, shouldn't that 'someone' be me?

As easy as 1-2-3, he took my bike down from the hook, replaced the tire, pumped the tires with air, and said, "There you go!"

Unbelievable! After five long years, the repair turned out to be so easy. I took off on my bike and once again felt the wind in my hair, the warm summer sun on my face, and that wonderful sense of freedom.

As I rode, I remembered something I'd learned long ago: *Stay focused on what you want and where you're going. If you focus on where you want to go—and the end result—you can accomplish anything.* Somehow I'd lost sight of that knowledge as I allowed circumstances to sidetrack me.

There was another lesson to remember from this day as well: *No matter what happens in life, I need to get on my bike—physically and metaphorically. No matter the challenges or circumstances I face, I'll live my best life if I stay focused on where I want to go.* Unfortunately, with the passage of time, the awareness I gleaned on my graduation day faded away.

After high school graduation, life continued in the prescribed manner for women of my era. I went off to college, married, opened a restaurant with my husband in Breckenridge, Colorado, and in the midst of running our restaurant, I gave birth to our first son. When our business closed, we moved back to Michigan where I had our second son. Eventually, we returned to Colorado for my husband's new job. What a ride this time of my life proved to be. Looping back to Colorado reminded me of the circles I used to do on my bike in my parents' driveway. The only elements that were missing were that sense of freedom along with the wind in my hair and the warm summer sun on my face.

We settled into our new life, and my oldest son started school. My youngest wondered what he'd do all day without his brother around. That's when it hit me. Why not get back on a bicycle and share my love of riding with him? Off I went to Target to purchase a bike. On the way home, I stopped at a garage sale and serendipitously found a baby carrier. As I'd learned long ago, when I focused on the end result, everything fell into place. What a fabulous day we experienced when I introduced my son to my first loves—a bicycle, the feeling of flying, the wind in our hair, and the warm summer sun on our faces.

Life continued. The demands of raising two boys and getting them to all their activities—including competitive sports—were all-encompassing. Once more, my bike went up on a hook in the garage. It remained there for so long that it became like the picture over my couch—I knew it was there but hardly ever noticed it. Once in a while, I'd take it down and ride it, but not very often. My 10-speed was really no match for the hilly area where we lived. So, up on the hook it went along with that free-spirited part of me. I continued to ride through my obligations and responsibilities without those elements that breathed life into me.

Once my boys were in school full time, I desired to create something of my own—a piece of life that allowed more of me to shine through. I love serving, helping, and connecting with others, and I love working with my hands. Putting those two truths together, I decided to go to massage school. I've enjoyed being a massage therapist for the past 10 years, and I've met wonderful people, some of whom have become very close friends.

One particular friend, who's run the Boston Marathon six years in a row and is a triathlete, came to me one day and asked if I rode a bike. What a question! I told her I'd forgotten all about riding in the midst of my life, but I used to love it. She invited me to go on a ride with her. The excitement welled up in me while—with the help of another friend—we cleaned the rust off my bike and added new tires. As we prepared my bike, I began to anticipate the sensations I'd given up so long ago.

I decided to take my shiny, refurbished bike out for a spin and attempted the steepest hill near my home. I made it up that steep climb without stopping, something I'd not been able to do in years past. Making that climb—after years of not riding—showed me once again that with my focus on the end result, anything is possible. I felt that wonderful sense of freedom along with the caressing wind in my hair and the glorious warm summer sun on my face. What a gift riding was to me!

In spring 2010, my new cycling friend gave me my first road bike. Through her generosity and other friends' support, I completed my first cycling event, a 33-mile ride in Longmont, Colorado. I am entered to ride four other events this year, and will lead an all-woman ride through the Colorado mountains in fall 2011.

My little green Schwinn hung in the garage of our family's summer home for many years. Long ago, I begged my parents not to sell it. As

I'd envisioned, my little green Schwinn has now been enjoyed by four grandchildren, and my sons. They too have experienced the wind in their hair, the warm summer sun on their faces, and the opportunity to go to special places with that bike.

I now see that from the seat of my many bicycles, I've had a chance to reconnect to who I was as a child. In rediscovering my love of riding bikes and the way it makes me feel, I've reconnected with my childhood joy, courage, tenacity, and sense of freedom. I've seen that I can accomplish anything I put my mind to, and I've been reminded that focusing on what I want—rather than allowing peripheral circumstances to distract me—sets me free. Nature is always there to support and love me, no matter what. It serves as a reminder that there is something bigger than me at work in the world.

In the same way I left the safety of our paved driveway all those many years ago, my bike continues to propel me forward to new adventures, new learning, and a deeper appreciation of this wonderful journey on the roads of life. With fire in my belly and the voice in my head I continue to soar!

Dawn Cochlan, CMT currently lives and practices massage therapy in Highlands Ranch, Colorado. Dawn enjoys riding her bike whenever she can. She doesn't have a hook in her garage! When the snow flies, she enjoys snowshoeing, skiing, and scrapbooking/stamping. She also teaches essential oil classes. To learn more about Dawn, visit www.mydoterra.com/ dawncochlan. She can be contacted at dawncochlan@yahoo.com.

I AM WOMAN, HEAR ME ROAR!

Sara Nowlin

As a fearless four-year-old, sitting in the backseat of my parents' 1979 Toyota station wagon, I loudly sang along with the radio with complete joy and abandon, "I am woman, hear me roar. I am too much to ignore!" I didn't get the lyrics to Helen Reddy's song exactly right, but I embodied the heart of that song. It vibrated throughout my entire body. Even as a little girl with wispy blond hair and bright blue eyes, I was a force to be reckoned with and I knew it! I had a power and magnetism that could not be denied. I never would have guessed when I was four years old that as I grew up I could lose that sense of self, that I would lose that sense of self, that knowing who I was and my willingness to unabashedly voice it. My voice, my roar, would be silenced.

It was in kindergarten that the silencing of my voice first began. I was a talkative and expressive child and sometimes my kindergarten teachers weren't quite sure what to do with me. I was often punished just for talking too much, forced to sit in the time-out chair in the corner, embarrassed in front of the whole class. I know now that teaching boundaries to children is important, but I can assure you that a lesson about boundaries was lost on my five-year-old self. In order to be a part of the class, I had to be quiet. It was my first lesson in suppression.

Another lesson in suppression occurred during a fifth grade multiplication game. There I stood, side by side with Dino, the other top math student, waiting in nervous anticipation for the next multiplication problem. I thought to myself, "If I win this problem, I will be the best! I will be #1!" Just the mere idea of that caused my heart to beat faster in excitement. But my excitement took a huge tumble when I overheard a classmate say, "Why do they have to show off?" So, distracted and humiliated, I fumbled the next question. I lost and became ranked #2. Sitting silent for the rest of class, I thought to myself, "I just want to be the best. I wanted to prove I could beat Dino. Is that showing off?" I imagine now that my classmate was likely feeling insecure or jealous. Of course I didn't have to take it personally, either. But in that moment, at the age of 10, I didn't have that kind of insight or clarity of thought. Instead, I internalized another lesson in suppression: Don't show how smart you are. The lid on the box of conformity closed a bit tighter on me that day.

Similar small lessons in suppression continued, and I became more and more invisible, just to avoid teasing or ridicule, and to try to belong. I knew I wasn't the only one being teased, but it often felt like it. The self-expression I had felt when I was a little girl of four was shrinking rapidly as I grew older.

Middle school and high school were filled with more lessons in suppression. Like many young girls, peer acceptance and belonging was crucial to me. I often felt like I had to choose between acceptance and self-expression. I chose acceptance nearly every time because the teasing was just too much to bear.

My biggest lesson in silencing myself was learned as a high school freshman. On a typical day at school, I opened my locker at break for a snack. Inside I saw a note that said "Stop checking out all the girls in gym. You dyke." Shock, surprise, shame flooded my system. There was no way that I could possibly face it. I folded the note up and put it back in my locker, locking away all my feelings, all my fears, and all my questions. They stayed locked away for years.

In the early 1990s homophobia was rampant. It was not talked about at school, and especially not at the Catholic school where I attended. There wasn't anyone I felt safe talking to—not my friends, not my parents, no one. I tried to manage the aftermath of even more harassment and comments, all by myself, by pretending they didn't exist, and eventually pretending I didn't exist. At school, I tried to be as invisible as I could. It didn't matter that I wasn't gay; the rumors were more powerful than the truth. The lesson I learned: Who you are is wrong.

I tried so hard to fit in, to change into the person I thought I needed to be to gain acceptance and belonging. But no matter how hard I tried it never seemed to work. I felt so lost. I had lost my sense of self. I had lost the little girl who knew exactly who she was, and wasn't afraid to show it. I had lost my roar. My voice was all but silenced by the time I finally got out of school. I wish I had known then what I know now. All of us kids were just striving to fit in, trying to belong.

When I graduated college I decided to become a middle school teacher. I wanted the opportunity to give a voice to others, to give my students what I felt I had never had—a chance to freely express themselves, to be heard. I worked tirelessly to provide those opportunities for my middle school kids, in a phenomenal partnership with the organization Challenge Day. Initially, my participation was all for the students, ensuring them their birthright of self-expression. But then something occurred to me: What about my birthright? How long am I going to be willing to give up my own self-expression?

When I saw that I had a voice for others, but not for myself, I stood face to face with my hypocrisy. Unable to even look at myself in the mirror, I started to turn the process inward, facing the dark places where I had been impacted, in ways I had never imagined. Working with Challenge Day[1] I finally began to reclaim my own voice at the very spot where it was first silenced.

Facing all those times in my childhood when I had felt silenced and suppressed, the healing was incredibly powerful. I cried the tears I hadn't cried back in high school. I expressed the anger I had felt toward the students who had teased and harassed me. Years of suppressed emotion began to pour out of me. I was like a faucet that had been opened all the way and couldn't be turned off. Through this process my emotional wounds began to heal and my voice slowly began to return.

I started to become comfortable in my own skin in a way that I hadn't felt since I was four. I felt a sense of wholeness because I had found a way to belong by regaining my sense of self. When I started to stand up for myself in ways that I never had, speaking my truth despite fear of rejection, it became apparent to me that it was now more important to be self-expressed than to conform or fit in. Because of my newfound internal comfort, my fear of rejection began to fade away.

I found a community of people who appreciated me, who admired my self-expression and respected the authenticity with which I lived. I surrounded myself with this community, which provided me with continued strength to stretch my self-expression even further, continuing to step out of the box of conformity. As I continuously strengthened my voice and my capacity to speak my truth, it was only a matter of time before I faced my most traumatic and silencing experience.

---

1 Challenge Day is a non-profit organization that provides experiential youth workshops and programs that demonstrate the possibility of love and connection through the celebration of diversity, truth and full expression. For more information – http://www.challengeday.org

This experience had been so painful and unspeakable that I had repressed it from my memory for nearly 10 years. It was only until I had sufficiently reclaimed my voice and had a supportive community around me that I could even allow this memory to return to the surface and be ready to be healed.

At one particular Challenge Day workshop, I began to have an uneasy feeling that something big was rising to the surface of my consciousness. It was gnawing at me. Every time my friend touched me I felt chills run up and down my spine. My hair stood on end. Feelings of disgust and rage began pulsing through me. There was no logical reason for me to feel this way, but clearly something was not right. My fellow workshop participants supported me as I dove in deeper to see what it could be. Even the friend who was triggering these feelings stood by me.

We had just completed a powerful exercise called Angel Walk, where we were blindfolded and guided around the room by other workshop participants. I knew I was completely and utterly safe. In that moment of total safety, what had been gnawing me all weekend finally surfaced. Looking across the room at my friend, it hit me: I had been sexually abused.

Shaken to the core by my realization, I fell to the floor, curled up in a fetal position and began to sob. When I was finally able to peek out to the room, I saw that I was surrounded by the workshop leaders and my community, all sending me their love with their eyes, hands, and smiles. With that, I knew that I would be okay. I would survive this. I could even thrive because of it since I had a circle of people around me who loved me and wouldn't let me fall. For the rest of the workshop, I felt like a baby just out of the womb. Although I felt barely able to function, there was always someone there to hold me and reassure me that I was not broken, just broken open.

The healing process that followed this workshop pushed me into the darkest of places. I felt I had been shattered into pieces and somehow I had to figure out how to put myself back together. Many days I struggled just to get out of bed. I relied on my family and friends to emotionally hold me together, as I used all my tools to try to express myself moment by moment. I cried while sitting in the car. I screamed into my pillows. I prayed for the strength to make it through each day. And as I made each individual choice to express myself, to use my voice, I continued to heal. Step by step, I put the pieces of myself back together and became stronger than ever. As the song I sang when I was four years old goes on to say, "I am wise but it's wisdom born of pain. Yes, I've paid the price, but look how much I gained." In the darkest place, where I had been the most silenced, I reclaimed a voice that was loud and clear.

I still struggle sometimes to speak my truth, to be fully self-expressed, but I know that it is a practice, a choice in every moment. Before I needed to fit in; I needed to belong. Now I know I have the choice, and it is very real and conscious. I continue to search for opportunities to uncover areas where I may be suppressed and I can choose self-expression. With every choice I make to express myself, my roar is reclaimed, and I seize another opportunity to speak my truth.

Deep within my soul, I know I was given the responsibility of reclaiming my self-expression for a divine purpose. I know I am meant to share my journey as an example for others to reclaim their voices, to reclaim their own roar. Much of my work as a life coach and motivational speaker now involves empowering women and girls to speak their truth and roar. I am constantly inspired by courageous women who allow themselves to be vulnerable enough to look at where they have been silenced. I become energized as I watch them reclaim their voices, and speak their truths. I am honored to be part of that process. A self-expressed woman is beyond strong. She is invincible.

Sara Nowlin works in the field of personal development as a coach, speaker, and teacher. As a middle school teacher, Sara developed and led school programs to ensure students were given essential life skills. For the last 10 years, Sara has volunteered with Challenge Day, the non-profit mentioned in her story, by supporting program leaders, contributing to strategic planning, and writing curriculum incorporated into their manuals. Sara holds a B.A. in Sociology and History, specializing in social oppression, from Lehigh University. She also completed graduate work in Counseling Psychology, at John F. Kennedy University. For more information, visit www.saranowlin.com.

COLORING OUTSIDE THE LINES

Barbara Warner

Coloring between the lines has never been my strong suit. As a child my crayons wanted to go outside of those cold, black boundaries. I admired other kids because their pictures were neater and prettier than mine and also they were the kids getting the praise. My elementary school report cards often read, "Does not follow directions," and I still remember my 7th grade art teacher saying my tree didn't look like a tree. Was I just a rebellious kid with no artistic ability? Or maybe there was something deeper and more meaningful in my soul that needed expression.

In many important aspects my childhood was quite idyllic. My hometown of 8,000 people was laid out along a beautiful Lake Michigan beach. World War II had ended when I was an infant. I was the youngest of three girls. My dad owned an insurance agency. He was a leader in politics, the church and the community. Mom stayed at home, never missing a PTA meeting or a women's society meeting at the church. (Maybe "Leave it to Beaver's" mom was modeled after my mom!)

It was nearly impossible for my sisters and I to get lost in town. Everyone knew us as the "Boyer girls." We were on the floats in the 4th of July parades and played Mary in the Christmas pageant. My parents knew my friends' parents. Most of us had been together since kindergarten. If there was a party going on and a curfew was missed, it wasn't hard for parents to find their kids. We rarely missed curfew, as it was quite clear as to what was acceptable behavior.

Toward the end of my high school years I began longing for a wider variety of life experiences. Life was a bit vanilla and I was looking for some banana split experiences. My world did begin to get more flavorful during my junior year in high school. An exchange student from England came to live with our family in Michigan. I remember her bringing beautiful Wedgwood china as a gift to my parents and I loved her stories about being a teenager traveling in Europe. Traveling became my dream too. Between my junior and senior year in high school, I went to Germany on a student exchange program.

My oldest sister attended a large liberal university majoring in sociology. One year she came home on vacation declaring herself an atheist. My parents felt that they had made a mistake allowing her to choose her own college. My younger sister and I were then instructed to go to one of the more conservative state colleges and major in either nursing or elementary education. Living in a world where one did not question their parents, we did just that. My sister majored in nursing and I majored in elementary education.

I don't remember being excited about most education classes in college. I did enjoy the classes I took in foreign affairs and global thinking. Between my junior and senior year, I was able to go to India on another student exchange program. Upon my return I chose to take more classes in foreign affairs and global thinking. I began thinking about what it would be like to live in another country for a longer period of time.

One spring day during my senior year in college, I received a letter from Washington D.C. Before his death in 1963, President Kennedy had created the Peace Corps. Upon hearing of the opportunities to serve abroad, I applied immediately. The letter told me that I had been accepted to begin Peace Corps training in the fall in Portland, Oregon. I was to serve in a program to work with children in a preschool in Turkey. But where was Turkey? I hurried to the library to find out.

Prospective Peace Corps volunteers had to go through a stringent background check by the U.S. Secret Service. That summer two very official looking men went to the Five & Dime store in my hometown where I had worked the Christmas before. They asked the manager if there was any likelihood I would be of danger to the security of the United States of America. Having the reputation of being one of the town's "All-American Girls," he and other community members must have given me a good recommendation as I was accepted into the program. By the time September rolled around I just wanted to get out of Dodge. Life was feeling very suffocating and confining. Feeling like a bird being sprung from a cage I headed west to Oregon to begin Peace

Corps training.

Peace Corps training included an hour each day studying important elements of American culture as well as Turkish culture. We also frequently met with a psychologist to explore our reasons for wanting to spend two years in another country. I certainly wasn't completely clear as to my motivations and appreciated the opportunity to explore them. One day we were asked to line up according to what motivated us. We were to go to the right if we were going to Turkey primarily as a personal sacrifice to ourselves and to promote the American way of life. Those who primarily wanted to learn about the Turkish culture and enhance their own lives were to go to the left. It was fascinating to see how many of us who began at the right slowly move to the left once we began to explain our placement. Honestly, I wanted to know what was in it for me. Serving others would be part of that gift. Looking back I realize that the volunteers who felt most adamant that they were sacrificing themselves for others, burned out quickly and were the first to leave Turkey, never finishing their two-year commitment.

During Peace Corps training three hours of each day was spent studying the Turkish language. Up until that time I had not studied any language except high school level Latin. Turkish was a real challenge and I remained in the lowest ranking language class the entire time I was in training. Due to my enthusiasm and no doubt some naivety, this did not frighten me. I was relieved, however, when they allowed me to go in spite of my low standing in class.

Early in December, we arrived in Ankara, Turkey's capital and remained there for a week before flying to the area where we were to spend the next two years. For me that involved a flight to Izmir where I was to be met by Phil, the local Peace Corps liaison who would take me to Manisa, a provincial capital of 60,000 people.

When I arrived in Izmir, Phil was not at the airport. In fact, *no one* remotely looking Peace Corps-like was at the airport. There were, however, many American military personnel there. The American military had a reputation of being arrogant and treating locals with very little respect. Additionally, as Peace Corps volunteers we were not proud of America's involvement in Vietnam. We didn't want to be associated with "them."

Conflicting thoughts flashed through my mind. On one hand I was a Peace Corps Volunteer and didn't want to look like one of "them." On the other hand after a quick mental scan of my options, I humbled myself and asked one of "them" for a ride to the bus station in Izmr. Once at the bus station, I was able to communicate that I needed a bus to Manisa. Once at the Manisa bus station, I explained that I needed to go to the home where the other Peace Corps volunteers lived.

During the horse and carriage ride from the bus station to my new home, I was filled with thoughts. In Germany and India, English was spoken fluently. Life had been easy as I was living with local people who were willing to help me through any difficulty communicating. In fact, my German family primarily wanted an exchange student so their children could learn English. I had no responsibilities except to enjoy my time with them as much as possible. However, this commitment I had made to the Peace Corps and to Turkey was more complicated and would take all of the strength and sensibility that I could muster to make these two years work. I could only imagine what it would look like and here I was! The future was beginning now.

Yet another surprise awaited me! The other volunteers weren't at home. An older lady came down from the top floor and said she didn't know where they were but asked if I would like to have some tea. After a couple of uncomfortable hours attempting to chitchat in Turkish, I heard some American sounding voices. Two girls came running down the street and embraced me like a long lost friend. Receiving incorrect information as to my arrival time, they didn't find me at the airport in Izmir. They and the Peace Corps liaison had been scouring the streets of Izmir for several hours looking for me. They had heard that my Turkish was very poor and were afraid that I was lost forever. There was a little smile inside of me (and has remained there since), as I realized that perhaps it was beneficial to be unafraid to speak outside the lines. I had been able to communicate quite well through gestures, facial expressions, drawing pictures and other ways that didn't involve the correct conjugating of verbs.

Living in a country where it was necessary to communicate in a new language was the source of many interesting and sometimes frustrating experiences. My work assignment in Manisa was to create and teach (in Turkish) in a preschool at a girl's vocational high school. The girls who majored in child care were to do their hands-on student teaching in my preschool. My Turkish counterpart, Adveya, was a teacher who taught with me in the preschool and also taught the child care students in the vocational high school. It was a great Peace Corps assignment.

When I first walked in to the newly built classroom, the only equipment was 20 cots and some wooden blocks. I am not sure what I expected but I knew I wanted it to look more like those well-equipped rooms I'd seen in American education catalogs. In earnest I looked around for Cinderella's fairy godmother. I wanted her to get to work with that magic wand. She never came but the end result was nevertheless quite magical. Having very limited knowledge of one another's language, Adveya and I went to work to turn that bare classroom into quite a wonderful place for children. In a couple of weeks, we had children's books in Turkish, games, dolls, paper and crayons. There was plenty of outdoor equipment too. We ordered some supplies and others were available through the Turkish government and the Peace Corps. Some we made ourselves. The first day of school came and everyone was very excited. It was the first preschool that the community had ever had. I was very nervous wondering how all of our plans were going to come together.

There were children from several poor families who came tuition free. One of them was Ragip. Early the first day he came to me in distress, urgently repeating, *"cis cim var, cis cim var."* I smiled and nodded not having a clue as to what he was saying. After a short time Adveya came to tell me that Ragip was asking if he could go to the bathroom. I don't quite remember the details, but I got him to the bathroom quickly. Soon after I realized that the texts we used to study Turkish in Oregon were from the US Defense Language Training School and taught very formal Turkish. Ragip was communicating in the very raw and real vernacular! It was time for me to learn some of the raw and real vernacular!

Fortunately Suheyla, a darling four-year-old, was in my class too. She knew no English but could understand my Turkish better than most. She and I had a routine where I would say something to the children and she would then stand up and explain to the group in correct Turkish what it was I wanted to communicate. Being the only person who spoke English in a classroom of 15 preschoolers, I still remember how many times she was instrumental in getting me through a rough day.

Knowing that my own childhood would have been richer had I been encouraged to express my creativity with confidence, I did not want coloring books in my classroom in Turkey. I wanted to give these Turkish children the opportunity to create outside the lines. However, many of the Turkish parents and teachers, similar to those in my hometown in Michigan, did not see the benefits of children's art the way I did. For them the most important outcome for a child was an adult sanctioned "pretty" picture. If an adult felt a child's picture could be changed to make it more appealing, that adult would " touch it up."

This was an emotionally charged issue for me. I tried to explain my philosophy to the other Turkish teachers using my limited Turkish. No one understood. I asked a Turkish friend who did speak English to come to the school as my interpreter and speak to the parents and teachers. Nothing changed. I finally asked a psychologist from Izmir to come to the school and speak and still, no change. Several weeks later, Adveya, whose own son was in our preschool, came to me upset. Her son had brought home a picture he had drawn the day before. She didn't feel it was very good so she had torn it up and drew him another one. Almost in tears she said, "My son was so upset with me. He cried and cried. I won't ever change his picture again. Now I know of what you are talking about." The power of that event was that Adveya not only was a mother but also was the Turkish teacher who would remain in that school long after I left. Hopefully, her influence would have a long-range impact on the adults and children in that community.

Looking back on this experience 44 years and many jobs later, I reflect on how my living and teaching in Turkey was truly a life changing experience. As a 23-year-old new college graduate I was given the responsibility to create and teach in the first preschool in a Turkish community. I had the responsibility to model an environment for children, parents and student teachers that would exemplify excellence. I was able to give children significant opportunities to excel and to have their wonderful pictures mounted on the wall. I am confident that the student teachers experienced respectful interactions with children. Hopefully that has influenced them as childcare workers in other settings and also as mothers.

I sometimes wonder if the preschool is still going, how Adveya and her family are doing and if Ragip has ever forgiven me for making that first day of school so stressful. I also enjoy imagining that all of the children, who are now adults, are a bit more creative in many aspects of their lives because I encouraged them to color outside the lines.

When Barb Warner, MEd retired several years ago, she knew that her future was going to be filled with exciting events that couldn't even be imagined. Wanting to share this vision with others, she enjoys doing talks to encourage people in the second half of life to make creative life choices. She also enjoys writing and is currently working on a book, Save Your Fork: Dessert is on its Way. *Barb resides in Denver, Colorado and can be reached at powerfultools.barb@gmail.com. Her website is www.powerfulaging.vpweb.com.*

A MILE IN MY OWN SHOES

Mary Lockwood

I'd been doing it already for years—decades actually, when you think about it. But the summer I decided to walk across the country with a handful of friends from college, what I thought I knew—about the simple act of putting one foot in front of the other, about myself, about the world around me—suddenly shifted, then slid out of focus. You know how when you crack an egg on the side of a bowl, the yolk slips off the lip and sidles its way down onto the counter top, silently settling into a slick, gelatinous goo? That's what the summer of 1995 was for me. It started out with all the right ingredients you need to make such a trek, but somewhere between the golden coast of California and the Capitol steps in D.C., the eggs I was cracking in anticipation of my proverbial omelet somehow missed the bowl.

There's an old expression that admonishes the would—be critic in all of us to walk a mile in another's shoes before passing judgment. This is a principle I've tried to live by my entire life. Harsh judgment dissolves like sugar in water in the presence of compassion. And compassion is only possible when you silence the inner critic and really listen to the other's story. But what my walk across America revealed to me, step by step, mile after mile, were the layers of criticism I had carefully piled on my Self. These left little room for the compassion I normally reserved for the world outside of me. Silly as it sounds now, it took walking 3,000 miles—in my own shoes—to appreciate the magnitude of my mistake and to begin to make amends.

At the onset of our walk, my initial steps were fueled by one purpose—to complete a challenging adventure, something outside of the box and extraordinary. By the time I climbed the Capitol steps and freed my achy, blistered, twitching feet from shoes you would not see on a homeless person, it was clear that this purpose had been, if not abandoned, then at least moved to a place of secondary importance.

To the best of my knowledge, this shift happened somewhere along an endless stretch of Highway 40—most likely in Kansas—about six weeks into our three-month journey. Before Kansas, crossing into Nevada from California, then on through Utah we walked, 30 miles a day for a hundred days, through desert and snow and rain, that ribbon of highway forever wandering ahead of us, leading us on. At the end, I knew my walk was about so much more than adventure; it was about me negating the belief in my heart and mind that I was a failure.

If your U.S. Highways history is a little rusty, here are some interesting facts about Highway 40: It was one of the original U.S. highways built in the 1920s, and it once traversed the entire country. Today, the highway cuts through a total of 12 states, from Colorado to New Jersey. If you think about it, 40 basically bears witness to every so-called "flyover state." Highway 40 can be a climb (Colorado does not know the meaning of the word "flat"), but if I'm being objective, it's mostly long stretches of wide open, level spaces that speak of endless summer days and flat, grey winters. I bet 40 has seen its share of history, from the perspective of Native Americans and "Go West" pioneers to Depression—era laborers and boom-time capitalists. I doubt it has seen much of our kind, though: college kids sweltering on its black top when they could be riding in the van they slept in just the night before, full of piss and vinegar and themselves, ready to take on the world.

I had met my friends at Franciscan University in Steubenville, Ohio. Fresh out of high school, having narrowly escaped a long career on the stage as a classical ballerina thanks to an accident that involved a ladder, a loft, and—ironically—a misstep on my part, I came to my studies with no idea as to what I wanted to do with my life, but very strong opinions on what I didn't want to do. To many, I suppose, knowing what I didn't want might sound like half-way-there progress. At the very least, it afforded me a process of elimination that cleared the way for options that were sure to surface. But when you walk away from something as I did, something that many aspire to and very few actually grasp, as I did, you can't help but question your M.O.

If you're like many women, you may have spent at least some of your growing up years in a tutu, playing princess ballerina, lugging a pooka belly swaddled in tights and a leotard around your mother's living room, classical music on the stereo. And, like many women, you may have carried this little-girl obsession with you into adolescence, where it morphed and grew into something that cut through you with all the earmarks of a life's calling. Maybe you pursued this calling, filling your days with classes that left your back aching and blisters on the tips of your toes that looked very much like water balloons, and your head with dreams of *prima* roles and the spotlight. And maybe, just maybe, after one of those classes, someone took note, and kept taking note, monitoring your progress, challenging your limitations, asking you to reach, do, and be more than you thought was possible, until one day, after having moved up in the small world that was your training studio, gorging yourself on plum roles (but nothing else—there was a scale to make your peace with, each and every day), a world-renowned, professional ballet company tapped you on the shoulder and called you up into their ranks.

You'd have to be crazy to walk away from an opportunity like that, but that's exactly what I did.

On the road to Capitol Hill, I thought about my abandoned career. I thought about my motivations to leave behind everything I had spent my childhood working towards, about the investment of time and who knows how much of my parents' money, about the disappointment they must have felt but never voiced. I judged myself, too. What kind of person walks away from an opportunity very few are ever afforded? Who feels the blinding warmth of the limelight when it's finally turned on her, then willingly steps out of the circle it casts, and into the darkness? I had been given a golden ticket, a chance to pirouette my way to fame and relative fortune, and I chose to spiral instead into the unknown.

My first year of college, I gained more than the standard Freshman 15 (I had always been an overachiever), drank enough beer to make Sam Adams blush, and never once sat in my splits. I didn't know it at the time, but I was doing everything I could to bury the ballerina I had so carefully molded over nearly two decades of my life. I didn't want anyone to know she had existed. And I didn't want to be reminded of her every time I looked into the mirror. As far as I was concerned, she had taken her last bow, the curtains had been lowered, and the bouquet of flowers that had been thrown at her feet had long since withered away.

My reasons for leaving behind a career in professional dance are many and varied. On my walk across America, as I shed the weight that had padded me from the girl I was, I began what would be a years-long process of examining these reasons. But more important than the why, as I peeled away layers of judgment, I walked my way, step by impossible step, towards what I would later come to know as compassion for myself.

Not too many years before that walk, I had offered myself as a canvas on which masters of the ballet world would paint their vision. In their choreography, my body would become a work of art. I had walked away from that world, and was only just beginning to understand that it was now time for me to make my life into the work of art that I alone envisioned. At the time, I couldn't give you the first idea of what that vision entailed. Today, I see it more clearly, and there is still much to be discovered. But I now know how much courage it took for me to move away from something that my heart no longer desired, and I admire myself for that.

Throughout the walk, I realized how much low self-esteem, a distorted body image, and the belief that I had to be perfect to be loved played a role in every aspect of my life. I used to walk with my toes pointed in a classical extension, posture perfect, turned out at the hips. When we had walked the last of 3,000 miles across an entire continent and I had peeled my sorry shoes off and let my toes see the light of day for the first time in three months, there was nothing graceful in my movements. But I had glimpsed another kind of grace, something internal and eternal, and something that gave me permission to be me. Through all those miles I finally had the chance to heal that part of me that was so wounded from being a young star and all the shame that came from quitting. Healing and grace became the purpose of walking a thousand miles in my own shoes. And I have walked with that grace of thousands of miles, ever since.

As founder and president of Sirin Web Group, Mary Lockwood works with entrepreneurs and small business owners to create websites and online initiatives that inspire the Web with fantastic results. In 2010 Mary launched a coaching practice to help entrepreneurs realize their dreams of owning a thriving business. Through her unique approach to coaching, Mary helps clients unlock their potential to engage at the highest levels—both professionally and personally—and realize their greatest potential. Mary lives in Southern California and can be reached via email at inspire@sirinwebgroup.com.

Loss

THE GLAZED PENGUIN

Diana Dolan

"9-1-1, what is your emergency?" I had said these words more times than I could count during the years I had been an emergency dispatcher. Always, the voice on the other end of the line had the same tone; they were all having the worst day of their lives and anxiously, sometimes desperately, needed someone to help them. Over the phone, I had delivered babies, given successful CPR directions, calmed seizures, and soothed frightened children. Those times when the person in emergency passed on, the caller then became my patient; I took care of them until units arrived. Being an emergency dispatcher is one of the most stressful jobs there is, and the role a dispatcher plays in the overall success of helping the person who calls 9-1-1 is all too often underplayed and under recognized.

I worked the graveyard shift. From 7:30 p.m. to 7:30 a.m., my partner and I handled the calls. While most everyone is asleep during the bulk of this time, there is always one, or a dozen, intoxicated persons; or a baby who awoke with croup; or a house fire that started from a midnight lightning storm, a cigarette left burning, or candle left lit at bedtime—all part of an ordinary shift. But the night I remember most was a most *un*-ordinary night.

My partner, Annie Spring[1], and I were spending a typical night answering calls, dispatching units, working on reports, and conversing with our neighbor, Rob Mays, who was a dispatcher for a private ambulance company that was renting space from our agency. The three of us got along fabulously. Our nights were almost always filled with laughter and the occasional stuffed animal being lobbed over the console to one of the other dispatchers. "Yak Ball," we called it, because the toy happened to be a little stuffed yak from a Happy Meal. All of this joking and play in between emergency calls helped the night go much faster. More importantly, it relieved the tension that comes from

---

1 All names, except the author's, have been changed to protect each individual's privacy.

handling stressful calls and trying to calm people down. Believe me, when people are panicking, it can make your stress level skyrocket!

One cold, fall night, we were in the middle of a wonderfully heated game of Yak Ball when the 9-1-1 line rang. My partner, Annie, answered the phone. It was instantly clear that the person on the other end of the line couldn't breathe. Annie immediately started her medical protocols, known as EMD (Emergency Medical Dispatch), to assist the patient until the fire truck and ambulance arrived. Since the person on the phone couldn't breathe, Annie used alternate methods to verify the information that came up on the 9-1-1 screen. She read the address on the screen aloud to the person and asked if it was correct. Immediately, she had my attention. I knew that address. Then Annie read the apartment number, a number I also knew well. It was the apartment of my estranged husband's grandmother, Nellie. Startled and anxious, adrenaline beginning to course through me, I focused on every word Annie said hoping for any indication that everything was okay.

Nellie was a very formal, almost overly proper person, who carefully guarded her interaction with others, including her family. But she delighted in handmade things, as did I. She couldn't help smiling with a glint in her eye when she spoke of some new craft she had tried or object she had made. This gave Nellie and me a special connection at a level she didn't share even with members of her family, as we both loved to make things, all kinds of things, with our own hands. She had recently, although unsuccessfully, tried to teach me how to knit. She had also started glazing pottery, and we had planned to go to the pottery store together in just a couple of days. Of all of my estranged husband's family, Nellie was the one most interested in me as a person and who had wanted to spend time with me, to share special moments just between her and me.

With the address confirmed, I dispatched units as quickly as I could, then told Annie that I was taking the call as I picked up the line. "Nellie," I said, my pulse racing, "It's me, Diana. I'm here. We've got people coming for you." Nellie was having such difficulty trying to breathe, she could only make weak sounds. I knew from many years of experience this meant she had a very short time before she lost consciousness. Still, she was able to express gratitude that someone she knew was on the phone with her. My heart was racing. Still, my training held fast and I followed protocol, keeping my composure. "Stay with me, Nellie. We're almost there."

Luckily, the station was close by and literally seconds later the fire truck and ambulance came across the radio announcing that they had arrived. A wave of relief washed over me, and I reassured Nellie that we were just outside getting equipment off of the truck, and would be with her in just a moment. Then, the officer came over the radio with words that stopped my heart. "Dispatch, this is a locked apartment building and there are no keys in the Knox box. Do you have a contact who can open the door?" My heart dropped. Of all the times for the building manager to not have keys in the emergency access Knox box! Nellie was not doing well, not well at all. Annie and Rob jumped into action, calling all of the emergency contacts and the manager's number; the units on scene tried the buzzers for everyone in the building to get inside. Meanwhile, I stayed on the phone with Nellie, monitoring her condition, telling her to hang on, reassuring her that she was not alone. Suddenly, I heard the phone fall from Nellie's hand and hit the floor.

"Nellie? Nellie!" My heart felt as though it had just been strangled, as I knew what had just happened. She was now unconscious on the floor with precious little time left. I could hear her breath sounds fading. A feeling of absolute helplessness mixed with rising panic consumed me as I could do nothing but hold the phone and listen, calling to her repeatedly to stay with me and begging her to pick up the phone. Then I heard a noise on the other end of the line that turned my blood cold. It's what is known as the death rattle. And I knew what it meant.

"Pick up the phone, Nellie, *please just pick up the phone!*" But there was no answer. My mouth had gone dry and it was all I could do to keep from bolting out the door and rushing to her apartment. It didn't matter that there wouldn't have been anything I could have done. Still calling to her, I forced myself to just sit there listening, my fists clenched so tightly with anxiety and frustration that my knuckles had turned white and my fingernails had dug into my palms.

Mere moments felt like hours before the firemen were able to get inside. They broke down her door, immediately doing everything they could to revive her and get her breathing again. I listened helplessly on the phone as they coordinated their efforts. Intubation. Heart monitor. CPR. Drug kit. Each member of the crew giving it their all for this little old lady crumpled on the floor. When they announced over the radio that they were transporting her emergent, Annie, Rob, and I were ready with the hospital divert status, ready to contact the ER for patient prep updates, ready for whatever they needed—all the while taking turns handling the never-ending stream of other 9-1-1 calls. But it was too late. I had heard Nellie take her last breath over the phone just moments before the firemen broke down her door.

I put the phone down and stared at the console. Defeated. What else could I have done? Did I do everything I could have? Was there anything I should have done *differently*? I know that not everyone can be saved. Over the years I had helped save hundreds of lives, and I had also been unable to help when things were just too late. But this one didn't feel like the others. This one hit me hard and I found myself doubting if I had done absolutely everything possible.

For a dispatcher, getting a call from someone they know is very unusual. But to receive a call from a family member—and to have it turn out like this—is unheard of. Still, I was on duty. I didn't have the luxury of losing it. I had to hold it together for several more hours until the shift was over.

"Are you okay?" Annie was watching me. Without looking away from the phone, I replied, "I need to call Tony. Nellie was his grandma."

"Go," Annie said, "We've got this."

I got up from the console and left the communications center, going upstairs to the only other phone in the building I had access to after hours. Fingers trembling, I dialed my soon-to-be ex-husband's number. Our separation had been anything but friendly, and I had no idea how this conversation was going to go. A sleepy and somewhat irritated voice answered the phone.

"Tony," I said, "it's Diana. Listen, we responded to your grandma's apartment tonight." I stopped. How was I going to say what I needed to say? And how was he going to take the news?

"Is she okay?" Tony was awake now.

"No," I replied hesitatingly. "She...didn't make it."

I could hear Tony's breath start to shake as the reality of death set in. We sat on the phone for a few minutes, both of us crying for our loss. I told him I was sorry, that I had loved her. Tony said he would call his mother to tell her.

"Thank you, Diana," he said. "I'm glad you were there." Hearing these words from him came as a complete surprise to me. I struggled to absorb them.

For the remaining hours of the shift and the entire drive home, I replayed the call over and over and over again, trying to find the one thing that I could have done that would have saved Nellie's life. Each time, the call played out the same. Murphy's Law seemed to be in full force this time, as every possible thing that could have gone wrong, did: Nellie's attack was too sudden; the building was locked; there were no keys; who knows how long it took for someone to wake up and open the door; and so on. I knew there was more involved than just me, but I couldn't stop beating myself up. I had to figure out what I could have done to get the units in the door faster, or keep Nellie breathing longer. Somehow, it felt like it had been my responsibility.

When I finally arrived at my house, I went inside and closed the door. Standing in the front entrance, I took a few contemplative breaths, then went into the kitchen for some water. There, sitting on the back of the sink, was a glazed porcelain penguin with a little yellow beak that had a chip broken out of it, and a hole in its back to hold a dish scrubby pad. Nellie had made that penguin for me and gave it to me as a wedding gift years ago. Time had taken its toll on the little guy, and a yellow chip of broken beak had been glued on in an effort to mask the scar of my having accidentally dropped him into the sink sometime before.

As I looked at the penguin, tears began to well up in my eyes and a small smile touched my lips. I could remember the day Nellie gave it to me. She had been so delighted to give me something she had made herself. The memory of how proud she was of the little penguin had touched me, and I cherished him.

I picked up the penguin and looked him over, examining the chip on his beak, dusting off his little black head. Holding him in my hands, I just looked at him for a while. In his eyes, I saw understanding. I saw reassurance. I saw contentedness. Somehow, this little glazed penguin had allowed me a renewed connection to Nellie and I found solace in him. Through those glassy little black eyes, I was able to see the situation for what it was. I had done everything humanly possible for Nellie. In fact, thanks to the help of Annie and Rob, together we did more to help Nellie than anyone could have in that situation. The deck was just stacked against us was all, and Nellie's time had simply come.

After many moments, and many goodbye tears for Nellie, I placed the penguin back on the counter and took a long, relieved breath as I clasped the edge of the sink, dropped my head back and gazed toward the ceiling. I could accept the situation for what it was. Nellie was at peace, and thanks to the little glazed penguin, so was I. Now I could begin to grieve for Nellie without feeling that her death was my fault.

It has been several years since that day, and the little penguin still sits on the back of my sink holding a dish scrubby pad in his back. Every day when I do the dishes he gives me a memory. Sometimes I see Nellie's smile on the day she gave him to me; sometimes I see her struggling to be patient and then trying not to laugh at me and my attempts at knit one, purl two. Sometimes I remember the pain of hearing her last breath. But regardless of the memory, the penguin reminds me of special times that I had with a very misunderstood lady, the knowledge that in her last moments she was connected to someone she knew and cared for, and that she had found at least some comfort by not being alone. And I am also reminded, and reassured, that everything possible was done when she needed it most, and not everything was—or is—my fault. Sometimes, that is my most valued memory.

Diana Dolan lives in the suburbs of Denver, Colorado with her two cats and three dogs. She is a member of Rocky Mountain Women Writers and the Society of Children's Books Writers and Illustrators. In addition to writing, she enjoys illustrating children's books; creating one-of-a-kind stained glass / clay gift boxes; editing; consulting; photography; kayaking on the East Coast, and walking her dogs. Diana spent 15 years as a 9-1-1 dispatcher, achieving the level of Division Director, before embracing her creative side. You can reach Diana by email at ddolan911@gmail. com or by going to her website: www.lunapants.com.

THE WHIRLWIND

Maureen Hunter

In the beginning, all was calm, with the occasional turbulence on stormy days. Then it changed forever and ever.

The day started out as many others had; I had no premonition or feeling that it would be any different. On reflection that bothered me. I had always thought that when something catastrophic happened in life, I would get a nudge or a poke. "Oy! Look out! Boy are you in for it!" Nothing. Normal. ZILCH. I finished work that day oblivious to the turbulent winds swirling, sweeping, silent and savage, which were about to descend. They knew. I, on the other hand, was blissfully unaware as I nudged the blankets back that night and fell soundly asleep.

A thunderously loud noise interrupted the still. There was someone at the door. Heart beating, I rushed up, anxious but thinking it was probably someone drunk and disoriented on their way home from the pub. My brain, fuzzy and not completely awake, came to focus on the serious countenance of two young police officers. Even when they asked if he lived here, no alarm registered. My brain had already gone into denial mode.

Brain: Must have got arrested and they've come to get me to bail him out for driving under the influence.

Reality: Your son has been in a car accident. His condition is critical.

My world fell apart at that moment. I started shaking, I couldn't stop. I couldn't comprehend. I couldn't do anything. Even when I tried to talk, my mouth stuck together— there was no sound. The policeman made me a cup of tea.

The winds that were swirling above swept with savagery into my protected and uneventful world. The whirlwind grasped me in its claws, churned me up and spat me out—splat. I felt I was a splayed mess. Never had I experienced anything so raw, so powerful, so crippling. I had no control over this. I was laid bare at that instant.

The tears which had been too shocked to cry came unbidden when I finally saw my son, unaware, broken and bloody, on a narrow trolley, in a quiet hospital, in the middle of a night, following an uneventful day. My nightmare was just beginning.

That night I didn't care if there were dishes in the sink, the unmade bed didn't even rate a glance. I threw a few things in a bag and went with him, on his flight to salvation or something too terrifying to think about. As the Royal Flying Doctor plane raised its wings, I sat cradling his bandaged head, smelling antiseptic and screaming inwardly through glistening eyelashes. I had sugar in my tea this time.

Sitting at his bedside, the whirr of machines fractured the still, though nothing could muffle the crying that came, and came, and came. I held his hand, kissed his unresponsive mouth, and cried some more. The crying lasted for five days.

When I at last said goodbye, I cried even more. When I cradled his body, the sound was brittle and I could smell the rose I had placed on his chest, releasing its scent between us both.

In an instant, I was no longer the me I knew. My son was dead. DEAD! I couldn't believe this had happened to our family. I couldn't comprehend or accept the reality that I knew to be true. I could not believe I would never see him again, smell him, touch him, or hear his voice. I cried even more.

The world stopped that day for me, but surprisingly not for anyone else. It still ticked along; people went about their business, complaining about nothing of any real significance. The world just carried on as if nothing had happened. Didn't they know my son had died? Couldn't they see on my face the grief, pain, and agony I was living through every single minute? No, the world carried on regardless.

My mind became an alien being. Concentration flew away, memory lost one minute and then the next. Life became a piece of time-lapsed photography, one millisecond at a time. Sleep was the only peace I had. When I woke in the morning, if I was lucky I had about two seconds of peaceful awareness before I remembered again that my son had died. I remember thinking of him every second, every minute. I remember thinking I had only cried twice that day, or that the wrenching tears had spent themselves after 30 minutes and not an hour or more. I remember thinking I hadn't cried for two whole days. I remember thinking, this week he would have been 19. I remember thinking and thinking and thinking.

No one could tell me how long this alien being would stay with me. I wanted to know timelines. How much longer would I feel like this? How long? HOW LONG? Silence! Finally, a lifeline…a friend passed a battered old paperback to me one day and said, "Here, read this. It'll help." I found what I wanted. Three months. It took three months to process a crisis. There, in black and white. I waited. After three months had passed I had given up on the tea; I was drinking wine.

One night I'd had enough. I couldn't do this anymore. I couldn't live with this excruciating pain of grief, with the terrible emotions that rocked my very being. No more. I took charge, of me, my life, and my future. At that moment, I made the decision that what had happened to me with the loss of my son, would not define my life anymore, not in the way it had. I would not allow myself to become a victim of circumstance. I would not allow my son's death to be for nothing and I would not allow myself to die while still living, a worse death still.

I fled. I fled from the memories, from the cold, from life, and took my battered body and soul to some comfort, a quiet beach many miles from home. Time stood still as I spent many sunsets in reflection and contemplation. I wrote out my life and planned my future. Tears fell quietly on the paper. The hurt came spilling out in droves, peeling away the shimmy of pretence and excavating the real of my life. I explored my existence and that of my son, of our two worlds and what it meant now in our new reality. My new self came into being.

I found my business in my journal one day, forming words out of letters. From my son's initials, SDR, came Esdeer, a new word that would reflect all that I would be and do from now on. I was healing, slowly. I was ready to reintegrate into life. I was ready to make a difference to others, to give back. The alien being was tamed and I was back to drinking tea.

Out of devastating loss my life had changed forever, in ways I could never have envisaged. I never ever thought I could or would survive. I never ever thought my life could go on. I never ever thought I would smile again. I never ever thought there would be a moment I wasn't thinking about Stuart. I never ever thought I would ever stop crying. I never ever thought anyone could help me. I never ever thought I could ever be happy again. I certainly never thought anything good would come from such a tragic loss.

I was given a gift, an opportunity to use that experience to give to and help others. It wasn't an easy concept to grasp initially; in the early days of my grief, I dismissed it with anger and disbelief. Yet it formed slowly in my being over time. I reclaimed my life. I reclaimed my power, the power of resilience, the power of intention, the power of commitment, and the power of passion to make a difference to others. Stuart helped me to truly be me, and that is something I will always cherish.

Maureen Hunter is passionate about using her own experience to make a difference to those experiencing the loss of a loved one. She is widely known for providing comfort, hope, and inspiration through her writings and grief programs. She writes regularly on grief, healing, resilience, and spirituality, and is the creator of Stepping through Grief: The 7 Steps Pathway, *a step by step process that helps individuals find meaning in their lives once more. If grief has touched your life, please accept Maureen's free inspirational guide,* Opening the Door to Hope, *at www.esdeer.com/hope or visit www.esdeer.com.*

ORGANIZING FOR A NEW LIFE

Anne McGurty

Since 2002 I have spent my professional life being a productivity consultant and professional organizer, working with executives and other busy people helping them strategize and organize their businesses and their personal lives. Little did I know that I would have to use my skills of helping others create balance in their lives with my biggest life challenge to date: breast cancer.

It was 2010, and lives and businesses were beginning to rebound after the recession. I was a single, female, 48-year-old, self-employed consultant. I had been having a rough enough time of it, like everyone else, but I felt the turn in business. I decided 2010 was going to be the year to get back into the routine of taking care of myself.

I was going to take a vacation, catch up on dental care and doctor's appointments, and enjoy the Colorado outdoors. In May I took a wonderful, relaxing vacation, visiting one of my sisters in eastern Massachusetts. One of the highlights was taking a drive to southern New Hampshire, spending the morning picking blueberries.

As I was moving forward on my goal to take care of myself, I scheduled my annual mammography. I had been ruthless about mammograms as my mom had been diagnosed at 52 and died at 62 of breast cancer. I was living my life very differently—healthy foods, exercise, and no smoking or drinking.

After my mammogram, everything changed. The routine was not routine. I received a call to return for a biopsy. I'd had an ultrasound in the past, but no big deal. A biopsy sounded different. I had lost a lot of weight (about 45 pounds) over the last couple of years, so for sure I thought it was a fat deposit floating in my breast somewhere. I was feeling more inconvenienced than concerned.

The experience of the biopsy was freaky. I remember lying in what felt like an upside-down massage table with holes for my breasts to hang down, not a nurturing massage table, but much more clinical. The doctor's assistant was trying to be comforting and assured me it was most likely just a calcification. I was lying there wondering, *What is a calcification, really? Who knows these words? Why am I wasting my time if it's no big deal? How much is this costing me?* I didn't mind catching up on medical stuff, but I certainly wasn't planning to use my entire $5,000 deductible in one month! I was starting to fear that this biopsy might be a bigger deal than I realized.

The next day I was with a client. We were at a perfect break point when the phone rang. I answered the call and a woman introduced herself. It was the call everyone dreads. All I heard was, "Dr. blah blah blah ... was out and felt we needed to call you right away." The voice proceeded to tell me, "We have your results. DCIS ... blah blah blah ... cancer ... blah blah blah ... you need to make an appointment with a surgeon right away." I'm listening and thinking, *Who is this person, and how does she know this information? This can't be true. Yeah, my mom had cancer, but not me!*

My emotions were running rampant, from anger to self-pity to panic. I was angry because I was healthy; I did everything right—hot yoga, bike riding, eating all the right foods. The self-pity showed up as *Why me?* I flashed through my life wondering what I was doing wrong. Then panic set in. *How will I be able to pay all these medical bills? Will a man ever love me if I lose my breasts? Will I be able to serve my clients and maintain a professional business? It's really happening. I've got breast cancer just like Mom. But I'm not married with a husband and children to support me. How on earth am I going to manage all of this drama?* I realized I needed to get present, be in the moment, and deal with the client at hand.

At the end of the call, I was frozen with all these emotions and also totally aware that my client was in the next office. My mind was racing how to find the words and body language to be the strong, collected consultant maintaining her composure. After all, I'm all about "looking good." I had to move on.

I took a huge breath and walked into Whitney's office, perched my butt on the edge of an adjacent desk, and said, "I need to tell you something shocking that just happened." My body was tight and trembling. The desk supported me; I could feel every bone in my body, even the little facial bones, ready to snap. Here it was my client's first day with me, it was only me and her. I was supposed to be this image of professional excellence. I silently chanted a prayer, "God, please say and do for me what I cannot say and do for myself!"

As I told Whitney of my call, I completely broke down crying. I couldn't get the words out. She jumped from her chair and hugged me and consoled me as I cried like a baby in her arms. At that moment, it was impossible not to accept the reality of my news. Here the journey began with an almost total stranger supporting me as I sobbed and trembled. She helped me pack up my computer and belongings, so I could go on my way to start my new project to strategize and organize my crisis of cancer. How on earth I drove the couple of miles back to my condo is beyond me. I was in complete shock. I knew I was not in enough control to use my cell phone, so I focused my eyes on the road and held the steering wheel as tight as I could on the drive home.

I quickly realized that I didn't have a lot of time to wallow in fear and self-pity, as there were so many things to do. The pragmatic part of me kicked into high gear. I told myself I could cry while I'm doing all of these things, but I had to keep moving. In the midst of my vulnerability and absolute terror, I knew that focusing on the business part would help me deal with what needed to be done. Or was that just my way of denying my feelings? Either way, it was time to start making lists.

I needed to gather a support group and find others who could relate to what I was going through. I called my insurance company and found out what my options and coverage were, and what resources were available to me. I created a notebook to organize all of my doctor's information, receipts, insurance paperwork, and claims. I found a breast surgeon. I made the decision whether to have a lumpectomy versus a mastectomy. Because my mother had a lumpectomy and radiation and died, I chose the mastectomy, followed by reconstruction.

I then had to find a plastic surgeon. All I kept thinking was that my new breasts had to be perfect. What size should they be, bigger or smaller? In a sick kind of way, I was excited. I kept thinking that one of the reasons I didn't want the lumpectomy and radiation was because I didn't want my breasts to be scarred from the burning of radiation. The vanity was overriding the fear of the surgery, which in retrospect may have been protecting my feelings of actually losing my breasts, or even acknowledging the reality of the cancer diagnosis.

I also needed to find an oncologist. I became so preoccupied with the surgery and the reconstruction piece I had forgotten to choose an oncologist. Oddly enough, no one else had mentioned seeing an oncologist. I had this strange underlying feeling that maybe this diagnosis was a mistake and I was being too trustworthy; therefore, I interviewed several oncologists. I fell in love with Dr. Acharya Radhika. This may have had something to do with the little necklace she wore. It looked like it was a gold angel and made me feel protected. I felt that my mom was there with me. Dr. Radhika confirmed I had cancer.

I then got my finances in order. I met with an accountant and figured out a way to keep everything in order and explore possibilities for supporting myself.

I also had to figure out how to notify my clients. I wondered, *Will it devastate my business if they know I'm sick? Will I become known as "the consultant with cancer?" How am I going to make business decisions, prospect new clients? How can I help others when I don't even know if I'm going to be mentally or physically available?* I chose to deal with it case-by-case, day-by-day, and email-by-email.

People were more empathetic than I ever expected. I was not prepared for the outpouring of offers to make meals, run errands, and take me to appointments. I had no idea the depth of friendships I had through my business network.

The next item on my list was food. How was I going to eat? My healthy diet was a huge part of my self-care. I cherished my three daily meals, my abundant vegetables and fruits. How was I going to have the energy to shop every day? I was determined not to get slothful and start binging on ice cream and glue myself in front of the television with Diet Coke and bags of popcorn. I would not let this get the best of me. My food program was important to me, so I documented my needs and was explicit with everyone who helped me on how to prepare my food. I have been so gratified that my requests were honored.

Next, I recognized the need for mental, physical, and massage therapy. Through my network, I learned of a counselor who provided free counseling. I booked an appointment immediately. I was also guided to a physical therapist that specialized in breast cancer treatment.

I also needed a living will. Without a family of my own, I had never really worried much about a will; however, the living will became much more significant. The upcoming surgery was a powerful reminder of mortality. Who was going to help me function while I was bedridden in recovery, not after one surgery, but two? And if there were signs of more cancer, what would happen? It was all becoming so overwhelming.

Somehow there was a smile on my face most of the time. But when I was alone, the anxiety and tears, the panic as I hyperventilated, and the fear were almost paralyzing. I was supposed to be in control, after all; I taught people to take care of themselves. I finally succumbed to a couple of tear-crazed phone calls to friends and family. I'm grateful to my sisters, Catherine and Mary, for those times when all I could do was just cry into the phone.

The next phase of my breast cancer came post surgically. The blessing was that the pathology reports from the breast tissue and seven lymph nodes came back clean, meaning all cancer had been removed. No chemotherapy, radiation, or tamoxifen! I should have been ecstatic, but I was so focused on the reconstruction and what lay ahead, I could barely celebrate. Just a few weeks down and I should be back to work, or so I thought. Easier said than done. I remember mornings lying in bed feeling like I had a steel bullet-proof vest on my chest. It was a chore just to roll out of bed. I had help for three weeks, but I don't even remember the first two.

Initially, the reconstruction surgery was a huge dis-appointment. My support system that helped me with the first surgery evaporated. I was in denial and minimized my needs as I approached the second surgery. It was scheduled and I was in and out in almost no time, except for a week of anesthesia fog. There were no calls, no emails. In retrospect, I realized I didn't tell people what was happening. I fell back into my "looking good" mode.

Accepting my new body image was also hard. Big surprise here, the expectations the plastic surgeon set up were completely shattered. I was horrified with the lack of symmetry, the oddness of scar tissue pulling on my muscles. I couldn't possibly imagine how the doctor screwed up so much. He assured me it would all fall into place. Swelling affects the appearance and surgeries take time to recover from. I sure wish the plastic surgeon had told me this upfront.

The first month after the surgery, I cried every day and vented my anger to anyone who would listen. Yes, they're perky and tight, but the voluptuousness of my breasts was gone. I prayed every day for acceptance of my new body and gratitude that my cancer was gone. The reality was that here I was, almost 50 years old, and I was finally just accepting my wonderful body. I had to think that now that I had this new body, it may be time to embrace it and love it and take care of it. The good news is that the plastic surgeon was right; it took a couple of months, but my breasts came to look more natural.

Then there's dating again. How was this going to work? I couldn't even think about how long it was going to be before I felt accepted in this realm. No need to stop living though, so I updated my online profile and got back out there. I was quickly reminded that my clothes didn't fit quite the same. I was extremely frustrated, and still am at times, with how to be comfortable with my "look," as it is a different silhouette. Necklaces and scarves do lie on my neck and chest better. Finally, a plus! Mr. Right is still out there and he's going to love my new body.

Back on that morning of July 23, 2010, after my diagnosis, I remember stumbling into my kitchen to make breakfast, weeping and asking God for guidance as to what I needed to do differently in my life to walk through this new life. I truly believe in my heart that there are lessons to be learned by every experience and it is my job to be aware of what needs to be learned. If I don't learn something through this process, I believe another lesson will be presented until I figure it out. The rules of my life have changed, and I'm willing to be guided. Maybe the lesson is that I am more than a body!

The key to my success through this journey has been to practice the principles I've taught my clients over the years and apply them to my life. I no longer have the body I used to, and I still am almost afraid to look in the mirror or therapeutically massage my breasts as I've been instructed to practice daily. I know in my heart to be grateful that I have been spared radiation, chemotherapy, and tamoxifen. I am blessed.

I've been through a major life-changing illness. Have I been courageous? I've made it through; I haven't dug myself into a hole emotionally or professionally. I keep showing up and have chosen to take the high road. And I am cancer free today. I have cosmetic options to deal with the vanity. I know it is okay to cry sometimes as I build my strength and move forward. When I look at pictures of myself, I still have tears, as I am saddened by the frailness that I see in my body today. I know there is still pain in my heart as I move forward, but I know I don't want to stay in the pain and it's temporary. I'm looking forward to getting to the root of the transformation in my life as a result of this process, as I know I will have more to share with others on this journey of recovery.

Anne McGurty is the founder and CEO of Strategize & Organize, a productivity training and consulting firm, and the author of Lost in Your Own Office: Tips for Getting Organized. *Anne is a keynote speaker, using her own life story to teach organizations how to prepare their employees for high productivity by helping them streamline their productivity and business functions in a systematic and repeatable way. She is a member of the National Speakers Association and past-president of the Colorado chapter of the National Association of Professional Organizers. She lives in Denver. www.AnneMcGurty.com.*

LANDSLIDE

Aspen DeCew

There were only two words on the other end of the line.

"Shawn's dead."

On May 16, 2010, my 28-year-old nephew, Shawn André DeCew, hiked to the top of a mountain with two friends. He knelt down to photograph a flower, as he so often did, when the ground gave way. He fell 200 feet to his death.

It was incomprehensible. My brother, Larry, was in disbelief… his son was gone. By the time I arrived at my brother's home near Salem, Oregon, he was immersed in the preparations for the memorial. He asked if I would help him to create a playlist of songs to be played after the memorial, something that would support everyone in letting go and grieving. We chose song after song that would facilitate this and muddled our way through our emotions with each song that reminded us of Shawn and his amazing life.

I felt a song gnawing at me. I couldn't remember the name of it or the words. It was like the experience when there is a word on the tip of your tongue and you can feel it. I kept saying, "What is that song?" And then, there it was, in my iTunes library. Without making the connection to what the title was saying, I knew I had found the song. I hit the play button, and Stevie Nicks began to speak…*"THIS IS FOR YOU, DADDY."*

My whole body froze. Then she began to sing, *"I took my love and I took it down; I climbed a mountain and I turned around; and I saw my reflection in a snow covered hill 'til the landslide brought me down."*

I couldn't hit the pause button fast enough.

Suddenly, I was aware of the title of the song: "LANDSLIDE." Prior to that, I not only had no recollection of the title, I had no memory of the words, the musician, or the message, just a feeling that there was a song I needed to find. I instantly felt it was a message for my brother. *"This is for you, Daddy,"* not as a bad nightmare or a morbid description of his death, but somehow a description of the gift of his life AND the purpose of his death. *"I took my love and I took it down."*

For obvious reasons, the song didn't make the playlist for the memorial CD. It hit way too close to home, but it most definitely made my playlist of "Shawn's Songs." I listened to all of the songs over and over. They were my healing, and I was compelled by every one of them. But the one I listened to the most was the one that began with, *"This is for you, Daddy."* The more I listened to "Landslide," the more the message for my brother seemed to come through. What I didn't realize was that there was a specific message in this song for me and my life—a different one.

In fact, the message had begun to emerge at the memorial. As each friend spoke about Shawn, I was in awe. Story after story was shared about how large his life was and, especially, how he contributed to others simply by how he "took in" life and experienced his own to the fullest. The uniqueness of his soul was palpable and his reverence for life undeniable. As I listened, something unexpected happened within me; I had this unsettling feeling that my life didn't have a lot of meaning.

This made no sense. I had been living my passion for years, helping people uncover the barriers to their lives. My work truly was my play. I loved speaking, teaching, holding retreats and seminars, and I had always known the life-changing impact I had on so many. So why did I feel that my life was less than meaningful?

I was now back in Colorado, two weeks had passed since Shawn's death, and Memorial Day was approaching. There was no question that I wanted to be in the place Shawn loved the most, the place where I would feel the closest to him. The mountains. So I booked a condo in Aspen and set aside the weekend to do nothing but connect to Shawn and his extraordinary life.

Partway there, I was mesmerized by what I can only describe as a cathedral of tall mountains. They were the backdrop to a beautiful lake just off the road, but what caught my attention was that these mountains were covered with snow. In an instant, I was taken back to the words of "Landslide." *"If you see my reflection in the snow covered hill...."* My heart began to pound and I had to pull over. I scrambled through the tracks of the CD and the song began to play. I couldn't take my eyes off of Shawn's reflection in the snow covered hill. The tears began to fall, and they fell in buckets. I now had the space to connect to my own grief and loss and be present to the reality of what had happened to Shawn. He was gone. Yet, as I listened to the song, it was as if he were right there speaking the words to me, telling me what happened.

I took my love and I took it down;
I climbed a mountain and I turned around,
and I saw my reflection in a snow covered hill,
til the landslide brought me down.

As the song continued, it was as if I was hearing the questions that Shawn had asked of his soul about the life he so loved.

Mirror in the sky…what is love?
Can the child within my heart rise above?
Can I sail through the changing ocean tides?
Can I handle the seasons of my life?
I don't know.
I've been afraid of changing,
because I built my life around you;
but time makes you bolder,
children get older and I'm getting older too.
So take this love…..and take it down.

As I played the song over and over, the words that had been a message from Shawn about his death began to morph into a direct message for me about my life. This was about my own landslide. I didn't know exactly what that meant at the time, but I could feel it.

In the weeks prior to Shawn's death, I had become aware that something inside me had changed abruptly. Throughout the past eight years, there had been a natural evolution, growth, and recognition of my work. I had just launched a major project in the Denver area, and everything was expanding. Yet I had hit some kind of a wall. Everything I had worked towards suddenly had this air of completion. I had no tangible evidence of this, but my heart sank into my gut that day on the mountain, and I had this strange but certain feeling I was being called to let go of everything I had created.

There had been years of cultivating awareness around my work, almost a decade of developing significant and solid relationships with my clients and students. And, now, as a result of my influence, over a hundred of them had gone on to train and pursue the powerful work I had brought to them, so they could bring it to others. My work had just reached the peak of a momentum I had been cultivating for years so it didn't make sense why I felt like my time in Denver was complete. And yet what occurred to me was that perhaps this was all I was to do. The work could be carried on by others, and maybe my time in Denver was done.

Underlying all of this something else was going on. I had this feeling of not wanting to expand any further. In fact, I found myself wanting to retreat. I felt depleted but didn't know why. Was it that menopause thing I kept hearing about? Was it some kind of burnout? Had I given too much? Was it that I didn't have enough support? I had no idea where this was coming from, but it was clear that I no longer wanted a big life. I wanted a quiet, simple one.

I've been afraid of changing,
because I built my life around you;
but time makes you bolder,
children get older and I'm getting older too.

As the summer months passed, I found myself feeling more and more lost. The question that emerged at the memorial remained unanswered. Why, with all I had contributed, did I feel that my life was less than meaningful? I kept wondering how I could feel such little inspiration about something I had always been so passionate about and how that could seemingly change over night. I was scared, but all I could do was surrender to what was happening within me.

In early July, I traveled to Southern California to find solace at the ocean. I spent hours in Yogananda's Gardens overlooking the vast and open sea, contemplating my life and reflecting on Shawn's life. I realized the kindred spirits that we were. I was all about helping others to truly live, to truly feel and experience their lives, and I did this by helping them remove the inner barriers to their happiness. Shawn did nothing but show people life, and it happened by virtue of his contagious enthusiasm for life and his eagerness to share it with others.

He was wide-eyed and awestruck about everything. His thirst for knowledge and the adventures he created on a daily basis were magnetic. He showed people life and what it meant to live, especially through nature and with what he saw through the lens of his camera.

Shawn was so clearly living his passion and I was living mine, but there was something powerful his life was reflecting to me. There was no question that my work excited me, fulfilled me, and had my attention on every level. Whether I was teaching a seminar, at a speaking engagement, or working privately with clients, I was in my bliss. The massive changes that were happening in people's lives were so fascinating and rewarding to watch and to be a part of that I hadn't noticed how much of life I wasn't living.

But that wasn't the only thing. The past eight years of developing my work resulted in speaking on bigger stages, working with a number of high-profile individuals and experiencing my own heightened visibility. The expansion, while exciting, came at a velocity and with an intensity that required ALL of my energy. There was nothing left for living. Contributing certainly brought purpose to my life, but my interests and my experiences had become very narrow. I was missing so much of the joy and diversity that life has to offer. Here I was, bringing life to others, but I wasn't living.

It was when I was looking out over the ocean in Yogananda's Gardens that I began to understand why my life seemed less than meaningful that day at Shawn's memorial. My thoughts returned to the trip to Aspen on Memorial Day weekend, sitting in my car and staring at the snow covered hill. I recalled hearing the word "sabbatical" repeatedly and relentlessly, as if Shawn were suggesting to me to take one. I remembered taking one deep breath after another. My whole body relaxed as I imagined what that would be like. I felt a deep longing for that kind of rest and spaciousness, and I recalled on that day seeing myself walking in beautiful, peaceful gardens, perhaps the gardens that I was in now by the ocean.

I knew it was time for me to step back and pause and rest. It was time for me to discover if I could contribute to others in the big way that my energy seems to generate and still take care of myself—to discover if there was a way to do this and maintain balance in my life. I teach that there is, but now I had to discover if this could work for me.

Can I sail through the changing ocean tides?
Can I handle the seasons of my life?
I don't know…

The idea of a sabbatical continued to come into my periphery into the autumn months. I wondered if it was just a fantasy, a nice place to go in my mind. I couldn't conceive of how I could leave everything, especially all the people I was committed to. And I couldn't see how this could happen from a practical and financial standpoint. It didn't seem possible. But I knew this place I had arrived at wasn't just about taking a vacation or making some adjustments. This was about a radical change. I knew that I needed to create enough space to truly step back and discover what I wanted for my life, and not just do tomorrow what I did yesterday, simply because I did it yesterday.

Could I really walk away from everything? And what was I walking towards, if anything? I knew that in order to find out, I had to step into a bigger void than I had ever faced.

Mirror in the sky…what is love?
Can the child within my heart rise above?

A switch had been flipped inside of me and I knew I couldn't go back. Nothing about this was logical. I had no idea where I was headed, yet I had this sense I would be taken to a better place, as Shawn had been. It was clear on so many levels that he was not afraid.

At the memorial, Shawn's friends told us that as the ground gave way and he fell backwards, they tried to reach for him. They said that as he fell, he looked into their eyes, and that as they looked back into his, there was nothing but incredible peace and surrender. The funeral director said in all her years of taking care of those who had been in accidents, she had never seen such an "aura of peace" on someone's face.

I vowed to transition into this new place in my life with the same peace and surrender that Shawn transitioned into his. One thing was very clear. I was no longer willing to bring anything into my experience that would take me away from my joy and from truly living.

I am deeply grateful that "Landslide" forced its way into my consciousness on the day my brother and I created the playlist. I have returned to it many times. Not only had the words that seemed to be about Shawn's life and death morphed into a direct message for me about my life, something else had emerged in the final lyrics. In the last verse, the entire song shifted. It was like an invitation, as if Shawn were saying to me:

So take my love and take it down.
If YOU climb a mountain...and YOU turn around.,
And if YOU see my reflection in a snow covered hill,
Well maybe...maybe the landslide will bring YOU down.

It was Shawn's landslide and death that showed me my life. Shawn gave me the courage to fall from the mountain I had climbed and to allow my own landslide to occur so I could transition to a new place, a new life. It is now day 27 of a year-long sabbatical. I write the final words of this chapter from a secluded cabin, surrounded by nothing but winter snow, towering trees, a river, and, most importantly, the solitude my soul needs.

I am listening to my inner rhythms. My days are filled with walks in the snow, discovery, meditation, organic food, music, yoga, candle-lit salt baths, lots of reading, writing, dancing, and just space. Every activity has been a ritual of self-care, and I have made inner peace my priority.

By the time this goes to print, I will have moved to a remote cabin in the pristine mountains of Aspen for the second phase of my sabbatical, and this chapter...will be the first of many I will write.

So take this love and take it down. If you climb a mountain and you turn around, and you see my reflection in the snow covered hill, well maybe...maybe the landslide will bring you down.

Excerpts from "Landslide" by Stevie Nicks.

Aspen DeCew is a speaker, facilitator, writer, and teacher of consciousness. She is known for her unique transformational work and is a mentor to many who are following in her footsteps in the U.S. and abroad. Aspen has been a featured speaker with Peak Potentials, the largest success training company in North America and on numerous "new thought" stages including the Chopra Center. She works with influential leaders, celebrities, and all consciousness-seeking individuals. Aspen holds international retreats and is currently on sabbatical in Aspen, Colorado. She can be reached at www.TrulyConscious.com/aspen-in-aspen.html

MY FATHER, MYSELF

Mira Rubenstein

The phone rang after 11:00 p.m. on November 2, 1995. I was deep in a dream; my daughter Willow answered the call. She came into my room and woke me up. With a worried expression on her face, she said it was Uncle Chucky calling. When I took the phone, my brother told me our father had died a few hours earlier. He'd taken a nap after dinner, and when my mother came in to wake him up to watch "Jeopardy," he was gone. There were airplane tickets waiting for Willow and me, and my brother asked if I wanted to write a eulogy.

I went downstairs in a daze, poured myself a glass of cabernet, and sat down at the dining room table. I found myself softly singing a favorite Leonard Cohen song, "Bird on a Wire":

Like a bird on a wire
Like a drunk in a midnight choir
I have tried, in my way, to be free.
Like a fish on a hook
Like a knight in an old-fashioned book,
I have saved all my ribbons for thee.
And if I, if I have been unkind,
I hope that you will just let it go by,
And if I, if I have been untrue
I hope you know that it was not you…

By the time I got to the last verse, I was crying without restraint.
But I swear by this song
And by all that I have done wrong
That I will, I will make it all, all up to you.

I was crying as much for his death as I was for the relief that he *had* let me make it up to him, and that I had let *him* make it up to *me*. I had lost my father more than once in my life, and though this was the final loss, it was only the physical one. We had found our way back to one another before he died, and I was very grateful.

I was pulling apart albums, taking out photos and other artifacts, letting memories wash over me. There were letters he'd written to his mother in Pittsburgh, my grandmother Sadie, telling her about my birth. He wrote about the first thing he'd noticed about me, that I had hands like my mother's and that, born one month before my due date, I looked "smaller than the chicken we had in the refrigerator."

There was the picture taken in our one-bedroom Bronx apartment, the drapes closed and my brother and I in our pajamas, sitting on the floor with my father kneeling between us, my arm draped around his shoulder, all of us with big smiles on our faces.

There was the photo of my father and brother and me, in the big four-foot-deep swimming pool at Castle Hill Beach Club playing the "whale" game. We'd all be in the pool and my father would dive under water, trying to grab our feet, and we'd be splashing around shrieking, "The whale! The whale!" trying to escape, laughing and breathless.

There were memories of my father telling us made-up bedtime stories, rubbing our backs, telling us his pun-filled "daddy jokes" as he tucked us into bed. I remembered him helping me with my jacket, pretending to be annoyed at the long braid hanging down my back, saying, "Get that old ponytail outta here!" There were postcards from vacation road trips through New England, memories of my father relaxed and enjoying the drive, despite his kids' backseat shenanigans. This was the father I'd loved without reservation, the one who'd loved me the same way.

Then I unearthed my high school literary magazine. The beginning lines of the poem I'd written in it were:

My father
sees my imperfections
as reflections
of his failures.
And in me he seeks
the perfection he lacks.
My shoulders hurt.

We shared so many similarities—the emotions held just beneath the surface, threatening to seep out at vulnerable moments, the inability to stay quiet when things seemed unfair or unjust, the enjoyment of wordplay that prompted grins and giggles in us and groans in others, the shared insecurities about not quite fitting in. So many connections. But by the time I was in high school, my father and I had become locked in a series of escalating misunderstandings and hurt feelings. I was "trying in my way to be free,"which almost blew our relationship apart.

By age 12 I'd started feeling restricted by being a member of the "Chosen People" and had begun attending my friend's church and temple services with them, in an attempt to find a more inclusive and personal path to God. My father's Judaism was his foundation, and it pained him that his daughter apparently found it lacking. By age 16 I'd become a vegetarian as a matter of conscience, and my father felt I was rejecting the food he and my mother had worked to put on the table. The multicolored, elaborately embroidered, ethnically patterned, and vintage clothing I arrayed myself in was an embarrassment to my mother, and it was up to my father to protect her from embarrassment. And so it went.

When I fell in love for the first time, not with a nice Jewish boy but with a Chinese-American artist and poet from my high school creative writing class, my father was not exactly pleased. When, on the eve of my high school graduation, my parents discovered that I'd been spending most of my summer weekends with this boy at his family's Fire Island summer house, and not at the summer house of a girlfriend, as I'd led them to believe, I experienced what it was like to have my father withdraw himself completely. It felt like I'd had all the breath knocked out of me. It was hard to take a deep breath without my entire chest hurting. It took an entire summer for my father to recover from what he perceived as my betrayal, and for me to feel like I could exhale.

When I was a senior in high school, my spiritual search had led me to a new teacher and initiation into an ancient meditation practice. I finally felt the inner connection I'd been looking for. But I tried to make sure my parents were asleep first before I sat down to meditate. The idea of my practicing meditation, of having an Indian spiritual teacher, was incomprehensible to both of them, especially to my father.

As dismaying as this was to me, when I learned that my teacher would be taking a group of his students to his ashram in India for a month-long retreat the following year, I felt an overwhelming pull to accompany him. I believed that, in time, my parents would come to understand. Though my parents understandably refused to give me permission, I nonetheless felt I had to go.

I worked all summer to come up with the $435 for the trip, obtained a passport and visa, and entered college in the fall. I made up a story about a college—sponsored study trip to French Canada that I wanted to take part in. My parents gave me permission to go, relieved that I'd put the "India business" behind me. I let a couple of friends know what I was really up to, just in case. When the time came, I packed a suitcase and had my parents drop me off at the Port Authority bus terminal, where I'd told them I was meeting the school group. When my parents finally left (after it seemed like they never would), I took the subway to a friend's house and he drove me to Kennedy Airport, where I got on the plane for India.

Being in India with my teacher and 3,000 other students was life-changing. The experiences I had in meditation confirmed and deepened every connection I'd ever felt to what I knew of God. I made lifelong friendships with like-minded students. I basked in the beauty of the rose gardens, the tranquility of the ashram grounds. When the month was finally over, I returned home to parents who looked as if they had aged 10 years in my absence… and a father who felt he could never trust me again. I had lied to them, I had caused them weeks of worry, and it seemed like I cared more about "the guru" than I did about them. My mother tried to understand my motivations and eventually forgave me for my deception. But my father was too wounded. We circled around each other for months before we could begin to connect again, however tentatively. Who was this daughter he no longer knew? Who was this father who didn't even try to understand me?

I returned to college and kept meditating. After changing majors three times, I somehow managed to graduate and moved to Denver for a Waldorf preschool teaching job. I met Bill, who was teaching outdoor recreation in the upper school, and we dated casually, enjoying the same books, movies, and music, sharing the same spiritual practice and political views. Then, despite our precautions, I became pregnant. Unplanned or not, I felt very happy to be pregnant. I was 24 years old, believed I was in love, was meditating every day, and trusted that even though Bill and I came from different backgrounds (he'd been raised Irish Catholic in Iowa), we had enough love and enough in common to make a marriage work.

I called my parents to tell them the news that I was getting married in a couple of months, and that, oh, by the way, they were going to be grandparents. Bill and I were planning a homemade, potluck, outdoor wedding celebration. My mother and maternal grandmother responded to the news by making plane reservations and buying new dresses. This type of wedding wasn't what they'd had in mind for me, but still, I was getting married! My father responded by following the old Jewish custom and sitting shiva for me. I was marrying a Catholic, and I was pregnant; as far as he was concerned I was officially dead to him.

Bill's family welcomed me warmly, and my mother and grandmother regularly called and sent me baby clothes and asked after my pregnancy. But if my father happened to answer the phone when I called, he'd simply say, "Just a minute, I'll get your mother." Only once, when I was about seven months pregnant, did he let the words slip, "How are you feeling?" I told him I was feeling healthy and happy, but that I missed him terribly. I held my breath. Then he said, "Just a minute, I'll get your mother."

After Willow was born and I would bring her home to visit, my father was enchanted with her. She had his grey-blue eyes and mischievous playfulness. They played peek-a-boo and hide-and-seek around the apartment; at night he told her the same bedtime stories he'd once told me. But I was still the daughter who had died to him, and he said as little to me as possible.

Meanwhile, after four years of marriage, I was feeling lonelier than I ever had in my life. Bill and I had little if any remaining emotional intimacy, and most of our conversations had become filled with sarcasm and misunderstanding. The differences between us that were once so intriguing were eroding whatever good feelings were once there. One night, when Bill was out with his friends, I called my mother and admitted what was happening in my marriage. Then I asked to speak to my father. "I don't know if he'll talk to you," she warned, but brought him to the phone.

"What do you want from me?" he asked. I broke down. "I want you to be my father. I need you to love me."

My father's next words were like a cold stake in my heart. "I can't. Whatever love I once had for you has died. You killed it." Then he put my mother back on the phone. I couldn't speak.

Bill and I divorced, and I went into therapy, gradually beginning to understand and have compassion for my father's pain as well as my own. My therapist also provided the practical direction I was lacking, encouraging me to enter into a graduate program in counseling psychology. I took his advice. The following Easter Sunday, Willow was with her father and I was working on a paper when my mother called and told me my father had just been taken to the hospital with a heart attack. I was on the next plane to New York.

When I got to the hospital and saw my father lying in bed, hooked up to tubes and catheters, looking old and small, I felt whatever grievances and resentments I was still harboring melt away. I stood in the doorway of his room while he slept and whispered, "I love you, Daddy. I want you to be happy. I know you've been doing your best, that your life hasn't been easy. I'm sorry I hurt you. I never meant to. Please get better."

My father did get better. He underwent months of cardiac rehabilitation, which included learning to manage his irrational thoughts, anger, and hurt feelings. He remarked to my mother, "I guess I need to get over being mad at my daughter."

I increased my visits home. My father told me he was proud of me for "straightening my life out," going to graduate school, becoming a professional counselor, and raising a smart, kind, lovely, and talented daughter.

One morning during a visit, my father took me shopping at the neighborhood EJ Korvette's. I was looking for an overnight bag to take to a family reunion we were all attending. As I examined one of the bags on display, my father made a comment about it in Yiddish. Never having learned Yiddish, I looked at him blankly. He turned to me and said, "You know, sometimes I think that maybe if your mother and I had made more of an effort to be more involved in the synagogue, like I'd wanted us all to be, you would have had something to hold on to and wouldn't have had to go to India to find your answers."

I looked at him and said, "Dad, I was really young. If I'd

known then what I know now, I would have done things a lot differently. I'm really sorry." And he looked at me and said, "I know." And I hugged him.

Grace comes to us in unexpected places. My father and I found it in the luggage department of EJ Korvette's. It was now eight years after his heart attack, and I was ready to write his eulogy. I started it this way: "Thanks for giving me another chance, Daddy."

Mira Rubenstein, MA, CCHt, NLP is a hypnotherapist with a private practice in Denver, Colorado. Born and raised in New York City, she moved to Denver after graduating from college with a BA in English. She received her MA in Counseling Psychology in 1988 and her MA in Education in 2000, and has worked as a professional counselor and teacher of English as a second language. Mira is the proud mother of Willow McCormick and is happily married to Stuart Tessler. Her hobbies and passions include singing, reading, language, taking rambling walks with friends, and traveling with her husband.

SPEAKING MY TRUTH MISSED BY JUST ONE DAY

✳ ✳ ✳

Mary Lou Johnson

"If I knew that today would be my last day, I would not be sorry for the way I had spent it."

My sister, Karen, said this to me at her front door when I was leaving with my family after a special evening together on her patio. I smiled and gave her a gentle goodbye hug. I did not realize its significance at that moment. The plan was to be together again the next day.

She had just been put on end-of-life hospice care after battling ovarian cancer for 13 years. After years of hope, reprieve, and denial, it was now indisputable that the cancer had won. Now it was a matter of time. She—and we—were told she had only weeks to months to live.

Karen loved many people, many things, and many places. One of the places she had wanted to return to was Kailua-Kona, Hawaii. She had tried to fit in a trip between treatments and doctor appointments over a period of several months. In one rare window of opportunity, she was thwarted by the news that there were no rental cars on the island. No available rental cars kept my sister from making her last trip.

This was a phenomenal denial of opportunity for a woman who had traveled myriad places for work and for pleasure. She had been a flight attendant for 30-plus years. Starting in college, she visited Europe. Then came Alaska and the climb up Mt. McKinley. Australia. New Zealand. Indonesia. Mexico. South Korea. Japan. China. New York City. There were many trips to tropical Hawaii: Maui, Kauai, Oahu, Molokai, and The Big Island of Hawaii. In contrast, there was the trip with me to stay in the Ice Hotel in Sweden north of the Arctic Circle. There were also numerous annual trips to explore the Boundary Waters by canoe. Perhaps her most special trip was to Bora Bora, staying in a little hut perched over the water, that had a glass floor for viewing sea life.

How could a woman dying of cancer be denied her chosen final trip of her lifetime? Since she couldn't travel to Hawaii, we brought Kona to her.

In a flash of inspiration, we convinced my mother, also a lifelong traveler who had not traveled in about eight years due to my father's physical difficulties, to make the trip from Ohio to Denver. She had to make arrangements for the care of my father who, 30 years older than my sister, had been put on end-of-life hospice on the very same day.

An invitation was hastily prepared on the computer: the clip-art palm tree was accompanied by the message: Kona Comes to Karen.

Everyone in the family was told to wear a tropical shirt. Everyone complied. Check.

Plates with a tropical motif were in Karen's cabinet, and appropriate napkins were bought. Check.

We brought over our neon-lighted palm tree for ambiance and wrapped the umbrella pole on the patio table with artificial hibiscus flowers. Check.

I sourced a floral shop on the west side of Denver with family ties to Hawaii that made hand-strung, real-orchid leis. I made the lengthy drive and bought three—one for Karen, one for Mom, and one for Karen's longtime partner. The other two females, my daughter and me, as well as my husband, our son, and our daughter's boyfriend, all wore fake leis from a party store.

Sushi was the featured food along with pineapple, edamame, taro chips, and Mai Tais. Karen's pain and reduced stomach space limited her to about three pieces of her beloved sushi. She had to take an uncharacteristic break for pain management before we indulged in dessert. She took a few bites while clutching a heating pad below her ribs.

After this festive and rewarding dinner together, we said our brief goodbyes and all went to our separate homes. We had made plans to get together on her patio again the next morning for a brunch with her favorite bagels.

I had bought a special card for her. Once home, I wrote her a note on this card that had a stylized "stairway to heaven" illustration on the front with the ocean's waves breaking lightly on the shore and a white dove landing lightly near the bottom stair. I don't recall when I had bought this note card.

My handwritten note said, "August, 2010. Dear Karen, We are thinking of you now and forever after your lifetime of climbing has taken you to the very top step. We join you in wanting an end to your pain. We will cry forever over losing you too soon. You will always have our love. I love you so much!" I added the names of everyone in my family.

We printed a photo from our "evening in Kona" which I included with the card. I also included this letter to her which I had written with much emotion:

Dear Karen,

I have written this letter to you several times in my mind when I am awakened by my thoughts and tears. The tears are with me as I write. I hope all of my thoughts represent themselves as I try to type them here. I don't want to leave out anything.

It is incomprehensible to me that soon you will be taken from our midst...into the mist of our collective tears. And you will be deeply missed.

You and I have always railed against unfairness. Cancer is an unfair adversary. It allowed you to fight, but it did not allow you to win. It doesn't, and it didn't, play by our rules of fairness.

Denial has been such a good friend to me until recently when she abruptly turned on her heel and walked away. With this companion at my side, I never allowed myself to think that you wouldn't continue to be here with me—with all of us—for at least the next 20 to 30 years.

As sisters growing up in northeast Ohio, I always thought we would grow old together. While fairly young, I pictured a cabin in Canada that we would go to for getaways. I didn't know anything about Canada. I didn't consider other options. I was just trying to imagine a place that would take us from our mundane, everyday lives. I guess that fantasy "cabin" became actualized by our visits to your home in Breckenridge, our trips to our Grand Lake cabin, and our stays in our "Hawaii House" in Kona.

I do understand why humans desperately want to believe in heaven—in an afterlife. People want to be with and around their loved ones forever. The opposite, not being together anymore, is incomprehensible and unbearable. I wish we believed in heaven. It might make this process easier.

But, there will be an afterlife of memories. You have helped us so much by putting together the creative albums of your life and ours. We can take out those albums whenever we want to and feel your presence.

And you will be included in the making of future memories. We will speak of you at our family gatherings. You will be included in our celebrations of birthdays, Christmas, and the times that bring joy, such as if and when there is a new grandniece or grandnephew, events you have mentioned you are sad that you will miss.

When we visit or pass by your home, the beautiful plants in your front yard will remind us of the care you put into selecting, planting, nurturing, and enjoying them. We will remember how much you wanted to see their growth each year.

Here are some memories and thanks from me to you.

I will always remember playing together — "buck buck" with a back-and-forth ball in your bedroom, jai lai in the backyard, ping pong in the basement, and riding bikes — even when we got into trouble for riding too far from home.

I will always remember wanting to do what you had done.

Some things I managed to do — like going to the same Girl Scout camps and unit. Remember Ken Jockety and the bicycle trip? I was so proud to have a bike (yours) to ride that had one extra gear for hill-climbing. It was unique and special at the time. It was amazing what one low gear could do. I was "special" because of you. I loved the primitive camping unit at Camp Ledgewood. I loved my full-summer travel in Europe on $10 a day. All of these things that I followed you in doing stretched me and helped me grow up and beyond what I knew from our little part of the world.

Some things I couldn't achieve — like keeping up with your athletic abilities. Golf remains something I still want to follow you to do. If, like you, I manage to retire from daily work while still young enough to learn new physical skills, I want to follow your example by going to a women's golf camp and then being able to play regularly — and decently. You always coached and encouraged me so much when I did try to play. I will hope to remember some of your encouraging words when I play again.

There is something I didn't want to follow you in — getting ovarian cancer. I was paranoid about it until I got everything surgically removed. I won't get OC, but I will get something someday. We all will die eventually. But we always hope that death will come at a time when we are ready. I wonder now, watching what is happening to you at age 62 and to Dad at age 92, if one is ever "ready" to leave the joys of routine and special life events.

It is so incongruous and surreal that you and Dad are both going through days of agony right now. I hate it for each of you and for all of us. I hate that you have been cheated out of the additional 30 years that should have been in your genes instead of that villainous ovarian cancer.

I had some more dreams and wishes for our future. I always hoped they weren't unrealistic fantasies and that I could actually achieve them. I wanted to show my appreciation to you for the wonderful Subaru you gave me by either paying you back monetarily in one big lump sum or by driving up to your house in a cute little yellow VW bug—like your first car—that you could use as your golfing/fun car. I wanted to succeed in my businesses, and I had wanted you to derive a decent income from the business you had built off of one of mine. These desires have all run out of time to produce the desired outcomes for you. Now I have to make sure that any additional time I put into my entrepreneurial efforts must pay off. I can see that life is too short to spend behind a computer and telephone. I must set a time goal to succeed at or end this work and then stick with it. If and when I do succeed, we will pour a glass of something bubbly for you, too, because I know you would want to share in the cheers.

But, right now, instead of sharing cheers, we are sharing tears. Great big tears of sadness. Rivers of tears of sorrow. How long will we continue to cry after your own tears cease to flow? I think it will be a very long time. You are very special to us in our family.

Karen, thank you for:

Being such a wonderful big sis to me.

Being such a loving, invested, and involved aunt to Katie and Andrew.

Showing us all how to live life fully.

I wish I could ease your physical, mental, and emotional pain. We are all powerless to do that. You and we will be glad to see your pain end, even though it means that you will have had *to give up your life to accomplish it.*

This is going to be so hard for you and for all of us. Tell us what you need if we don't figure it out. Leave us knowing that you have our thanks and lasting love.

With so much love from your heart-broken sister,
Mary Lou

I was all set to take this card, photo, and letter to Karen the next morning. Instead of heading off to our favorite bagel shop, when the unexpected call came, my mother and I headed to the hospice center where Karen had been taken early that morning when her intractable pain would not respond to oral morphine at home.

We found my sister unresponsive in a hospice bed. The hospice doctor talked with us to create a plan to manage her pain to provide her with some comfortable days and weeks. We waited a few hours for her to sleep off her last morphine dose so we could talk with her. Suddenly, the hospice nurse alerted us to a critical change in her breathing that he recognized but which we did not recognize or understand due to our lack of experience. This is what I learned that day: How does an active, vital woman end a full life that was invaded and interrupted by ovarian cancer? With a last shallow breath not followed by another.

What an inspiring woman Karen was to me, my family, her life partner, and her friends. She completely tied up every loose end of her life, literally the day before she died. Every photo was tucked away in special albums she had created. Her last album—the one chronicling her entire life—had just been completed. Her files were in order. Every piece of mail had been addressed. Every bill was paid. Her belongings were all organized and tidy. With help, she had completed all desired house projects: roof, gutters, new front and back doors. Her xeriscaped front yard was in year two. She loved each plant and desperately wanted to see each one grow and flourish over the years. She felt the same way about her niece and nephew—my children—wanting to see how their lives unfolded.

How many people have their lives completely wrapped up before they die? Not many, I think. Though she never gave up the fight, she concurrently moved steadfastly in the direction of completing her life.

I didn't recognize that she had reached the end when we parted at her door that night. I did not realize as I wrote my card and letter to her that night that I would not have the opportunity to give them to her and to tell her directly how much I loved her.

My love letter to my sister remains with me now. Out of the 21,480 days that we were sisters, I lost my chance to tell her my feelings directly by just one day. My advice to you is…tell your sister, or brother, or other loved one today how you really feel about her or him. Speak your true feelings while life gives you the chance.

Mary Lou Brecht Johnson is a daughter, sister, wife, mother, and also a speech-language pathologist, entrepreneur, and author. Her heart is in all of these roles. Truth-speaking is a quality and an activity she tries to improve upon over time. You can learn more at www. HelpYourChildSpeak.com about how Mary Lou guides parents to help their young children learn to talk better. Reach her at MaryLou@ HelpYourChildSpeak.com.

MOONLIGHT SONATA - A REMEMBRANCE

Wendie Batterson

There it is again—*Moonlight Sonata* by Beethoven, playing in the background. It seems to play at the most unusual times. Today it's playing at the coffee shop. Every time I hear that piece, it takes me back to that last time with my dad, being with him as he passed. In a heartbeat I go back, even though that was now almost 20 years ago.

Even before the phone rang that day, I knew it was the dreaded call. It had been coming for a long time. Dad had been physically ill for so long and now was not eating and basically starving himself to death. On top of his heart issues he had major digestive problems, suffering from acute acid reflux. It basically hurt him too much to swallow; he couldn't eat much of anything but clear bouillon and saltine crackers. He had become a shadow of a man and resembled pictures of the Nazi concentration camp prisoners. It broke my heart to see him like that.

My older sisters were handling Dad's illness. "Pops," as the grandkids called him, was close to the point of checking out. They had called hospice in several weeks earlier, and now the phone call came to say, "It's time for you to come." I was the only one of the three sisters who was long distance. My sisters were local and were taking care of our aging parents, both in their 80s and neither doing well. Dad had the physical problems and Mom the mental ones.

I caught the first flight to Pittsburgh, the place where we all had lived as a young family on the "farm" and where our parents' families had lived for generations. I remember thinking, *This is going to be one of the hardest things I've ever done.*

I had always been extremely close to my dad, probably because I was the "renegade child" who continually confronted all of his traditional ideas and values. We would get into heated arguments, "debates" as he liked to call them, about any and all issues, from political agendas to abortion to racial prejudice to whatever. These debates had started in the mid-60s and continued until his acute illness. If the truth be known, these heated conversations kept his mind alive and he enjoyed them immensely. I was the child who frustrated him the most, caused him the most gray hairs and the one he worried about constantly because I was such a rebel. He could relate to my non-conforming essence. After all, he had not exactly "fit the mold" of his parents' expectations either! There was always an underlying bond between us. We were kindred spirits on some level.

As we drove from the airport to our parents' home in the small town north of Pittsburgh, my sisters gave me an update on his impending death, as well as on Mom's stability. According to hospice, Dad's body had started shutting down and it would only be a matter of days until he passed. Mom was totally stressed, in denial and incredibly afraid.

We walked arm in arm up the old porch stairs that still creaked in all the same places, and through the front door of the old white two-story frame house. It was not a happy home anymore and hadn't been for a long time. Our parents were from that generation that naively believed that Medicare and Social Security would take care of them, so they had not planned at all for their retirement, or for any illnesses or normal aging issues along the way. They would have been homeless, or living with one of us and our families, if my middle sister and husband had not stepped in and bought this old home for them. They basically had nothing and it saddened all three of us to see them living their last years like this, even though "his girls" all helped financially as much as we could. Our parents spent what little money they got on their meds and there was nothing left after that.

I remembered the times I had visited and found the refrigerator totally empty, with no food in the house. I immediately would go grocery shopping and stock them up for several months, for as long as the refrigerator would hold the food and it would not spoil. Our parents had lived through the Depression, so I also knew that they would not throw anything away—even if it became a science experiment in the fridge! It was a fine line to walk. When I would bring all of the grocery bags home to them, Dad would be totally irritated that I had spent money on them. His pride would get in the way and, although grateful, he would never utter the words "thanks for helping." I knew he struggled with the pride thing, so the words weren't necessary.

Mom, on the other hand, was like a child on Christmas morning when all of the grocery bags came in the door! We were all concerned about her as well. She had grown more forgetful and childlike, which we naively thought was because she was so stressed about Pops. Shortly after his passing, she was diagnosed with Alzheimer's and we all realized how much Pops had constantly "covered" for her mental lapses.

As my sisters and I climbed the inside stairs of the old, creaky house, I felt the coldness and the sadness immediately. I went to Dad's bedside and he was asleep, drugged for the pain of his body shutting down. I held his hand and kissed him on the forehead. "I'm here now, Pops." I wasn't sure, but I thought I saw a faint smile cross his mouth when I said his nickname. It was so quick that I wasn't sure if I saw it or not, but the corners of his mouth seemed to have turned upwards. *Rascal*, I thought, *always kidding*. The only thing that was missing was the twinkle in his eyes.

I talked to the hospice nurses to make sure that he was comfortable and not suffering, and told them to increase the morphine whenever it was appropriate. I wanted them to know that I was on board with whatever choices they were going to make to help him be more comfortable.

It always astounded me when I went home, facing the austerity of the way my parents were living. For sure, financial planning was not one of Dad's strong suits. Always a "dreamer," he had grown up among the "privileged," thanks to his dad being in the right place at the right time. Grandpa was one of the luckier ones, considered wealthy, who came out of the Depression "smelling like a rose."

Being among the privileged, our dad had been sent off to military school in Virginia when he was only nine years old — put on a train by himself and sent away. I always thought how scary that must have been for him, knowing how vulnerable I had felt at age nine and also having seen my own children at that age. He was a peaceful, caring, and gentle soul, this dad of ours, and I always wondered how he handled the whole military environment. I had heard stories of "severe reprimanding of the lad" while he had been a cadet. He had no choice though; military school was mandated by his mother, a first-generation German immigrant who married very well, according to the standards of that time.

There was so much about Dad's life that made him seem like "a man out of his time"—his privileged upbringing that shaped his inability to deal with life's harsh realities, his pressured choice of career that really did not fit his talents and gifts. Ironically he wound up in a financial job when he chose not to manage his own finances. I had always imagined that he should have been a member of the English gentry in the 1800s—who knows, maybe he had been in a former life. I sighed to myself, such a "*misfit*."

And yet, in so many ways, Dad was truly our knight in shining armor, one of the really good guys, the one who would take on anyone that went against "his girls," the one who would always be there for us. But not for much longer, at least from this side of the human/spiritual experience.

As I walked into his bedroom, I noticed that something was missing—of course, it was his music. He had always been a fanatic about classical music. He would play his symphonies at full blast on his Sears console buffet record player whenever he had the opportunity, much to Mom's chagrin. Even when they could not afford anything out of the ordinary, he would order more symphonies through his "Concert Series of the Month" club. I smirked—those mail order concerts probably put them close to divorce court more times than they could count! Mom could never understand this "lavishness" on his part, but then neither did most people. I totally understood why. Music was where he sought his refuge when the realities of this hard world got to be too much for him. With his music, he could escape into his own world and let it all go by, finding some relief, even just for a few moments. His music was his passion, his addiction—that was so very clear to me.

I looked around for something to play his music on. His old console player was on the first floor, surrounded by boxes of dusty concert records, so that wouldn't work. I found an old radio, tested it to see if it worked, and by chance landed on a classical music station. I put the old radio on the bedside table and said to him, "Now you have your music." I wasn't sure, but I thought I saw that similar faint smile turn the corners of his mouth upward ever so slightly.

For the next couple of days, he lay there, high as a kite on morphine and listening to his classical music. One time, when I sat by him, I teased, "You know, this is a pretty slick way to go out of this world!" Was that another faint smile that crossed his lips? *Damn*, I thought, *a sense of humor right up to the end!*

I talked to him a lot during those last days. I wasn't sure he heard anything I said, but there were some things I wanted to say. I teased him about being so conservative, so narrow in his political beliefs. I joked with him about all the animals he had brought home to Mom on the farm, knowing that she was not an animal person. I told him I forgave him for the horse that he promised to get me, but never did. Probably the most important thing I did was to reassure him that we would take care of Mom, his "Betty Blue" as he affectionately had called her since they first started dating. I told him that it was okay for him to leave now, that we would all miss him, but it was okay—he could go get "the next farm" ready for the rest of us! All these things we discussed together and there was silent understanding. I always held his hand when I sat by his side. I could tell just by the texture and color of his skin that the time of passing was getting closer.

And then the time came. The hospice nurse said it was close; his body was almost totally shutting down now. We sat around his bed. Our Mom was so sad and so stressed. Little did we know that she may not have totally understood what was happening because of her own disease, but she must have been wondering what would become of her without him. I watched Mom's face as she tried to be strong for "his girls," and she just couldn't manage it. Her fears of being alone all surfaced at once and she couldn't stop fretting. None of us had ever been with anyone who had passed before, so this was all new, this magical moment between the two worlds.

As we were gathered and being quiet around him, *Moonlight Sonata* came on the radio. It had been one of his all-time favorite classical pieces. He had even tried to plunk away at the piano many times throughout his life, trying to pick out the major chords. I had always wondered how he had been able to squeak out of the piano lessons that Grandma mandated for all of her children—yep, he had been a sly rebel in his own right.

I looked at him and knew he was definitely at peace, listening to his favorite song. And, as the final chord and notes ended, he chose to end his life and take his last breath. It could not have been better orchestrated if there had been a symphony conductor standing over him in the room. This sonata ended on the last notes, Dad took his last breath, and both were over.

I looked at my family and all I could say was, "He's gone— but he went out on the last note of his favorite song! How in the world did he manage that?" I laughed through my tears. Of course he would figure it out to end it that way. It was his way of saying, "It's over, I'm done, and it's time for me to go now." It was a privilege and an honor to be with him at that last moment.

Yes, hearing *Moonlight Sonata* always takes me back to that place in time. It makes me smile when I hear it now because I know he's near then, filling the void that his absence has left on this side of the two worlds. And, even for just a moment or two, it lessens that distance between us.

Wendie Batterson has been a teacher in some way, shape, or form most of her life. She has taught French and English in the public school system, taught English to Spanish nationals while living in Madrid, and worked in corporate America for many years in Training and Organizational Development. Wendie holds a B.A. in French, English and Education, an M.A. in Counseling, and a second M.A. in Management and Human Relations. She and her husband live in Franktown, near Denver, where they have three horses and other rescue critters. She has a grown daughter and son, who also live in the Denver metro area. Wendie volunteers with Horseback Miracles, Inc., a life values equine therapy program for at-risk adolescent girls from local residential treatment centers, as well as with the Alzheimer's Association "Memories in the Making" art program.

Faith and Spirituality

A NEW VOICE

Paula Jayne Friedland

I stepped out of the audition studio onto the noisy New York City street, unable to restrain my exhilaration any longer. A friend of mine happened to be walking by right then, and I screamed out to her, "I just got the part of Sheila in the European tour of the musical *Hair*!" She jumped up and down with me as I squealed with glee. I ran home, not even feeling the ground beneath my feet, and called my parents to share the amazing news. They both laughed and cried with me as we celebrated the best role I had landed since coming to New York seven years earlier.

The next two years were some of the most fulfilling of my life. I performed on stages throughout Germany, Switzerland, Sweden, Austria, France, Belgium, and Holland, playing the lead in this amazing show. It was the thrill of a lifetime, to be performing, my favorite thing in the world, in these cities I had only dreamt about.

Then as I was talking to my dad one night from Holland, he iced the already amazing cake: he was coming to Amsterdam to see me in the show! The memories from that visit remain some of my most treasured to date. I felt so blessed.

Three weeks after returning from the tour, I was sitting in my apartment in New York and the phone rang. It was my dad. "Honey," he said, in an uncharacteristically small and shaky voice, "I'm afraid I have some bad news." I held my breath.

"I… have…cancer," he said. I gasped. *This can't be happening.*

"It is very serious, and I guess there is very little time left." *No! NO! How could this be?*

I remembered, just two months earlier, peeking out through the curtain before the beginning of the show, and beaming to see my dad's shining smile. I remembered the feeling after the show when he came up to me with tears in his eyes and hugged me so tightly, and with his voice overflowing with love said, "Honey, I'm so proud of you."

115

My dad had always been a very strong provider for our family, a rock of stability, and although he was a practical thinker, he always supported me in pursuing my dreams. He was the force behind the scene that gave me the courage to follow my passion, even when it was hard. He was the strongest man I knew. So how could this nightmare of cancer be true?

But it was true. And in two short months, my father was gone. My whole world turned upside down. I panicked. It felt like the time I was seven years old, experiencing the ocean for the first time; one minute I was giggling with glee and the next violently taken down by the undertow. Terrified, I felt I too was about to die.

My life was broken apart, out of control. My survival instinct kicked into overdrive, interpreting his early death as a wakeup call to "get my life together." To me, the message was that life is short, life is fragile, and my future needed to be much more conventional, more stable—enough of these frivolous pursuits. So I put my head in charge, because my heart was broken.

The next decade was a practical one. I moved back to Denver, got my master's degree, and became a counselor and life coach. I began coaching artists of all kinds to reach their dreams, to own the value of their art, and to share that art with the world. Helping these beautiful, powerful artists realize their deepest desires of creative expression felt wonderful.

But after a while something just felt wrong. I couldn't put my finger on it, but there was a sadness in me. Its presence was a mystery. I knew I was making a difference by helping other artists, so why did I feel so unfulfilled? When I left New York I decided it was time for me to move on, to put away my pursuit of art and be sensible. And like many actors, I was told at some point in my career that I was drawn to performing because I needed applause, and that as I matured, I would outgrow that need and could leave the drama fluff behind. So that's what I told myself when I left New York.

But as I sat in my home, having just finished a coaching session with a client who had landed a wonderful role in a Broadway show, I realized I had been living a lie. I had been living vicariously through my clients, when in fact I longed desperately to be performing. The craft that I had worked on my whole life, as a singer and actress, was not fluff. The calling that I always felt around performing was not a frivolous pursuit, it was my gift. It was in my blood. And I had sold my soul down the river for the false promise of stability.

I sat at my piano and started dusting off my dormant stacks of music. As I leafed through a book of songs by my favorite composer, Stephen Sondheim, I landed on one that cut straight to my heart: "Being Alive." I realized I hadn't been fully alive for years.

The floodgates opened. I cried a river of tears, grieving for my father, and at the same time grieving for my gift, the art I had given up so readily in the pursuit of practicality. Out of sorrow came the epiphany: I had to reclaim it. I had to sing again.

This time, I put my heart in charge. I began working on an original revue with my best friend about our individual creative journeys with art. Together we laughed, cried, sang, and wrote, and in three months we had a show—a beautiful, inspiring, rich, personal show. I wanted to jump out of my skin I was so excited. I was singing better than ever and was about to perform at one of the premier venues in Denver. Finally, I'd be back on stage, where I had always belonged.

Everything went beautifully—until a week before we opened. I caught a virus and ended up with full-blown laryngitis. My worst fear was realized: I'd lost my voice! We had to cancel. The little demon voices inside my head tried to tell me that this was a bad omen, that I wasn't meant to perform again. But I fought them, and after an excruciating five weeks, my singing voice returned. Hallelujah! We got the show back on its feet, and in a week, in my beautiful dress, with my beautiful co-artist, I stepped on the stage.

The crowd exploded with applause and screams. I felt that familiar adrenaline rush, the heat of the stage lights, that feeling of taking command of the stage. In a split second I had them in the palm of my hand. My talent lies in telling deep emotional truth through each song, and as the show went on, I knew that gift was stronger than ever. I made them laugh and I made them cry. My story guided them through something true: the rawness of life, both the pain and the beauty of being alive. At the end they were on their feet and I was in my element, giving my gift and receiving it right back from them. I was alive again. I was home.

But during the last performance, I started noticing a little glitch in my voice. It was a strange, grating sound that affected the middle notes of my range. Over the next few weeks, it got worse and worse. Like some kind of malicious thief, it began to steal more notes from me, until I could barely sing at all. I saw the doctor and he diagnosed me with Vocal Chord Paresis—paralysis of the nerve—caused by the previous virus. There was no immediate cure. However, he was confident it could be fixed through medication and short-term vocal rehabilitation.

I went to rehab for weeks, which turned into months, but my voice didn't seem to get better. I saw my doctor again and he did a scope of my vocal chords. I remember anxiously sitting in his office as he looked at the images of my chords. For several minutes I sat as he read them. Then, nonchalantly, he turned and—I will never forget this moment—said, "It is pretty likely that you will never get this back. You won't be able to fully sing again." Casually, with a few words, he pronounced the death of my singing voice.

I broke down right there in his office. After 10 minutes of gut-wrenching crying, I realized I had to get out of there. I dragged myself up, and I left. Inside my car, I continued sobbing. I wanted to die.

I felt the undertow again. I was being taken down. I looked outside my car, and everyone was still moving and driving around as if nothing had changed. But my whole world had been pulled out from under me. Time stood still and seemed to be moving at the speed of light at the same time. I was completely disoriented and devastated.

Finally some faint voice of reason came through and told me to seek help. Despite the shock and trauma I felt, I managed to reach out to my voice teacher and my voice therapist, both of whom felt that the evidence and my doctor's conclusion did not support this being a career-ending injury.

I found a different doctor, a true expert with singers, and began working with a new vocal therapist who had a reputation for helping even the most injured singers perform again. And thus my journey—the descent into the darkness I feared, the biggest spiritual quest of my life—began.

It was one of the hardest things I've ever done. Like learning to walk again, it was a slow and perplexing process. I would seem to improve, and then the next day it was worse; then a little better, then worse again. My recovery had no rhyme or reason; it was a cruel roller coaster. I could never escape because I could hear this glitch, this pathology, in my voice every time I spoke or laughed, hundreds of times a day. Every day.

Half of my waking hours were spent crying. I had to search every corner of my soul to find a place I could believe from. I fought against brutal demons who kept saying, "You will never get better. You will never sing again." Trying desperately to believe, I was haunted by the question *Who would I BE if I were no longer a singer?* I became deeply depressed.

I felt sick imagining my life without this gift. Even though I knew I was a talented coach and counselor, I felt empty and disconnected from any personal passion. I desperately grasped for something to define myself by. Being stripped of my voice felt like such a violation, like having a piece of me just ripped from my body. My art was like my child—my special gift to the world. What could this life be worth without it?

As the days ticked by, slowly, faintly, came the suggestion that I was more than just my singing. It was no Hollywood movie epiphany. But I was begrudgingly accepting that I had to find my value in some other way. I had to resign myself to a new identity. I had to try to find a new place in the world.

Then, as I was beginning to embrace the sobering notion of a new identity, something happened. My voice therapist suggested trying a medical procedure which might help my voice recover. I was terrified, but I had to try it. So I did. And a small miracle occurred. I did not recover my full range, but I could sing notes I hadn't been able to hit for some time.

My new voice had a limited range; my high notes had not yet returned. Being a soprano, singing high up the scale, had been very significant to me. I knocked people out with those notes. But in the new reality, those notes were gone: I was not a soprano anymore, and might never be again. But the redeeming factor was that I could—actually—sing. Even with fewer notes I could feel the love for singing like I'd never felt before. Again I cried, but different tears this time: tears of deep gratitude and joy to have my voice again.

Three years later we commenced to remount that original show. But to do so, I had to lower the keys of most of the songs or not sing at all, period—a crushing blow to my ego. The notes that remained demanded that I face, yet again, a new way of embodying my art. Who am I with this new voice, without the range I used to have?

Identity is a strange thing. It is always there, defining us; but until it is challenged, we never notice it. Then something terrible happens, and the old persona tries desperately to hold on to what was. But the new reality knows better. *There is no longer a place for you. Your time has passed.*

So here I sit, on the precipice of a new venture, singing from a new place, a place that feels foreign, sometimes sad, and certainly unknown. But what I've been learning is that we cannot find something new until we are willing to let go of the old. It's terrifying. You feel like if you let go, there will be nothing to catch you and you'll fall to your death. Or die of heartbreak.

But my friend reminded me that this show we are doing is about our truth. It is an autobiographical show about our relationship with art and it is about expressing our authentic voices. And from this new identity, I have to speak THIS truth. Otherwise, I am a liar. Otherwise, I go against everything I have ever stood for in my life: authentic voice, artistry, truth. I must express who I am now.

So who am I?

I am a truth teller. I am an artist. This is still my identity. The instrument may have changed, but the core truth is the same. And what I have come to know so intimately about the instrument is that I must love each note, from the depths of my being. Each of them, a precious, borrowed gift.

The reality is I don't know how long I have to sing. This demon that stole half of my range could swoop down at any time and snatch the rest of it. Or my legs, or my sight, or my life. If I have learned anything by the losses in my life, it's that nothing is guaranteed. So I'd better sing with the voice I have now. There is no time to waste.

Paula Jayne Friedland is a counselor, life coach, corporate trainer, speaker, and performing artist. Her mission in all of her endeavors is to help others connect to their authentic voices and to speak them in the world—in service to their higher purpose. Her own path as an artist includes public performances, as well as creating and delivering "Keynote Cabarets," inspiring speeches that use songs to punctuate the points of the spoken word. If you are looking for coaching in any area of your life, to connect to your deeper self, or a unique, entertaining, and inspiring speech for any type of event, visit Paula's website, www. paulafriedland.com, or contact her directly at 303-283-0083.

WHAT FAITH CAN DO

Renee Vejvoda

My day began like all the rest before it, full of sadness, loneliness, and heartache. But then came an unexpected knock at the door. The young girl standing there, a complete stranger, wore the biggest smile on her face as she said, with complete enthusiasm, "Hi, my name is Lana. I am here to take you to church with me." Unbeknownst to me, my mother had staged a spiritual intervention for me, whom she thought of as her deeply troubled teenager. It was the day that changed my entire life. Becoming a Christian that year, at the age of 16, is a memory that will be forever ingrained in my soul.

The foundation of my life since that time has been spiritual. However, as time went on and the years were molded with marriage and raising two beautiful children, I drifted away from the dedication of my faith. Never did a day go by that I failed to give praise to God for the blessing of a wonderful life. But parental and family dynamics entered my world which left me with many unanswered questions surrounding my beliefs that were not developed or based on Christianity as a child. I spent years dealing with the ghosts from my childhood and facing all of the untruths as a young adult.

All my life I also have struggled with periodic bouts of depression. It is something that is imbedded that cannot be controlled. I experience feelings of worthlessness, loneliness, sadness, and an ache that takes over my heart. Sometimes the pain is more than I can bear or explain. I suddenly have a pivotal realization that something big is missing, absent from my heart. I struggle with these feelings of unsettled emotions and they come crashing down on me unannounced and without warning. *Why does it feel like my heart is broken and full of sorrow when my life is so blessed and wonderful?* I find myself weak, feeling heavily burdened, always tearful, and extremely vulnerable.

My day today began like all the rest before it, full of sadness, loneliness, and heartache, except there was another knock at my door. This time, it was God and He wanted ME!

The knock came on a hot summer Sunday afternoon, August 8, 2010. I always try to stay busy, to distract myself from feeling or thinking. I live just outside the reality of the moment. I felt drawn to leave my house and walk, which was part of my daily routine. There was a feeling of urgency. God wanted my attention and at that moment, He was speaking LOUDLY. Without hesitation I put on my tennis shoes and grabbed my Ipod that was fully loaded with inspirational, spiritual music that I downloaded just the day before. I am a creature of habit and usually walk the same route, but today I found myself moving in a different direction and heading toward the neighborhood park. As I listened to the music, one song after another, all touching my heart, the words of this song played softly in my earphones. My pace became slow, thoughtful, and focused on every word.

Lord, I'm really glad you're here. I hope you feel the same when You see all my fear, and how I have failed. I fall sometimes. It's hard to walk on shifting sand. I miss the rock, and find there's nowhere left to stand. I start to cry. Lord, please help me raise my hands so You can pick me up. Hold me close, Hold me tighter.

God was speaking to me. His whisper was so powerful that my surroundings became virtually invisible. It was time to listen, time to heal, time to make my way back to where I started at 16. God was leading me back to a place where I felt safe and loved, back into His healing hands. Was today going to be the day I made a choice to listen or was I going to keep right on walking? Did I have enough strength to admit and recognize the person that I am? Could I dig deep and take back what had been absent from my life for so long?

Not realizing my own presence or my surroundings, I walked into the park and fell to my knees. I bowed down with a stream of tears and said, "Yes, Lord, I hear you! Yes, Lord, I hear your whisper. I feel you hover over me, and I feel your presence as if you are walking right along side of me, holding my hand. I am here. I finally met you in this place." Still on my knees, the song continued to play.

I have found a place where I can hide. It's safe inside Your arms of love. Like a child who's helped throughout a storm, You keep me warm in Your arms of love. Storms will come and storms will go. Wonder just

*how many storms it takes until I finally know You're here always. Even
when my skies are far from gray, I can stay; teach me to stay there. In
the place I've found where I can hide. It's safe inside Your arms of love.*

"Arms of Love" sung by Amy Grant

Removing my headphones I began to pray, stronger and
louder than I have ever prayed before. Asking and praising.
Coming back to my Lord open and broken. "Lord, take away my
pain and help heal my heart. Please fill the gaping hole with your
love, grace, and comfort as only You can do."

Our God is about second chances and I found myself in
complete surrender. Praying as if He would not hear me even
though there was not a doubt in my mind that He was listening
to every word that came from the deepest part in my heart. "As
best as I know how, God, I am humbling myself before You. I am
bowing here in Your presence and saying, Lord, by faith show me
Your wisdom. Nothing is off limits, too big or too small."

There is no escaping the Lord. There is no hiding from Him.
He knows every intimate part of my soul before I even speak
it out loud. He always answers prayers and gives power to the
weak. He has anticipated this day, this moment in time when He
created me. Words cannot begin to describe the feeling when you
are ONE in the presence of GOD. The feeling is overwhelming
joy!

Who knows how long I was in this position. When I opened
my eyes and looked around me, the park that is usually FULL
of people, playing summer soccer, walking the bike path with
kids and dogs, was totally empty. I was immediately present. I
looked 360 degrees around me and still saw NO ONE. Then I
paused and listened. The air was totally silent. I listened again.
I heard nothing. The sound of peacefulness was unbelievable.
Everything was completely still. Dark storm clouds filled the sky
behind me, but in front of me was a magnificently deep beautiful
blue summer sky filled with huge white clouds. The grass was
soft beneath my feet and looked greener than I had ever seen. The
leaves on the trees that lined the creek were still and motionless.
Humbleness and peacefulness filled my heart. I have never been
so aware of all of the beauty that surrounded me.

I was completely alone, yet I was not alone. I may have been
the only person in the park at that moment, but I was there
sharing this moment with God. He was surrounding me with

His love, His protection, His promise! "When my life was ebbing away, I remembered you Lord and my prayer rose to you, to your holy temple," Jonah 2:7. The heaviness in my heart was instantly fading. "Please Lord, let me stay and rest." I did not want this moment of healing to end. All I could do was praise God for His presence with me. He was giving me peace. He was granting me grace. "Praise God from whom all blessings flow."

Realizing I had been there for more than an hour, I finally decided to exit my bubble of comfort and joy and head home. It seems my Ipod is on a "God shuffle" today because the next song that awaited my heart had these words:

I long for your embrace. Every single day. To meet you in this place and see you face to face. Will you show me? Reveal yourself to me. Because of your mercy, I fall down on my knees. And I can feel your presence here with me. Suddenly I'm lost within your beauty. Caught up in the wonder of your touch. Here in this moment I surrender to your love. You're everywhere I go. I am not alone. You call me as your own. To know you and be known. You are holy and I fall down on my knees.

"Here with Me" sung by Mercy Me

At that very moment, it started to rain. Not just a few drops, but it started to pour down buckets of rain. For the first time in a very long time, I smiled and laughed out loud. I was so smack in the middle of a God moment! Looking up at the sky, I saw it was entirely dark and it continued to rain and rain. This was my cleansing! This was my gift from God. The physical answer to my prayer. I was on a close walk with Him being blessed with His presence and His love was pouring down on me. I was drenched from head to toe.

I was nearing the end of my walk, just a block away from home, when I looked up at the sky directly in front of me to notice the reappearance of bright blue sky. It seemed my God moments had not ended. I praised God and thanked Him for taking me on this walk, whispering to me and bestowing His promise of love upon me. It was a reminder that all that is wonderful and beautiful was just waiting for me in the days to come. *You knew the moment I was born that I would need a Savior in my youth at age 16 and today,* I thought. This is a new day. I will forever refer to it as "Day One of my Healing and my deeper walk with God," Sunday, August 8, 2010. *Thank you, Lord Jesus, for loving me so much and orchestrating this wonderful experience for your glory.*

I am not sure that I can put into words my days since my walk with God. I know He had never let go of me for 30 years. He had been present through every high and low of my life and I have worshiped Him all of those days. But today was different. Magnificent. I received the healing hands of God.

Even though Christianity met me when I was 16, my life experiences, maturity, and trials and circumstances have made me appreciate and see my relationship and commitment to God in a whole new way. Since I have committed to having Him "first" in my life, above all things, my life today has been an enormous encounter of blessings. One right after another. It is like God has had a bucket of blessings with my name on it sitting at His feet just waiting for me to lift up my eyes to Him and say "Here I am." It is profound to think that the Lord of all the earth would care so much about the smallest detail of my everyday life. Who I am, the hurt I bear, the happiness I feel. His love for me is so much bigger than me and His presence in my heart is so apparent and fulfilling. I pray that His glory be seen in my life as never before. To describe my walk with God and the rain He brought down on me as amazing and humbling, would not give it the magnitude it deserves. My life is forever changed. That's what faith can do!

"Come to me, all you who are weary and burdened, and I will give you rest. Take my yoke upon you and learn from me, for I am gentle and humble in heart, and you will find rest for your souls. For my yoke is easy and my burden is light," Matthew 11:28-30.

Renee Vejvoda was born and raised in a suburb of Chicago with two older brothers until she was 15. Moving to Colorado she met her husband, Karl, and has two of the greatest children, Bryan and Emilie. Renee works her creative magic in two jobs, providing custom embroidery for All Stitched Out and serving as manager for CampExperience™, An Amazing Women's Educational Retreat. You will always find Renee making or creating something. She loves hanging out with her kids and being a special part of their lives. To learn more about Renee and her businesses, or just to connect, contact her at reneevejvoda@comcast.net.

LETTING GO

Tryna Cooper

It was early spring 2001, and I was 44 years old. Life had been glorious. Now I found myself in the midst of many life changes. The last few years, challenges had presented themselves and I had experienced more dark in working with others than ever before. Lessons in detachment seemed to arise at every turn. And even though I had taken many risks and learned many lessons in my life as an entrepreneur, little did I know I was about to face an experience that would profoundly change my views of life—and death.

A few months earlier, on December 31, my husband Larry and I had celebrated our 25th anniversary. Actually, we had been together for 28 years. We met at age 14 in junior high, began dating at 15, and soon became inseparable. I was the shy, quiet girl from the Catholic school; he was the wild, outgoing class flirt. Opposites attract, they say, but I knew he was my soul mate. I knew it at the very core of my being. So many friends and family members thought we were crazy, but we didn't care. We knew we were meant to be together. At the age of 18, six months after our graduation, we married, much to the dismay of our parents. In their minds, marrying at such a young age was taking a foolish risk.

Our son was born that year and so was our first business. When Jon was three months old, Larry came home from work and announced that he had quit his job and was going to start his own business. Fear gripped me. Was he crazy? We had no money and were in school. Again it was crazy, foolish risk in most people's minds, but I was beginning to see that together we were up for the challenges that many wouldn't face. Larry had a unique strength, a belief in himself and that he could create whatever he desired. His strengths began to open me up and expand my belief in myself as well. I believed in him and I believed that together we could conquer anything. It was the beginning of our life together

129

as creators and entrepreneurs.

During the next four years, we had two daughters. By the time we were 24, we had three children, ran a thriving business with employees, had bought our second house, and were deeply involved as leaders in our industry. As the years passed, we created several other businesses and became community activists. Larry entered local politics, and we were involved as a driving force behind the creation of a new county in Colorado. Life was fun, challenging, full of risk, and so rewarding.

In 1997, our lives began to change. Our kids went off to college and to lead their own lives. We were becoming "empty nesters." Let go, I thought. It was my job, but it was hard.

At the same time, we sold our main business. We thought we would have money and free time together. We were so wrong. The man who purchased our business decided not to pay. This led us into a four-and-a-half-year journey of court challenges, law suits, and disappointment. It was an experience that cut deeply to the core of our beings. In less than a year, we lost dear employees and watched over 20 years of work and creation driven into bankruptcy and liquidation. Court battles continued for another three years as the man who "bought" our business tried to blame us for his failure. It was a time of emptiness, sadness, and disillusionment, yet it was a powerful lesson in detachment for both of us. We needed to release and let go.

In 1999, after 10 years of political office and community service, Larry also suffered a painful loss in a political race. It was painful to witness an ally who had at first chosen not to run and had given Larry his blessing to seek his office, change his mind and become the opponent. It was painful to see someone who at one time called himself our friend turn to unethical tactics in the race as he was driven by his fear of losing. It was painful to hear that many of Larry's supporters, believing that he was going to win by a landslide, hadn't taken the time to vote. And it was most painful to watch my best friend and partner suffer so much through the experience. Again, it was a time of emptiness and sadness, and another powerful lesson in detachment, for both of us.

Then we found ourselves in the early spring of 2001. My work had become a full-time focus on the workings of the legal system, as we were still involved in the lawsuits surrounding the sale of our business from almost four years before. We were still unable to work in the industry to which we had dedicated our careers because of the non-compete covenant we had signed. We were cut off from community and political activities because of the continued blackballing that occurred after the political race.

Most disheartening for me was to see the toll the past several years had taken on Larry and his spirit. His strength and belief in himself had been bashed and battered; he had lost his passion and direction. To reinvent ourselves, we had decided to devote our energies to several new business start-ups, but the same enthusiasm wasn't there.

My heart hurt. I had to face the realization that while I had supported Larry behind the scenes for so many years, I had always been in the background and had relied on his strength and creativity for my support. At this time, he had little to give.

I wasn't sure where to start to pick up the pieces and start over. For me, the saving grace was that we had both turned to spiritual studies during this trying time. Our newfound faith and awareness of Spirit is what we relied on to move us forward during this time. Little did I know how we were to be tested.

We had spent a few days in Grand Lake snowmobiling. On our return, Larry left for a business trip to the East Coast. He was gone a few days when he called to tell me he wasn't feeling well.

Day 1. Larry began to run a fever and thought he might have the flu. His fever rose to 104 degrees. He left his meeting to find a doctor. The doctor also thought he might have the flu and told him to rest.

Day 2. Larry decided to catch a flight on Friday and return home early instead of staying the weekend for the rest of the meeting. His fever was still 104 degrees. On the flight home, he fell asleep on the plane and found that the flight attendants had moved all of the other passengers out of business class while he slept just in case he was contagious. He was so sick when I picked him up. I tried to get him to go to the doctors on his return, but he was convinced it was the flu and decided to wait out the weekend.

Days 3 and 4. Larry's fever never broke. He continued to run 104 degrees throughout the weekend. I was getting worried because the fever wouldn't break. He was getting weaker by the day.

Day 5. Monday morning came and I finally convinced him to

go to the doctor. I drove him there and waited in the room while the doctor saw him. He still showed no other symptoms but the 104 degree fever. After much debate, the doctor finally persuaded him to check into the hospital to run tests. As soon as Larry was admitted, he was put on a broad spectrum antibiotic. Blood tests and scans were run, but the results offered no explanation. Still the fever persisted. I felt a bit more comfortable with him in the hospital, but alone, so alone at home.

Days 6 and 7. Larry grew weaker each day and the fever hung on at 104 degrees. There were still no other symptoms and no explanations. He was not responding to the antibiotic. He was cranky and I was beginning to get scared. I couldn't imagine what was wrong with him, but I was reassured of his strength when he ordered a nurse out of his room. He told the doctor that he would not allow her back in because she didn't want to be there and had no compassion for her patients. His spark was still there and I felt some relief. I felt like I needed to stay with him, but our work was getting behind. I wanted to do something and I felt so helpless because there was nothing I could do.

Day 8. It was now Thursday and Larry was not improving. The fever stayed consistently around 104 degrees. The doctor decided to call in an infectious disease specialist, who ordered another series of tests. They were looking for everything and anything, and nothing showed.

I looked at Larry and he was wasting away before my eyes. He was tired and worried, angry and scared. I felt the same. I couldn't understand how someone could run that high of a fever for so many days and not have something show up. My sense of helplessness grew, and I kept telling myself I had to be strong, but the ache in my heart was growing more each day.

Day 9. There was no change in Larry's fever overnight so another scan was run in the morning. Finally, after all these days, the hidden devil showed itself. There was an abscess on his right kidney! My feelings were so mixed—relief and worry. I didn't know which to embrace. The doctor placed the order to drain the abscess, but Larry refused to go in for the procedure without me present. It felt so strange to have him lean on me so heavily after all the years that I had leaned on him. The role felt strange and awkward. I could feel his fear and I could truly feel mine.

The doctor gave permission for me to be in the room with

him during the procedure and I held his hand. He was so weak, but his grip was tight, just hanging on. My relief was short-lived as I found out that as they tried to drain the abscess, the poison entered his system and he went septic. We were told this abscess was really a Staph infection. Thirteen cultures were grown to test 13 antibiotics to see if there was one that would treat the infection. I was told, however, that Staph was quite resistant and there would be no guarantees. No guarantees?! What were they saying? They are supposed to treat these things! Larry's fever climbed to 106 degrees that night. He was moved into intensive care.

I went home, swearing to myself that everything was fine. There was no way this was happening. They had found the cure. Nothing to worry about. I was sure of it. Or was I? My denial ran deep. I wasn't willing to look at any other possibilities. Think positive. Everything was fine. I wouldn't allow myself to cry. No need.

Day 10. After a night of little sleep, I returned to the hospital. There was no change in the fever, still 106 degrees. And then came the news—not good. Only one of the 13 antibiotics showed any sign of treating the Staph. I was grateful there was at least one, but the true message hit hard. "The prognosis is not good," the doctor said. "Chances of survival with this condition are less that 10%. We have done all we can. It is all up to Larry now if he is going to survive." Was he going to die? No way. He was fine a few days ago. It's just a fever. Yet I looked at him and he was growing weaker. I had to be strong, yet every ounce of my being wanted to cry. Our kids came to visit and sat with him. We all sat that day with Larry drifting in and out of consciousness. I didn't want to leave, but I told myself I needed to sleep to keep my strength to help him get better.

I went home that night not knowing whether I would get a call in the middle of the night or if he would be there when I got back. I was so afraid. The fear welled up in me from a depth inside that I had never known. How could I live without him? He was my best friend and my soul mate. We had been partners in everything for over 25 years. What would I do without him? How would I survive? He had always taken care of me. The fear was gripping me. I had never felt such terror. I sobbed and cried myself to sleep that night.

Day 11. Still no change. The fever raged at 106 degrees. First he was lucid and then he would fade out. The waiting was agonizing. He wouldn't let the nurses touch him unless I helped. He was so dependent on me and I couldn't lean on him. I didn't know where I would get the strength.

I went home that night scared—but angry. How could he do this? How could he be leaving me with everything? It wasn't fair. How dare he get sick! The anger bubbled up from everywhere in my body. Why was I angry? How dare I be angry when he's dying? Dying? How dare he die and leave me! I raged and cried. Again I cried myself to sleep.

Day 12. Again, no change. Still 106 degrees. He was lucid, then unconscious. No response to the antibiotics and fading away. I was tired. As I watched him dying before me, all I could do was hold his hand, rub his legs, and tell him I loved him. And that was it. What was going to happen? We talked and I waited. I felt so alone. Even with the kids there, I felt alone.

I went home exhausted and cried again. I prayed and asked why. I was tired, so tired. I cried hopelessly.

Suddenly, the realization hit me that I had no control. It was what it was. I couldn't fight it. There was nothing to fight. I couldn't even grasp it. No matter how hard I tried to get control, I couldn't. All I could do was let go. Release it and trust. So, I asked Spirit to take it. Whatever it was, I would trust.

With that surrender, with that release, a peace came over me that I had never felt before. It was like a warm, loving embrace with such a sense of security I had never known. Such a love, and the knowingness that I would be okay. And he would be okay. No matter what happened, it would be okay. Just as it should be. I had no control. I wasn't supposed to. I knew it deep in my soul. The peace was deep. All was good. I slept.

Day 13. Still, there was no change, at least not in Larry's status. But in my heart and my being, change was profound. I knew that to really love him I had to let him go. I sat with Larry, held his hand, and told him I loved him. I told him not to stay for me and to go if he needed to go. I would be okay. I blessed him in his choice and loved him. The peace was profound. I didn't know if he heard me at that time. He was not lucid or awake, but about an hour later he began to show some signs of change. His fever began to drop. I loved him, trusted Spirit, and let him go. It was by far my greatest lesson of detachment and trust.

It was a long way back for Larry. He had lost 35 pounds and could hardly walk when he was finally released from the hospital. It was months of recovery at home. Larry told me later that he was given a choice to stay or go, and he chose to stay. His experience of near death was profound for him and changed him immensely. My experience of his near death was profound for me also. I learned that releasing and letting go allows Spirit to work wonders. I learned I really have no control, so I might as well flow and embrace experiences with love. The peace I felt that night gave me the strength to move forward and carry the load for both of us. It has continued to resonate in me each day for the last 10 years. Letting go changed me, and I will carry that blessing with me the rest of my life.

Tryna Cooper grew up in Colorado. She is married to her husband of 35 years, Larry; they have three children and five grandchildren. As a life-long entrepreneur, she is currently co-owner of several small businesses, including Textile Consultants, Inc., and Meetings and Events, LLC. Tryna has also been on a path of spiritual study, teaching, and service for years and holds a Master of Metaphysics Certification through the Self Actualization and Enlightenment Center. Her newest business venture is as a partner in Journeys For Conscious Living, Inc. (J4CL) in Arvada, Colorado. Through J4CL, she hopes to help others create balance in their lives in order to reach their fullest potential as spiritual human beings.

I'M READY TO LISTEN NOW!

Marie Kirkland

I am a listener. I listen to the rhythm and flow of life and all that it shares. I listen to my life and go where it guides me. It's this rhythm of life that makes me dance with joy, laugh out loud and gives my life momentum. I listen to the presence of Spirit and live my life aligned. However, this hasn't always been my truth. There have been times when I've been lulled to sleep by its steady beat while I tucked my passion safely away and searched for purpose. And there were other times when I've left my past behind, much too quickly, in search of what already existed within me. Along the way, I've found that true alignment exists when you connect with your divine source, know your purpose and live your passion.

We all have an inner space within us that allows us to connect with our Source, our purpose and our passion. I was fortunate to recognize this inner sanctuary at a very early age. This sanctuary then and now is a quiet awareness of God within and a passion for the written word that I shared with my father who was an avid reader. In this sanctuary, I came to understand three things that would shape my life: I was divinely connected and would never be alone, I was a witness to my life and became my own best friend, and that I would one day share my voice. However, it would take family tragedy, a few detours and many years before I would fully realize the vision and passion of my youth and so much more.

Around the third grade, I noticed a shift in our family. There was less laughter, less music, and a different family dynamic. In particular, there were frequent visits from my uncles who would have long talks with my mother as my two younger brothers, my sister, and I played nearby.

It wasn't until a conversation with my two cousins that I understood why. My whole perspective changed in one weekend visit. While they were unpacking their suitcases, I noticed that they hid their insulin kits in my top drawer.

"What are you doing?" I asked.

"Mommy told us to hide it," they said.

"Why?" I asked. "I'm not going to bother it."

"We have to hide it from your dad." As my heart sank and my eyes swelled with tears, I asked why, once again. In a whisper they said, "So that he won't steal it, because he uses drugs."

This conversation between 9 and 10 year olds is etched in my heart and mind with indelible ink. I can't remember if I asked my mom about it right away, but I do remember that everything changed almost immediately. While I never saw my father under the influence, I did notice frequent absences where he was "away." Ultimately, we packed up our lives and moved away in the middle of the night. My siblings and I grew up very quickly.

In 1970, a year after our move when I was in the 6th grade, my family was happy to hear that Dad was in recovery and living and working in Cleveland, Ohio. But our joy was short lived. On Valentine's Day, our world changed again. I returned home that evening, after babysitting, to find my mother on the phone in tears. She just learned that my father was attacked and killed as he was leaving Western Union, just moments after sending Valentine's Day wishes to her and my grandmother.

I was devastated. I felt a myriad of emotions. Part of me was absolutely sure that I was connected to a Source filled with Love and that I was on the journey I needed to travel, but I also felt lost, lonely, and abandoned. I held on to the parts of my dad that felt like love. I thought about how much he loved us, his humor, his gorgeous smile, his passion for the written word. Once again words became my refuge and books my friends.

Over the next six years, we moved from place to place, city to city, and school to school as my mother raised us, worked hard, and filled the void as best she could with love. She was assisted by a crop of strong women in our family who watched over us and kept us safe. However, it was my grandmother's heart and love that was home for me. She loved us unconditionally and although it was impossible, the four of us seemed to fill an unfillable space in her heart after my father died. No matter where my travels took me it was to this space that I always returned.

I continued to listen to my life and at 18 years old I joined the Army. I was bright eyed and ready for adventure but most of all,

I was excited to start a life of my own. I knew from the moment I arrived at basic training that I would make the Army my home.

It became just that, but it wasn't the home my soul longed for. I longed to live a life of purpose and be the writer I envisioned as a child, painting a picture of the world with my words. Like my favorite authors, Maya Angelou, Pearl S. Buck, and Ralph Ellison, I longed to create, travel, and live abroad. The Army provided plenty of travel, especially to foreign lands, but mostly it meant growth, security, and a life to feel good about.

My life purpose of helping people to live life fully and connect with their divine nature began to cultivate while training and mentoring young soldiers. I felt full and complete as I taught them military and life skills that helped them build successful careers that are still thriving today. In 1995 I retired.

Nobody tells you what the transition from the military to the civilian world is really like. Of course, there were pamphlets and required out-briefings, but they don't tell you how long the transition will take or how you can lose yourself in search of yourself, no matter how prepared you are. They simply say, "It is a transition." There were retirement parties and parades, but on the very last day, December 1, 1995, when I signed my papers and received my retirement pin, the 20 years, five months, and two days were over in a matter of minutes.

In the years since retiring from the Army, my path of discovery has been to live both in and out of alignment. I created a cycle of shifting from focus and direction to being divinely guided, then multitasking myself into such overwhelm that I would push myself to exhaustion, all in the name of finding my way.

As with any transition there are defining moments. I vividly remember when my journey to oneness began. It came on a chilly February night driving on I-95 with my husband, just outside of Washington, D.C.

"I've got to stop the car, I can't breathe," was all I could say. I quickly exited the highway at the next off-ramp, pulled into an empty parking lot, and slumped over the steering wheel. In an effort to help me inhale and exhale, one breath at a time, my husband unfastened my bra. Leaning over the steering wheel, I felt as if I could breathe for the first time since we got the news that my grandmother had made her transition. As I settled into each breath, I realized that her last ancestral breath was my first breath into a new life without her. What I didn't know was the path this life would take me.

For years, I had been searching for a spiritual path that embraced the common truth of love found in most religions. This discovery came after months of grieving and a complete surrender of the soul. My husband introduced me to Religious Science from a *USA Today* article he read about the Agape International Spiritual Center. I searched for a center in our area and found that the nearest one was in Raleigh, North Carolina, over an hour away.

The day we walked into the Center for Spiritual Living, I knew I was at home. I could stop searching and begin listening again with an open heart. I embraced the teaching and immersed myself in classes. Learning about spiritual principles and how to consciously apply them to my life through affirmative prayer allowed me to create positive change in many areas of my life.

The two biggest changes in my life were being fully present for myself and my family and changing careers. Empowering others and being of service were already so much a part of who I was; transitioning to life coaching allowed me to live from my heart source and empower others to do the same.

To support my business growth I began working at Toyota. True to my old pattern, this moved me out of my life once again and I stopped listening to my soul. I became a wife and mother by phone, rushing to school events and some days not seeing my family at all. Until another chilly February afternoon when my body spoke one simple word—STOP!

This particular day, I walked into work and knew immediately that something was not quite right. Not sure of what that "something" was, I made a mental note of feeling outside of my body, but I continued managing, solving problems, putting out fires, and, of course, multitasking. Still feeling out of sorts, I contacted my doctor for an appointment; with no appointments available I made my way to Urgent Care. The two miles to Urgent Care felt endless. Arriving just before closing right after sunset, I walked into a building that felt as alone as I was scared.

"Ma'am, with your symptoms we're going to have to do an EKG," was all I heard the physician assistant say. After three EKGs the doctor came in. The look on his face alarmed me. "The results worry me," he said. "We are going to send you to the hospital from here. You are not to drive or be driven—the risk is too great."

After calling my husband, I waited. While they were hooking me up, I watched. And in the back of the ambulance, I was still. As the roar of the motor and the sound of the siren filled my consciousness, all I could say was, "God, I'm ready to listen NOW!" The response radiated in my consciousness: *You are Perfect, Whole, and Complete.* Somehow, the meaning of these words became crystal clear. *You can stop searching and do what you are here to do.*

What followed was months of doctor's visits, tests, and prayer. I wasn't prepared for the array of emotions I felt when I found myself confined to bed. In addition to being mentally and physically exhausted, I was afraid, angry, and relieved. I was afraid of what the future would hold. Would I regain my capacity to breathe without chest pain and walk without dizziness? Would I regain control of my muscles? Would I be there for my family or would I always be in their care? I was angry that I let myself get so out of alignment that it affected my physical being. I was angry that I temporarily lost the ability to earn an income. And surprisingly, I was relieved that there was a reason for me to step away from what no longer served me.

I would love to share that the road to recovery was as easy as changing my mind. But it was also a matter of letting go of fear and illusion, and raising my consciousness through affirmative prayer and spiritual practice. I continued to see my doctor and a team of specialists who tested me for stroke, heart ailments, multiple sclerosis, lupus, and depression. This was the perfect time for an inward journey. I became my own ideal client and made self-care a priority.

After years of study, I answered the call to be a spiritual practitioner and stand in loving service and support of others and hold their highest truth in consciousness. Classes were beginning the first week of April, three hours away at my new spiritual home, the Center for Spiritual Living - COLORS, in Charlotte. I had no idea how I would make the six-hour round trip each week; all I knew was that I was not alone. No matter how I felt throughout the week, I was able to make the trip each Tuesday. One day turned into two, then three, and soon I was up and about all week.

In October, I received the results from months of testing. I had experienced a mini-stroke, had developed high blood pressure, and was being monitored for the possible onset of MS. My new lifestyle of loving self-care, exercise, and diet more than regulated my body, and my symptoms ceased to exist.

One of the biggest gifts of aligning my life is remembering to listen and go where it guides me. Paying thoughtful attention to your truth and listening to the quiet whispers of your soul is necessary to align your life with Spirit, live your purpose, and enjoy your passion.

Marie Kirkland knows how to listen to the truth of who a person is while guiding them in realigning their lives and living their truth. Marie's systematic holistic approach provides a unique blend of coaching, spirituality, and business. Marie is a Centers for Spiritual Living Licensed Practitioner trained in spiritual philosophy, universal principles, and affirmative prayer, a Certified Spiritual Life Coach and radio host of Conversational Journeys. For more information about Marie and her services visit http://inneralignmentliving.com.

FAITH AND SECOND CHANCES

❊ ❊ ❊

Maylin Lue Pann

Some people believe they're "lucky" to get a second chance. If second chances have anything to do with "luck," I've had a lot of luck in my life. But I believe something different. I believe second chances are created from the power of your thinking. I am living proof that it's never too late to find that much needed second chance, in life, in health, or anything else that you desire.

Loss and devastation began for me at any early age when my parents' family business vanished right before our eyes. We were living in Jamaica at the time, where I grew up, when a fire destroyed everything that my family had worked so hard for. In that fire both the business and my dreams literally went up in smoke. The burned down business meant no money for me to attend college and to fulfill my dream of becoming a teacher. As a young girl, I was devastated. I was awarded a college scholarship for teaching, but due to our family's financial situation it was impossible for them to send me off to school, provide money for board and lodging, and buy clothing for a cold climate where I would attend college.

As the years went by after the fire, I made the decision to believe that my choices in life were limited and felt that I had to settle for less. The Big Story I told myself was, ***"I can't get what I want."*** I carried that belief into adulthood where it caused me many years of pain and anguish. I had given up my dream to become a teacher and worked as a secretary.

Years later, after delivering my third son, I thought that was the end of my life. Immediately after delivery I started hemorrhaging profusely; I was fading out but could hear the desperation and panic in the doctors' voices. Someone was crying out "Lord Jesus!" over and over again. In that instant, I knew I was dying. I saw my life flash before me—I saw their little faces, my three-year-old and six-year-old sons. Thoughts ran rapid through my mind. *Oh, I will never see them again! We never said goodbye! They were so happy that Mommy was bringing home a baby brother or sister. And now, I will never see them again.*

In those moments, I remember surrendering my life to God. I knew He was the only Source that could help me at this critical time. I totally turned my life over to Him and had the faith and knowing that things would be okay. I began the Lord is My Shepherd prayer; halfway through it I was gone. I woke up nine and a half hours later to someone repeating my name, "Maylin… Maylin." The priest was standing beside me administering last rites. It was touch and go for three days before I finally was in the clear.

That experience changed me profoundly and was just one of my many second chances in life. I learned that having strong faith and, more importantly, letting go and trusting God is the most powerful tool to creating miracles in my life. That's exactly what saved me and gave me even more second chances in the years to come.

My family and I immigrated to Toronto. During one of my secretarial jobs at an IT organization, I was responsible for distributing staff paychecks. When I looked over a few of the checks, I noticed that some people were paying more money in income tax than I was making every week. Realizing this, something inside of me started to bubble up. I felt this restless feeling. Once I got past my amazement and shock over what these other people were earning, I realized that I could start looking for better opportunities for myself. I didn't know how, but I knew these people were not smarter than me; they just had an opportunity to get a college education when I didn't.

Soon after I enrolled in a personal development workshop that taught how to get what you really want out of life. I did everything they said to do. I wrote down my goals, and even though I had no idea how my goal of making more money was going to come true, I knew for sure that I wanted to make more money. I set a goal to increase my income by 50% by the end of the year. Miraculously, in 15 months I had achieved that goal—and this was in the public sector, which was highly unusual. It was truly a moment in my life that I knew and believed that *I could get what I want*! I realized I was being given another second chance.

Through the years I built my career and became a successful computer training manager. Although I was monetarily successful,

I once again had that same restless feeling that I wanted to do more with my life and see what else I could achieve. My great desire was to coach people how to break through limiting beliefs and move forward to achieve their dreams and goals without struggling and to do it more quickly than I did. I wanted to quit my corporate job and create a successful full-time coaching business.

By now, I had the golden handcuffs tying me down—a secure job, good pay, and five weeks of vacation time. I knew that quitting my job, without an additional income, would prove difficult. I wanted to find another option that would allow me to earn money and focus on where I was passionate—teaching, coaching, and speaking in the personal and spiritual development area. I decided that I simply needed a detour or an exit strategy.

That's when I decided to buy a franchise in the salon industry. It seemed like the perfect opportunity: a turnkey business that could produce income, in which I could work part-time hours while building a coaching practice on the side. Little did I know that the franchise would end up being one of the most difficult and challenging periods of my life. I soon realized that I needed to work 12-hour days to make things work, that people and employees demanded my attention, and despite doing everything I was told to do by the franchisor, the business was hardly breaking even. Once again, I was devastated.

The failure and loss was unbearable. I had given up my secure job. I was so stressed that I could hardly eat or sleep. To top it off, I was beating myself up constantly. I couldn't believe that I had made such a horrible decision. I was angry. I stopped believing in the power of positive thinking, in goal setting and visualizing success. All I could do was compare myself to other owners and seek outside validation that I was not stupid. The experience depleted everything I had inside. I was empty. There was simply nothing left.

As I did what I could to hold myself together and pick up all of the flailing pieces, I started to recognize a deep hunger for spirituality. I realized that I needed to believe in something, and that I might as well believe in God again and resume my spiritual practices. And that's exactly what I began to do. It was my next second chance.

Through my renewed belief, I started moving into action

again. I put the franchise up for sale and started looking for freelance computer training work. Within two weeks I attracted my perfect training contract, and my new career was launched as an independent computer trainer and consultant.

From the franchise experience I learned to celebrate my wins, however small. After we sold the franchise, we had a celebration dinner. I was able to let go of the business and felt a deep sense of freedom and gratitude for yet another second chance.

I discovered from that loss that there are many great lessons to learn from adversity, and that despite the pain I can always come out stronger on the other side. I also had to learn to forgive myself, and learn to move on. I even had to feel the sadness and grieve for my losses. I had lost $100,000 with that business, and looking back I could have spent all of that to pursue my dream of creating a full-time coaching practice.

Two years later I founded my own training and consulting firm. Just when I thought things were going great, I got cancer!

When I was diagnosed with cancer my reaction surprised me. I remained calm and positive, knowing that my ability to control my emotions was crucial to controlling my health. I was confident in my ability to create yet another chance at a healthy life if I held onto my faith and persevered. At the time I was running a successful computer business, and also following my passion for personal development. The lack of passion for what I did always manifested itself eventually in some type of failure, as if God was pushing me to a place where I might find another chance to get it right.

When I was diagnosed with cancer again three and half years later, I was devastated. My faith in second chances and even in God was growing weak. I struggled to keep faith in reaching my goals. Not being able to get out and work made me feel like a failure. I felt so empty inside that I wanted to give up the fight.

I consulted my best friend (my journal) in whom I could share my darkest secrets, my deepest joys and deepest sorrows. I wrote, "Dear God, what can I do to move through this?" The answer was, "It's not your fault. Just forgive yourself and love yourself. You've come too far to stop now. Don't give up. Success is just around the corner for you."

Through the answer I realized what I had been missing. For all I had learned about self-talk and mindset, I had not been integrating them into my relationship with God. God had always been the one to open doors. It was just that now I was better at asking Him.

I delved into the healing process to keep my thoughts where I knew I needed them to be. This time, I was painfully aware of how critical my belief was to my ability to overcome this life threatening disease, not only in the process but in myself. I was terrified of the treatment but agreed to take chemo and radiation. Using self-talk for guidance, with God and my journal by my side, I navigated my way through the treatments unscathed.

I also set the intention to increase my income to six figures while decreasing my work load to make time for treatments. At the end of the year, I achieved my goal. I actually worked less and earned more during that time! This was the defining moment that made me want to share with others how they can also manifest what they want using this simple and easy technique I was using.

After all the second chances, I looked back and saw faith standing by my side in every single one of them. It was my faith that pulled me through and led me to where I am today, helping others reclaim and rebuild their lives and take advantage of second chances. Success came for me in the moment I got out of my own way (and God's way, for that matter). My soul had been crying out for more meaning in life. Little did I know this meaning was inside of me all the time just waiting for me to create an authentic life. I forgave my failures, embraced my deepest desires, and trusted and loved myself enough to manifest them. I was now living more than a successful life—I was living an authentic one.

Through all of this time I was leery of incorporating God into my teachings, but now I embrace it head on. I finally chose to open the door to fulfillment that had seemed locked for so long. I also embraced all the circumstances in my life. Successes and failures, rights and wrongs, good experiences and bad—I saw them all simply as circumstances, no more, no less. My self-love grew to become my empowerment to manifest the vision I now believed, wholeheartedly, I could create. And so I did.

Through it all I realized that I needed to know exactly what I wanted and what direction I was headed in to create that kind of success. I needed to be clear and hold the intention steadfastly, and not let anyone else get in the way. Most important I had to take inspired action every day.

As I healed from cancer and dove deeper into my life's meaning and purpose, I answered a calling that led me to create Dynamic Results, a Mindset and Spiritual Life Coaching Institute dedicated to helping women worldwide live more authentic and fulfilling lives. Through all of the difficult times, the heartbreak, the devastation, and the second chances, I learned that by loving ourselves unconditionally and allowing God to guide us, we can find the stamina to never give up and create all the chances it takes to live our dreams.

Today, I know that the greatest and most authentic expression of my life is to live in my purpose and to serve others with it. Every moment of my life leading up to this point has put me right here in this place where I needed to be. The only thing that ever kept me from this magical place was the clouds of doubt and fear. With the right self-talk and positive affirmations, those insecurities have dissipated and I have discovered and opened the door to a second chance, and even a third, fourth, and more.

The choice to become unstoppable is our own, with every thought we think, word we say, feeling we feel, and action we take. We must learn to forgive our past, love ourselves for who we are and all we desire, and embrace and trust in the amazing power each of us is capable of generating.

With that, anything becomes possible.

Maylin Lue Pann has been conducting workshops and trainings for 20+ years. Today, she is an expert in Neuro-linguistic Programming, The Silva Method, The Spiritual Laws of Prosperity, Coaching & Leadership International (CLI), Coaching from Spirit, and is a certified Law of Attraction Practitioner with the Law of Attraction Training Centre (Canada). Her mission is to guide women entrepreneurs to their inner passions, to remember who they are and reclaim their lives so that they can achieve their dreams and goals easily and effortlessly. To learn more about Maylin and her work, please contact her at Maylin@ dynamicresults.ca or visit her website at www.dynamicresults.ca.

DUM VITA EST SPES EST

Serenity Rey

Dum Vita Est Spes Est is a Latin phrase meaning "while there is life there is hope." It is a saying I consider my lifeline. Just before I embarked on the most important journey of my life, my leap of faith, I realized that phrase meant more to me than just a line of ancient script. It anchored my conscious thoughts to my core being. So I would not forget it, I had it tattooed into my left forearm. Looking back now I am filled with wonder and pride at how far I have come. I still have so many roads left to travel, but standing here, looking back at the path I have walked thus far, makes me proud. It never ceases to amaze me, the amount of strength I have in me. We are all so much stronger than we know, than we will probably ever know. While there is life, there is hope. My story is a true testament to the strength of the human spirit. If I can inspire at least one person to hang on, it will all be worthwhile.

My childhood was pretty similar to many others. I have plenty of joyous memories, but there are just as many painful ones. My father left when I was barely learning to walk and disappeared from my life permanently when I was five. We were left, my mom, my older brother, and I, to fend for ourselves with no other family. She moved us to Colorado where she provided the best life she could while still battling her own demons, her own pain from a life of neglect and abuse. We struggled for many years, but while we had little as far as material possessions, we had each other and that was all that mattered. The rest of my childhood was uneventful, but not having my father around took its toll.

I learned very early to self-medicate. At about 13 years of age I began experimenting with drugs. I tried just about everything under the sun, as long as it could be smoked, sniffed, or swallowed. I found a way of filling the hole in my life that my father left. My experimentation was a way to numb the pain. A way to forget that nagging suspicion that maybe I had something to do with him leaving. When I was high I was numb and that's all that mattered. It was simply my personal formula for survival: no feelings equaled no pain. Every summer was spent trying a new drug and every new drug was a new addiction. There was no moderation with me. No recreational fun. I was an addict, constantly replacing one addiction with another.

I spent my teenage years jumping around from house to house. I never struck out on my own to become an independent woman. I was not happy alone. Being alone was torture. I could not stand who I was. So I surrounded myself with men. And drugs.

I managed to graduate high school and attended a couple semesters of college. I found my first passion in life helping animals. I began working at a kennel on weekends, walking, feeding, and caring for the animals. From there I began training for and eventually landed a job as a veterinary technician. Most technicians had to go to school to get a degree, but I was lucky enough to get a job on my smarts and experience alone. Things appeared okay on the outside. Inside was very different.

My job became nothing more than a means to an end. The passion was gone. Soon after my 23rd birthday I became addicted to what would eventually become my undoing: a drug named "coke" and a man named "Dan." When I smoked it I felt better than I ever had, but five minutes later I would fiend for more. I became hopelessly and recklessly hooked, more than I had ever been to anything in my life. I came face to face with the devil that year and he had me wrapped around his little finger.

This was one of the worst years of my life. To describe the pain and worthless, helpless feeling I was left with is impossible. I could not hold a job. I lost all of my friends, save for Dan and the "friends" who partied with us. I sold, pawned, or traded everything I owned that had any value. I lost weight. We didn't eat, didn't sleep, and didn't leave the house for days on end. And to my complete and utter shame, I stole from my own mother. My mother, who had given up everything so we would not go without, who worked day in and day out, so we would have a place to live, food on the table, and toys to play with.

This drug brought out a side in me I never knew existed, a side I never want to see again. We would wake up after a binge and the feeling of guilt was so great I felt I could not go on. The only survival method I knew was to mask the pain, to numb my feelings. I was stuck in a vicious, endless cycle and knew that if I did not quit I would die. But how could I quit? How could I feel? The pain of life was unbearable. I saw no options. Only Hell.

It was in this dark place that an angel came to me. I was pleading for help, for a reason to quit drugs, a reason to live. My prayers were answered: a gift from the universe in the form of a child.

On June 13, 2006, my daughter Trinity Ann was born. She was perfect and healthy and the best thing that ever happened to me. She brought light to my world that was once so dark. She brought me a reason not only to live but also to thrive and to chase my dreams with an enthusiasm I had not had since I was a child. Her eyes pierced their way straight to my heart, searing my soul with unconditional love. No matter what I did, this child would love me. She would continue to look at me with wonder and admiration. It was then I made a vow that I would never let her down. That I would be the best mother I could be and provide her with the life she deserved to have.

I left her father and we moved in with my mom. I found a job working at an ER for animals. Things were finally as they should be, but I would still have my sobriety tested. And I had yet to truly FEEL.

When Trinity turned three, I began to get restless. I loved helping animals, but it wasn't as fulfilling as it once was. I started to feel like there was still so much more out there for us to explore and experience. And Serenity, the co-dependent, had yet to actually be on her own. I began to feel a pull towards my creative side. I began writing poems, journals, and stories. The thought of writing music filled me with such longing that I knew it was my path. I heard that anyone who wanted to make it in the music industry needed to be in California or New York. While I had never been to New York, I had been to California several times and had always enjoyed it. I loved the beach, the weather, and the extreme diversity.

I began networking online until I found someone who lived there. His name was Steve and we began to correspond regularly. He had dabbled in television and had a successful season of his own show. He explained that he had once been in my position—a lost soul looking for an opportunity to make it in this world, when someone came along and offered him that chance. They brought him to California, gave him a job, and helped him get on his way to the life he had always dreamed of. Now, he explained, he was returning the kindness by offering the same opportunity to me. He told me he had job for me. It would just be something in the administrative field, but I could use it to survive while getting out and meeting people in California. This was it! This is what I had been waiting for! This was the opportunity of a life time and I was not going to let it pass me by.

The next few months were spent preparing. With Steve's help I was moving to California. The plan was to go out there alone at first, find an apartment, start my new job, and then I would fly back for Trinity. Four weeks didn't seem too long.... Little did I know it would be the longest four weeks of my life.

When I arrived in California I was immediately hit with doubts about Steve's credibility. His house, I noticed, was much more humble than he had led on. I decided it didn't really matter. Money was not an issue for me and if he led on to having a little more than he actually did, that was no big deal. But then he started skirting around the questions I asked about work. He would tell me, "Don't worry about it, just enjoy yourself for a while." When a couple weeks passed with still no straight answer, it hit me. There was no job. I had been duped. Lied to. Completely betrayed. I had even signed a 12-month lease, although I only brought enough money to buy a car and pay a couple months' rent.

The realization was devastating. I confronted Steve and it ended in a screaming match. I knew then, I was on my own. The pain I felt was deep. I was in a completely different world now. And my heart, my soul, my Trinity, was hundreds of miles away. I had an overwhelming desire to numb the pain. To drink or smoke myself into that old state I had become so familiar with. What would I do? How could I not only survive this pain, but face it head on? I didn't think I could. I went into an extreme state of depression and cried myself to sleep every night.

The area I had moved to, unbeknownst to me, was not the safest. There were sirens constantly screaming, dogs barking, and people everywhere. It was in complete contrast to everything I had known in Colorado, which was quiet, safe, and calm. I had nothing and knew no one. And now, for the first time in my life, I had to face this incredible pain with no support from a substance. It had to come from me. My strength had to come from within even though I was not sure if I had it.

I had always been the spiritual type and decided that was what I needed to draw on right now. I saw that getting in touch with Spirit was the only way I could make it through. I did an online search for a spiritual center in my area and quickly found one that appealed to me. I arrived one Sunday morning, lost and scared, and sat through a service. I felt like I was on the right track, but still felt as if I needed more. This church was very small, the crowd was a bit older, and I didn't feel like I would make the connections I needed here. On my way out a man stopped me and we started talking. He asked about my story and after telling him, he mentioned a very popular spiritual center in Culver City that I should check out.

The following Wednesday we went and I immediately knew THIS was where I belonged. This was where I would find my strength. I began to attend regularly and met some amazing people. I was getting stronger and things were getting easier emotionally. I was finally able to pick up Trinity and feel whole again. I had made it through the worst, but things were still hard. I still had a family to worry about and no means to take care of us.

One day at my spiritual center they mentioned a group called the Sacred Service, a group that regularly went out to do volunteer work in the community. I knew right away I needed to help. We met on a Saturday morning at a beach in Newport and spent several hours picking up trash. I worked along side a woman named Cynthia, who happened to be a prayer minister. After hearing my story she immediately offered her services to me, free of charge. From that day forward we began praying. Every single day, we prayed I would find work. We prayed I would make rent. Only two weeks in, I had a complete stranger hand me $300 and I was able to make rent that month. The universe was answering my prayers, as it always does.

After that my funds were drained again and I was out of options. I continued to pray with Cynthia day in and day out. My daughter and I were on the verge of eviction and I still had no job. One night after prayer I looked down at my tattoo and was reminded of hope. A strange sense of calm came over me that I cannot explain and I knew then—with my heart and soul— that everything would work out. Two days later I went on an interview and was offered a position on the spot.

Today I can look back and not only forgive Steve, but thank him. He gave me that extra push needed to get out to California, and it took that experience to show me it was time to start depending on myself. Being in California now, I see that there is something big waiting for me. I know with utter certainty that there is a reason I am here. I know that the Universe will never lead me astray. I also learned that I can face any challenge head on. I can take care of myself and my daughter. I know now that the strength within me is enough. It has always been enough. And in the words of a wise bear named Winnie the Pooh, "You are braver than you believe, stronger than you seem, and smarter than you think."

Serenity Rey was born on November 19, 1981 in Rockford, Illinois. At the age of two her family moved to Denver, Colorado, where she spent the rest of her childhood and early adult years. She is the mother of a four-year-old girl and they reside just outside of Los Angeles, California. Currently she is in the administrative field but plans to continue on her creative path, writing stories and creating music. She also wants to continue spreading her message of hope to anyone that will listen. Serenity can be contacted by email at serenityrey@gmail.com.

Surviving to Thriving

OUT ON A LIMB

Kathy Cagney

My story of overcoming abuse and alcoholism is riddled with intensely deep and dark painful memories. At least, it used to be. You see, that deep and dark place where the memories were held has been exposed to the light for so many years now, it has lost its power.

I attempted writing this story many, many times. I tried over and over again to put the pain and anguish into words. I wanted you to know what I'd been through so that we could make a connection. I do know that pain is pain, regardless of how it's inflicted.

My pain came about in the heinous act of being sexually molested on the kitchen table of my mother's best friend's husband. He was someone my family trusted and he violated that trust. In fact, he violated me until I was 12 years old. As a way of coping, I dissociated. It was far too devastating to stay present and thus, as a way to survive, I went "out on a limb" on the tree outside the kitchen window. That tree saved my life and I will never forget it.

~~~

Saturday morning was finally here. It was a beautiful, breezy summer day. The sun was shining so brightly through my bedroom window I could see little dust bunnies on the floor. I was so happy the weather was good because it was a perfect day to wear my blue cotton pastel-striped dress. The two little pockets in the front were my favorite part of that dress. I could keep my little troll doll in there, the one with the bright yellow hair that was so different from mine.

My mom called me from downstairs telling me it was time to get in the car and go; we were running late. We were going over to the big beautiful house a few blocks away where my mom's best friend, Josephine, lived. Their street was much wider than ours and lined with big trees and manicured lawns. In the front of this big white house with green shutters, the flower garden was amazing. It was so colorful, filled with flowers I didn't know the names of. The stairs leading up to the front porch were wide—I'll bet 10 people standing straight across could all go up at the same time and still have plenty of room left over. Inside, the floors were covered with oriental rugs in deep rich, dark tones. The little table in the front hallway always had on it a vase filled with fresh flowers cut from their garden.

When we arrived everyone began talking all at once; we were excited about what the day ahead would bring. Mike said he was taking his glove and baseball to play catch, and Nick was frantically looking for the Frisbee he wanted to bring along. Everyone started loading bags of food and stuff to play with in the cars. Our picnic was going to take place at Fort Monmouth, a nearby army base where my dad was finishing out his service. It was so beautiful there with the rolling green hills of the golf course and the giant swimming pool. Even the drive in through the gate was amazing. We always felt so special upon arrival because the soldier standing guard at the gate saluted our car. We had a special sticker in the window denoting my dad was a Major. We always watched with anticipation waiting for the soldier to salute and we'd all salute back. It was so cool!

Amidst the mayhem of everyone getting in the cars to leave, Josephine's husband suddenly announced that everyone should go on ahead without me and him. He said we had a special stop to make and would be just a few minutes behind them. We were going to pick up a very special dessert for the outing and he wanted me to go along for the ride with him. Our downtown bakery had just started making special butter cookies shaped and decorated like Snow White and Cinderella and Tinkerbell. He said you just won't believe your eyes when you see them! I was giddy with excitement; he must know how much I love cookies!

The boys couldn't care less about the cookies and they rushed out to the car ready to go. Everyone was shouting their goodbyes and saying, "See you in a little while, don't be long!" My mom, dad, and brothers got into our station wagon and drove away, followed by Josephine and her sons in their car. That's when my life changed. Little did I know that my fairy tale day would suddenly turn into a nightmare.

I knew by the way Mr. K was looking at me that something

was not right. He took me into the kitchen and lifted me up onto the kitchen table. He started doing things to me that I knew were wrong. I was so confused. Why was this happening? He tried so hard to convince me that this would be our little secret and I should never tell anyone. He said that this was special and magical just for the two of us. The fear and shock coursed through my six-year-old body. My heart started racing and then it started breaking. The confusion was overwhelming. My voice was screaming inside but nothing was coming out. He was too big to push away. I was too little to fight back. I turned my head, looked out the kitchen window, and saw a big tree with lots of branches and leaves. I started noticing the thick brown branches and the bright green leaves swaying in the breeze. The sun was shining on them and it looked like they were dancing. I wanted to be out there dancing on those branches, too. And, then I was. I was out there among them, in my mind anyway. That's where I went, out on a limb. It was all I could do to survive the horror that was taking place on that cold, hard table beneath my frail little frame.

Everything that happened the rest of that day is a complete blur to me. There is no recollection of seeing or picking out princess cookies covered in colorful frosting. The day that started out so bright and sunny turned out to be devastatingly dark and stormy for me. What the weather did, I have no idea.

Years later, in therapy I learned that what I was doing is called "dissociation." It was a gift my spirit gave me that day, to be able to keep my sanity and compartmentalize the trauma.

Does anyone really understand the soul-stripping pain, confusion, and humiliation of childhood rape unless it's happened to them? How could they? Do the words "pain," "confusion," and "humiliation" even begin to adequately express what it feels like? For those of us that it's happened to, we can hardly explain the depth of despair we felt. I don't think we have words for something that's never supposed to happen in the first place.

But it did happen and I needed to heal from it. So with the help of a good therapist, I slowly, and I mean slowly, found the words to use, and I spit them out. I spewed forth all the ugliness I felt inside. I knew on some level that it no longer belonged to me. It was time to release it. And release it I did. Through all kinds of means: art therapy, music therapy, drama therapy, group therapy, you name it. I was going to do whatever it took to release that ugly ogre inside me.

For five and a half years, I went to group therapy every Tuesday night. On one particular night, my therapist asked me to start giving voice to the pain I was holding in. I couldn't find the words. I stuttered and stammered and struggled to get them out. It took what seemed like an eternity for me to finally release, one syllable at a time, the truth and ugliness of what had happened.

Speaking about it was like being stuck in the undertow in the middle of an ocean storm. I felt like my legs were struggling to find the ocean floor. I was desperately trying to find a way to feel grounded and steadied so that I could keep talking. Just when I thought I was ready to say more, another wave would come along and knock me off my feet. My chest felt heavy with the pressure of the waves of emotion. My mouth would slam shut for fear that I would drown in sorrow. The taste of salty tears running down my cheeks was impossible to ignore. Little by little, one wave at a time, the storm settled and I found my way to the safety of the shore. I finally got it all out and sat there in sheer exhaustion. I felt at once the relief of being free from this deep, dark, ugly secret. Moments later I felt the sheer panic of now what? What do I do now to put the pieces of me back together again?

I continued going to therapy and began to feel whole again. My therapist, Karen, whom I affectionately referred to as my "giant gluestick," was a pivotal person in my life. I know that divine intervention led me to her so she could help me heal in so many ways. Karen tried to explain the process of peeling back the onion, the many layers to my pain that needed to be healed and revealed. However, at one point along our journey, I was paralyzed with fear about going back into what I called "the black hole" of pain. It seemed terrifying and daunting to me, so much so that I lost my voice again. I was not able to speak, not even stutter or stammer the words.

Karen asked me to draw a picture of what I was feeling. I drew a stick figure that had no hands or feet, crawling up to the edge of a precipice looking down into a long, dark, deep hole filled with a massive amount of sticky black tar. I feared it would never release me. Karen said it was up to me to decide if I wanted to go in and that she would go with me. She promised she would help me find my way up and out again. By the grace of God, I found the courage to go in. When I say I feel like I went to hell and back, I mean it! The journey changed me, healed me, and restored me to the beautiful, precious child of God that I was born to be.

Karen kept that drawing and still uses it to this day in her talks and workshops. She recently told me about a client who was feeling the same fear that I had. She showed this client my drawing and told her my story. The client took the drawing and added a ladder to the picture. She said she'd be willing to go in but needed to see that there was a way out before doing so. What a beautiful idea! This was such a powerful gift to me because I got to see the connection we all have and how we can add to each other's journey in ways that we can't even imagine.

It took me 25 years after the molestation occurred to seek help. The abuse started when I was six and ended when I was 12. I have no recollection of my life between the ages of 12 and 16. My little lost self was just going through the motions. Then, at the age of 16, I started drinking and didn't stop until I was 34. I got sober through the help of AA, a good sponsor, and a wonderful support system. I'm proud to say that, as of this writing, I celebrate 20 years of sobriety!

I am truly, deeply grateful that I had the courage to get help when I needed it most. The last 20 years have been filled with the most exciting discoveries of the power that self-awareness brings. I feel so blessed to be living at a time when there are so many people, like you and me, who are passionate about finding our true path and being the fullest expression of ourselves. I love being fully awake and aware to all the possibilities that life holds. I am especially enjoying being in midlife. It feels like a great time to give birth to new ideas and adventures. I am excited to see what I will create next. I know that with pure intention, focused thought, and courageous action anything is possible!

Kathy has enjoyed great success as an entrepreneur and reinvention specialist. She has owned and sold several businesses and has traveled the country as the host of a TV show. As a member of the Screen Actors Guild, she has performed in television and theatrical productions for 30 years. Finding herself in midlife with another chance to reinvent herself, she is now a speaker, author, and Creative Coach. As an Interior Diviner, Kathy helps women redesign their lives from the inside out. When you coach with her or attend a talk, you'll discover how much fun it can be to make midlife suck less and rock more! To contact Kathy please visit www.kathycagney.com.

THE POWER OF LOVE

Hailey Wiseman

Once in a while, we are given just the right circumstances where practicing the art of love, of being loving and being in loving service with gratitude, flows naturally and without hesitation. In November 2010 my mother passed away 11 days after crashing her car into a culvert. God called me to be with her each of those days and when God calls, I listen and act.

My mother and I were not close. She had spent the majority of our life together verbally and emotionally abusing me but I knew, without a doubt, I had been called to her bedside to facilitate assisting her with whatever it was she was working out with God. I knew she was not done. Each time I was at her side, I would lay my hands on her and pray she would come to know what it was God was asking of her. I would pray all the anger, hatred, and resentments she felt be released from her heart and that she would truly know she was loved and experience and accept the essence of being loved. She had been searching for love her entire life.

Rewind 26 years. I was not sure how long I had been asleep when I heard a soft voice beckoning me to wake up. I opened my eyes but the light and images in the room were bright and distorted, creating four horizontally stacked carbon copies of one another. I could not focus my eyes but I could hear a lullaby voice whispering, "Can you hear me?" I nodded and the soft voice told me she was glad I had decided to come back and that she had been sitting with me for three days. She said, "I'm so glad you decided to stay. You are young and beautiful and have your whole life ahead of you."

I suppose I really did not want to die but I did not want to live either. It was rather difficult to find joy in anything when on the inside I felt so tired, beat up, and disillusioned. As a teenager I couldn't wait to get away from my mother and now at 21, even though I didn't live with her anymore, I was still trying to get away from her. Her constant demoralizing litany spiced with her favorite phrase of "God damn you Hailey Lynne" had been set on replay in my mind.

I was not consciously aware of these tapes running over and over, placing roadblocks in front of every positive choice I tried to make. Anyone paying attention would certainly have noticed the dramatic curves of the emotional roller coaster I was riding, but nobody was paying attention. I struggled to survive but could not hold on. I finally let go, threw my arms up in the air, and rounded the last curve before that final drop into a silent, almost breathless sleep.

There I lay, confused about how to feel or what to think but soothed by the kind nurse who encouraged me to hang on. What the nurse did not know was I had made the decision "not to die" before I even arrived in the ER, much less the ICU.

I had been in the park for several hours but no longer could hold my head up or keep my body upright. I had taken every sleep inducing pill I had saved for the past year along with about 50 aspirin and anything else sitting on the glass shelves of the medicine cabinet. For a year I tried to fool myself into thinking I was not planning suicide, telling myself *You are just saving those pills in case you need them.* But I could feel I was becoming extremely weary and uncertain of my ability to hang on; I could no longer overcome the overwhelming feeling that time was running out. I also was acutely aware that I could barely hear the internal voice that had so often saved me. Since I was little girl, when things would get bad, I would hear from somewhere within my psyche, *You are going to be okay.* I would then know on a profound level that I was worth so much more than I was feeling.

I obviously was not really fooling myself by saving those pills. I was consciously waiting until I felt I had exhausted every choice and I was absolutely sure I didn't care if I was alive or dead. I thought that smiling, exercising, eating healthy, and working towards a career was joyous living. It never occurred to me the euphoric feelings that had kept me attached to life were induced by my addictions to sex, drugs, and alcohol. Having dropped the addictions I was living the illusion that I was "healthy and getting my life together," but really I was only showing up with a smile. The part of me that knew I was worth investing more faith and love into, was numb.

After taking the last of the pills, I staggered away from the outdoor water fountain, zipped my light-weight jacket a little closer to my neck, put my purse over my head and across my body so I would know I had it, walked over to where the St. Augustine seemed plush and laid down. My purse had seemed very important to me. It had a wad of cash in it along with a note I had written with all the information needed to identify me. I'd tried to get a hold of several friends from a pay-phone before I ingested that last handful of pills but nobody was home. Getting from the pay-phone to where I decided to lay down had proven to be a dizzy moonwalk along the bank of the creek, and I knew there was no way I would be able to call for help again once I laid down. I didn't want to risk falling in the creek and drown. I had always feared drowning and I didn't want everyone to think it was an accident not a suicide, especially my mom. I wanted her to know I had killed myself so maybe then she would love me.

As I lay in the cool grass, the combination of drugs rushed through my veins inducing a deeply relaxing state of consciousness. I began to feel as though I was being cradled. I became aware that I was suspended above my body in a sphere of light. I could see beings around a table. There were 12 of them. The being at the head of the table came forward. It was a heavenly being of pure light and I was delighted to be in its presence. I knew this energy.

The being spoke to me saying, "As your council we have come to take you home with us if that is what you want." I thought, *If that is what I want, what do you mean?* It replied, "If you want to come with us you can." I thought, *What, I can choose to die or not?*

The being then said to me, "Yes, but if you choose to leave your body and come with us, you will still have to do what you came to the earth to do and it will be difficult."

I could not imagine life being more difficult than what I had been going through. *What, life will be harder than it is now?* The being replied, "Yes, you will have to finish your mission without your physical body. It can be done but not as easily as it can be in your body."

I thought, *I can't possibly endure anything more difficult than what I am already going through,* and with that the being smiled and turned to leave. The other 11 beings around the table began to rise, flank the being I was communicating with, and they all began to ascend into the light. I felt as though I shouted, "Wait, don't leave! I haven't made my decision."

They turned back and the light being said, "You made your decision."

No, I didn't, I thought.

The being then replied, "You feel as though you cannot endure anything more difficult than you are now. That is your decision." I pleaded, "Don't leave."

I felt weightless and filled with the pure essence of love. I didn't want this feeling to ever go away. I felt no pain in my physical or emotional body. The being then said, "Hailey, we are always with you and always will be."

I was sad they were leaving and whimpered, "When will I see you again?"

The light being said, "We will come again when the time is right. You will know it is us and in the meantime know we are always with you."

Again they turned and ascended into a soft but radiant light. They became the light, they were the light. I was still floating above my body and could still feel their presence. I felt as though I was wrapped in love. I wanted to experience this feeling for as long as possible but very abruptly I felt myself re-entering my body. I knew I was because I could no longer look down and see it and I felt heavy, not weightless as I had when I was hovering above. All at once, I could feel the physical and emotional pain again.

Waking to the soft voice of the nurse was soothing to my frail body and mind. I could literally feel the energy of the love she was sharing when I opened my eyes. The nurse got a call and said, "Hailey, I will be right back. Someone is asking to visit you and I have to go see who it is." I nodded.

Soon she returned, sat down in the chair next to my bed where she had been before, took my hand, and in her beautiful voice quietly said "Your mother is here. She is yelling and demanding to see you. Hailey, she is agitated. You don't have to see her if you don't want to. You are 21, an adult, which means you can choose not to see her and I can ask her to leave. Do you want to see your mother?"

I said, with my eyes closed, "No."

The nurse said, "Are you sure?"

I then felt indecisive. I was so disempowered and with the question "Are you sure?" I doubted my initial response of "No" and said, "Okay."

The nurse said, "Honey, you don't have to see her, I'm just making sure I understood you. Your voice is barely audible. It is okay to nod your head rather than speak." I nodded my head "Yes."

Just before my mother came in the nurse asked, "Do you want me to stay with you while your mom is here?" I nodded "Yes."

She said, "Okay, but if you decide you want her to leave, you just let me know. You are very fragile right now and need to rest."

Moments later I heard my mother loudly saying, "Hailey, open your eyes." I tried to open my eyes, but I was still seeing multiple images. It was mentally assaulting. I was trying to say, "I can't open my eyes" when she said, much louder than before, "Hailey, open your eyes! Look at me, it is your mother!"

When I didn't instantly respond to her demand, she screamed, "Hailey, I said open your eyes and look at me right now. I said look at me. You are not going to blame this on me, this is not my fault. Look at me!" I tried, but the vision of this maniac bouncing around with four mouths yelling at me was robbing me of the sweet moments of love I had experienced only minutes earlier.

Then I heard the nurse say, "Hailey, you don't have to talk to your mom right now. Do you want to wait until you feel better?" I nodded "Yes" and with that she asked my mom to leave. The nurse got up and walked to the door and opened it. My mother stormed out. I could hear her giving everyone a piece of her angry mind.

Synchronistically, 26 years later I found myself in the ICU lovingly holding my mother's hand just as that nurse had done for me. During one of those evenings, a beautiful being of light came into the room behind me and embraced me. I felt calmed and loved. I could feel the healing light moving through my arms and hands into my mother's right hand. A moment into this healing I felt my deceased brother Shane come into the room and stand next to me. I said to my mother, "I think Shane is here." She nodded "Yes," in reply. I asked her if she could feel him and she nodded "Yes" again.

A few days earlier mom had told me her "Daddy," "Shaney," and "God" had been in the room visiting her. I knew they had, they were now. I felt honored and blessed to be able to trust and know the feeling of God when it is near.

As I engaged in this act of loving service I could feel I was being healed as much as my mom was. As the energy of love increased I could feel my heart opening and moving closer to the source from which it came; God. I sensed a spark of healing for all of humanity being ignited. I could feel the hearts of every person near and far, those I know and those I don't, expanding with love. God was revealing the power of love to me.

In her last conscious moments my mother was able to tell me she loved me. I told her I loved her and forgave her and asked her if she forgave me and she said "Yes." She told me she loved me again. I was overwhelmed. My mother had rarely told me she loved me over the last 20 years and had only recently done so a few weeks before her accident. Now she was able to say it freely and lovingly.

Through the years of rejection and disdain my mother exhibited towards me, I learned to love with a greater capacity than I am able to understand at times. And during the last days of her life, gracefully and with a relaxed ease, I loved her and she accepted the love I offered. My life with her taught me that the practice of speaking one's truth, setting healthy boundaries, being committed to an open heart, being patient, moving into service, being grateful, consciously connecting to the breath, being prayerful to reveal God's will, accepting it, acting on it and not being connected to the outcome is a powerful cocktail called "LOVE" and it works every time!

Hailey Wiseman, M.A., is the creator of "Soul Talk Therapy," a transpersonal approach to psychotherapy designed to reveal one's true Soul's calling and the workshop "Loving Through Forgiveness" inspired by the passing of her mother. This powerful workshop teaches one to live and love in the present without attachment to the past. She is also the author of the newsletter "Blessings for Your Soul" featuring her popular "Soul Advice" column and the host of the Blog Talk Radio program "Blessings for Your Soul." Hailey's life work is centered on empowering folks to make the journey home to their heart where they can find the courage to turn their dreams into reality and live with the intention of inspiring change and fostering love in the world. You can learn more about Hailey at www.haileywiseman.com.

ARE YOU SAFE?

Laura Jacob

I was mortified driving to the marriage counselor. The week prior he had indicated that he would need to meet with me privately to tackle my issues…MY issues! I had spent the week replaying all the old messages I had gotten as a child and in my first failed marriage. *Not worthy of unconditional love, not worthy of a faithful, clean and sober partner*…blah, blah blah. The list was long.

When I arrived, my head hung low but a small voice within was denying that I was the crazy one! How could I defend myself? How could I explain the anguish I was experiencing from this mite-sized man who controlled everything about me? My husband had interfered with my work, controlled my money, insisted I change my name to his, and eliminated familial, professional, and friend contact. I couldn't even have a garage door opener—he would always be there to greet me. I couldn't have a key to the mailbox—he would get the mail. I could spend only 50 dollars a week on groceries to feed a family that often included four adults and three pre-teens. Of course every dinner had to include mashed potatoes and no vegetables. I hate mashed potatoes and I love vegetables. I was allowed to have a glass of wine in my home as long as I hid the glass and bottle.

The examples raged through my head. Of course I was allowed to share my opinions, but then I was ordered into his car and driven to a place where I wouldn't dare escape. He would speak at me with his finger pointed in my face and tell me how I could or should feel. He was always quick to remind me that since my mother didn't like me and I had been cheated on before, it was excusable that I didn't know how to love him. Of course, I needed to be in bed at nine and ready to make love to him. That is why he got married—so he could have sex every night. He really told me that!

I was so embarrassed. We had gotten engaged after 10 weeks

and then married after 10 months of dating. My twins were 11 years old and his son was a class behind them, but also 11. I had been around him for years at two different churches, but had not really ever spoken to him. I adored his older daughter who was 18 at the time. She had lived with her mother near the mall that we frequented and we saw her regularly. She was so cute and always so kind to both me and the twins.

If I'd taken any notice of him, it was that he was always very serious, very sad, and always alone. After speaking with him once at a fundraising event, he asked me out probably 10 times, to which my answer was always no! I had absolutely no attraction to this man. I am 5'9" and he was 5'6". I was more inclined to be attracted to the big guy in the back of the bar who left his wallet at home. This guy looked like Barbie's Ken and his shoes were way too shiny! He was an extreme introvert and I was a bubbly extrovert. He was black and white and I was all the colors of the rainbow plus a few more purples!

He tricked me into our first date and it was relatively painless. Before I knew it we were out to lunch as a blended family. It was there that we found common ground with prior spouses. His first had cheated on him with his best friend; his second had gone to prison for embezzling funds and using drugs. Mine was an unfaithful, recovering alcoholic and drug addict, both prescription and illegal. We had a connection because of our pasts and the challenges of single-parenting. I still wasn't attracted to him, and in fact he would describe our first embrace as icy!

He conned me into going out of town with him, as all he had done for two years was work and he just wanted to get away with another adult. I wish I had a video of what happened that night in Vail, as I still can't believe that I fell for it. A spiritual coach suggested he knew my weak spot and nailed it. He suggested he would and could take care of me and my twins the way we deserved! I had longed for those words all of my life. There was no emotion or love in my family. I still have never seen my parents embrace or show affection for each other. No one ever told me they loved me or anyone else, for that matter. At 18 I guided my younger sister to Planned Parenthood for birth control. When my mother discovered this she called us both tramps and locked herself in her room for days. No wonder when I was raped at age 19, I never told a soul! After all, I was "a tramp" and probably deserved it! Any sign of neediness would not have been tolerated and I learned to be independent from a very young age. I usually describe myself as independent to a fault, which makes my life story that much more unbelievable!

When the marriage counselor greeted me I entered, prepared to be annihilated. *I must not be able to see the truth,* I thought. *All these others must be right and I simply don't get it.* Yet I'd thought of myself as quite bright. I have a master's degree in Communications with a certificate in Dispute Resolution from the University of Denver, for God's sake. How could I have fooled so many people with all of MY issues?

As I sat down and prepared myself to accept my shortcomings, the counselor looked deeply into my eyes. He stated that he had needed to see me privately to ask me one question. *Only one,* I thought. *Whew! Maybe I'm not as bad as I was imagining.*

"Are you safe?" he asked with a look of grave concern. It was as if he had popped a large balloon that had reached beyond its capacity. *Safe,* I thought...*NO! No, I have not felt safe since the wedding.* The honeymoon was horrid. We stayed at a five-star resort in Kauai but I was not allowed to have breakfast. He stated that I wasn't worthy of breakfast. I found myself sneaking to the gift shop with cash to drink Gatorade and eat peanuts. I had lost 25 pounds in the 10 months prior. He always said I looked better that way. I look at pictures of my bathing suit hanging off my bottom, I was emaciated. I guess he felt more manly since he couldn't surpass my height at least he weighed more.

By now I was sobbing. The counselor apologized for being deceiving in front of my husband, but he knew it was the only way he could get me alone. He was right. If my husband thought for one minute we were going to talk about his shortcomings, I would have not been allowed to return. Just the week before he had accused me of having an affair with a friend with whom I worked. Nothing could have been further from the truth, but he twisted and turned things so threateningly that the man did not attend a meeting we were both supposed to attend. I had to call my husband every hour from the hotel room phone to prove that I was alone and in the room. I still can't believe that I succumbed to his insanity, but I feared for my friend.

The counselor proceeded to ask me if I as familiar with the term *misogynist.* Honestly, I was not. As he began to describe the

171

disorder I felt as if he had been spying on us. He characterized my husband's behavior with frightening clarity. He suggested I read the book *Men Who Hate Women and the Women Who Love Them*, by Dr. Susan Forward and Joan Torres. I highly recommend the book, especially when I suspect control/abuse to be present. To this day I owe that counselor my life. I'm not sure how far the abuse would have gone, but I am certain I would have been emotionally destroyed before long. That insightful man gave me tips on how to exit the marriage without letting my husband know that was my intention. He guided and supported me out of a very dark hole.

The counselor explained that the misogynist's underlying fear is to be abandoned by his woman. It typically results from an untrustworthy relationship with his mother. My husband was so fearful of losing me that he acted insanely to control me. In essence, he lost me because he tried to control me. I felt like my head would implode and by the time I escaped I was as angry as a caged cougar! I cried several times a day. I continued to lose weight. My eyes became sunken and distrusting. My breath had turned to small sips.

The night I realized I had to get out or die was the night he was being honored as president of his Optimist's Club. Earlier he had raged at my daughter and, when I tried to discuss it with him, he had raged at me in the car. As I watched him muddle through the ceremony, I had an out-of-body experience that told me I had to leave. It was also the first time I realized the man could not read. I later figured out he couldn't write either. He was a brilliant business man who was illiterate. Being passionate about education and communication, I suggested he get a tutor to overcome the situation. He angrily got in my face and told me no one would ever know this. I didn't blame him for his illiteracy, for I believe the school system failed him. What I couldn't accept was his complete unwillingness to reach out for help. His pride was bigger than his desire for self-improvement.

By God's grace I was able to sneak ten dollars a week from my menial budget. That is what I needed to have my credit approved and rent another home. Sadly, yet thankfully I had rented our previous home to tenants. My twins and I could not return home for nine more months. Guided by angels I rented the home behind ours. It put the kids back at the same bus stop and neighborhood.

It put me close to everything I had previously known. I asked my kids' father to take them while I made this transition. When he understood that I feared for our safety he cooperated.

As I was guided, I told my husband that my issues were so deep and unresolved that it would be better for him if I took the children and moved out. Although he didn't like it, since there was no blame, he too eventually cooperated. We stayed up all night as he begged me to stay. It was sickening to take all the blame and put on the facade, but regaining my life was well worth it.

When the movers appeared the next day, they knew it was a possible domestic abuse situation. They laughed with me privately wondering who the "little guy" could hurt? I enjoyed their humor and the close eye they kept on me, but inside I was scared to death. This man had humiliated me and made me doubt myself. The move was quite easy as I had never unpacked the boxes of my personal belongings. Maybe intuitively I knew I wouldn't stay or maybe it was his control over every item in our home that kept my things boxed up. Foolishly I had donated every piece of furniture from my home. I had to start from scratch. Living in that icky rental home with no furniture was better than living in constant ridicule and fear.

By his pleading, I had cut my work as a dental hygienist down to two days. That allowed me to be completely controlled by him five days a week, to work by his side as his business partner. Thankfully my employer of 19 years gave me back my full-time position when my husband fired me. Again, I was so embarrassed, as I had shared with patients about my new fabulous life with this wonderful man. The humiliation was deep, but my desire to provide for my children and regain my life kept me going hour by hour, patient by patient.

It took me another four months to work through the separation and pending divorce. I had never felt so alone in all my life and yet never been happier! Whether he was bending my wrists backward to achieve my submissiveness or pinning me against the wall as I exited the shower to chastise my thoughts or actions, his behavior was all fear-based. I am so grateful that I get to choose my own thoughts and behaviors today. It took me years to regain this confidence and it wasn't without a few more negative relationships, but I have found my voice again. The chance to share and possibly prevent one more woman from the horrific experience of bondage and captivity that I endured gives me the strength to share my truth.

Laura Jacob is the proud mother of amazing twins, Garth and Veronika. She is a life coach and Religious Science practitioner. Laura also practices dental hygiene in Denver and is currently the president of the Colorado Dental Hygienists Association. She is the founding president of the Mothers of Multiples Society and forever a strong advocate for women and children. She is currently in a wonderful, loving relationship and is crazy about elephants since her return from Thailand. Laura is passionate about speaking your truth and advocates always saying what you mean and meaning what you say! Contact her at LauraJacob@comcast.net.

JOURNEY INTO THE LIGHT

Linda Wasil

I heard the door knob turn slowly, so slowly. My heart raced and I held my breath. It was pitch dark and I was waiting for the familiar shadow to appear. *What will happen now? Will this be the last time? Should I scream out "NO! Leave me alone!"* Familiar body tremors took over my body as I knew this wasn't going to be the last time. Tears rolled down my cheeks as my breath shortened. *How could this be happening again? Why do I have to live in fear?*

This existence was all I knew. I often looked out my bedroom window and dreamed of being a happy, carefree kid playing on the swings I saw outside. I thought to myself, *isn't this what life should be like for a six-year-old?*

For many years I poured all of my energy into my career attempting to suffocate memories of childhood sexual abuse. I thought this was something I could control working endless hours striving to be a perfectionist. Most of my value came from receiving promotions or accolades for my work. Finally, I had the answer for a successful life, or so I thought. I could erase my childhood memories if I was a "success" in the corporate world. Although I was making great money and had "the title," I was miserable inside, always doubting myself and fearing that the other shoe was going to drop.

One day driving my car in a heavy rain storm in Northern California, I suddenly felt like I was in a trance. Suddenly the windshield wipers and their motion became very present to me, as if the blades had magical-wiper-powers, whispering a secret message... back and forth, back and forth, back and forth, back and forth; a message sent to my heart from a mystical, rain-drenched heaven. The rain and the wipers forced some kind of miracle of awareness as if, while whisking sheets of water away, they were also clearing my vision to give me hidden truths about myself which came bursting from my subconscious into the light of day. All the memories came flooding back, memories I had of all those unhappy days and nights. Memories I had tried so hard to wash away by burying them deep inside and simply ignoring them. Inside the cloud of unknowing, I saw myself: the door opening, my body trembling and all the raw, familiar scenes. I was able to pull the car over to the side of the road, my head buried in my hands as my body shook. *How could I have repressed all of these memories of childhood abuse for so long? Am I dreaming? Is this real? Why was this coming up now after all of these years? Is this part of the reason for my unshakable depression and lack of will to live? What do I do now? How will I sleep? Is there anyone I can confide in?*

The next week I started intensive therapy. At first I couldn't even speak. The body trembling continued as if with each new memory, before it exited my body, left with an earthquake-type tremor. I cried until my sides hurt. How could I talk about all of this? It all seemed jumbled in my mind. Was it really true or was I making it up?

Slowly, over weeks and months, words replaced tears. Every week I dove deeper and deeper into the darkness. Nothing seemed to stop the endless depression and hopelessness. My therapist suggested medication to ease the pain. I refused to fill the prescription, desiring to be present to every emotion and feeling coming up from inside of me.

Years passed and I progressed into more intensive treatment programs. Pounding pillows and recounting my story seemed to make things worse at times. Was this pain ever going to end? None of this seemed to help much as I was just replaying the story over and over again. It was a relief to be heard initially but I desired something more. I continued searching.

I read and studied every self-help book I could get my hands on. I took intensive weekend courses that gave me a temporary "high" that lasted a few days then stumbled back into hopelessness and depression. Again, I didn't understand why I was still feeling this way. After all, I owned a beautiful house in the Bay Area, had two cars, took luxury vacations, had a great job and friends, made great money, yet I still had these negative feelings and self-doubt.

One day, as I looked out into the rays of sun through the pine trees in my newly landscaped backyard, I said to the Universe, "If things don't change I'm outta here, and I mean it! You have one month to show me a different path, or I'm leaving this planet for good."

The very next day I was in my kitchen ironing when I received an intuitive message to turn on the radio to an AM station. What? I never listened to the radio in the house and if I did I listened to FM. Yet the knowing was so strong, I didn't doubt it this time. I quickly walked over to the stereo and turned the radio on. My fingers stopped at a station where I heard a man speaking about verbal clearings and energy work that could transform any area of your life that wasn't working. Even though this sounded too easy I kept listening. He talked about asking questions to unlock limitations. This process, he said, allowed people to have an awareness of what is true for them. The work is called Access Consciousness.

For example, he spoke about one of his clients who was unhappy in her marriage of 25 years but unable to leave her husband. She had recently been diagnosed with breast cancer and was going to begin chemotherapy. Through a series of questions he helped her to see that she had created the cancer as a way out of her marriage. When she became aware of this, she made the choice to leave her husband.

As he recalled numerous successes with clients, for the first time in a very long while I felt excitement and my body was at ease. I called into the radio program and asked a question on the air and booked a session the next day. I wondered, *could this be what I had been asking for?*

Over the course of several weeks, all of the stories that had been locked inside me started to unravel. I felt lighter and the depression started to lift. At one point, I told the facilitator about my childhood and he asked me a question that blew my mind: What if I knew everything that was going to happen in my childhood before I was even born?

What?!? Instantly I felt lighter, but a part of me didn't want to believe I actually chose my family situation. What a bizarre concept! It took a while to sink in but there was something to this.

He continued, what if I chose this because I knew I was strong enough to survive it, and it may have prevented someone else from being abused? Wow, could this mean I was actually a powerful being instead of a victim?

This awareness shook my very core. I had played the victim role so well and it had served me in many ways. Could all of this self-doubt and sadness be a cover-up for the potency and joy that I truly am?

I continued having private sessions and taking classes. My life started to get easier and more fun. As the layers peeled away, I started to see where I had chosen abuse in my life.

For example, I had been addicted to work, overeating, abusive relationships, shopping, etc., to dull the pain and check out. I started asking questions that unlocked these areas in my life where I felt stuck.

For instance, I began to see that I was in an abusive relationship with my boyfriend that had slowly eroded my self-esteem. It's interesting that when we first started dating, I would sense that his comments weren't kind but I didn't say anything because I believed deep down that I didn't deserve to be treated any better. On the rare occasion that I would stand up for myself and state that I didn't appreciate his sarcastic comments, he would tell me that it was all in my head and that I was being too sensitive.

Over time, his cutting remarks would be coupled with pinching or slapping. Even if I asked him to stop, he would continue until I was in tears. When I showed him the bruises on my body, he would deny that he caused them and claimed that again I was "too sensitive."

One night as we were arguing, he twisted my arm as he threatened me. With tears running down my cheeks, I begged him to stop as the pain in my shoulder intensified. Eventually, he let me go when I promised to never raise my voice to him. That evening with an ice pack on my shoulder, I held myself in a fetal position as I tried to sleep. My mind raced as I replayed the events of the evening.

The next morning my boyfriend apologized and said that he didn't mean anything by his threats and wouldn't hurt me again. This time I didn't believe him and knew that I had to leave. The violence was clearly escalating. More importantly, as I started to value myself I KNEW that I deserved better. I made a decision to never be in an abusive relationship again, and with that I ended the relationship. With the Access tools and questions I had learned, I could unlock myself from this tangled web of abuse and choose differently.

Ending that relationship was a pivotal moment in my life as I started having gratitude for myself and realized that I had the power to create my life and what I desired. I now have a sense of peace and gratitude for myself that is beyond what I could have imagined.

Now I enjoy working with clients to assist them in seeing that they are a gift and that they can generate a joyful life. What would the world be like if each of us recognized the gift and contribution we truly are? How does it get even better than this? What else is possible?

Linda Wasil, B.B.A., C.F.M.W., is a coach, intuitive counselor, speaker, and practitioner of Access Consciousness. For over 13 years she has facilitated clients all over the world in living their dream of a happier, more fulfilling life through individual sessions, workshops, and presentations. She is a Certified Bars Facilitator and teaches this hands-on body process that can reduce stress, help with sleeping, and assist in unlocking stuck patterns in any area of your life. She is expanding her energy work to include animals and shares her life with her dog Coco and horse Misty. To learn more about Linda, visit www.Lindawasil.com or contact her directly at Lindawasil@gmail.com or 650-400-6128.

THE BOTTOM LINE

Charlotte Purvis

It was about 10:40 a.m. when I arrived at the dentist's office for my 10:50 a.m. appointment. Considering my schedule and that I am "creative" in my approach to time, arriving early was a big deal. Those extra 10 minutes allowed me the pleasure of scanning a copy of the first edition of *Speaking Your Truth*. I quickly found my way to the back of the book in search of contact information for the editors. The next day I sent an email requesting submission guidelines for this edition.

While visiting my mother's home about three weeks prior, she and my brother gave me a framed photo of the three-room "shotgun" house in Tuscaloosa, Alabama, where I was born in 1951. Upon returning home, I placed one of my business cards in the bottom right corner of the frame. I pause often and stare at the house and the card and wonder, *How did I get from there to here?*

The desire to tell my story has been like fire shut up in my bones the last several years. With the framed photo, the fire was beginning to burn out of control. When I saw *Speaking Your Truth*, it was as though I received the message, "Charlotte, you are invited to speak your truth." This chapter is my RSVP.

The community off 15th Street where the shotgun house was located was called "The Bottom," also known as "Lonesome Bottom." Though a young child when we lived there, I recall that our house was a reminder not to judge a book by its cover—the inside was clean, the furnishings were nicely appointed, and everything was organized. I also remember the sound of the train on the tracks just a few feet away from the house and our strong sense of community. Our Big Mama lived just a few doors down, so it definitely wasn't Lonesome Bottom for us. It was a starting place for my parents' generation—the first generation in our family to live in the city. When you think about it, you have to start somewhere. My family started at The Bottom.

Our life beyond The Bottom was in a lovely new place called

McKenzie Court, a public housing community. When we moved there, "You couldn't tell us nothing," as we say in Alabama. We went from three rooms to three bedrooms. Hot water. Light switches. Laundry area right off the kitchen. Bricks. Front yard. Backyard. Community building. Large playground for the whole community. A small playground just for us young'uns. What more could we ask for? Looking back, we often refer to McKenzie Court as "the suburbs." Luxury living at its best—especially when you're looking at it from The Bottom.

I recall being quite excited about moving to McKenzie Court—so much so that I wanted others to move on up with us. My first prospective residents were my best friend and his family. I told him—in great detail—what to tell his parents to do. Sadly, his parents found out they were "too poor" to qualify for McKenzie Court. I recall thinking something could be done to persuade those decision makers. I eventually gave up on my bright idea and my friend did, too. Oh, by the way, this all took place while I was in elementary school.

Yes, at an early age, I was deeply concerned about others. I knew that I was put here to help people. And I was blessed with a big dose of humility, whether living in The Bottom or the suburban public housing community. Of course, I didn't have the fancy adult words to express that as I do now. It was a feeling inside, a spiritual unction, a calling—and it brought me great joy.

I set about helping other classmates and being a listening ear for them. Several of my male classmates still recall being able to tell me anything without worrying about hearing it again. I was passionate about being confidential—I saw that as the ultimate way to show respect for others and to show appreciation for their trust in me. My role model in this regard was my high school guidance counselor. I wanted to be just like her.

Being born in The Bottom didn't prevent me from having sky-high dreams. I learned by observing my parents and all the adults in my community that to make my dreams come true would require work. They worked without complaining and believed that it is a privilege to have work to do. They taught us that whatever we did, we were to do it with pride.

Thankfully, no one in my village seemed concerned that my dreams were too big. My very dedicated parents, my supportive Big Mama and extended family members, those sweet people at my beloved Elizabeth Baptist Church, the watchful and caring staffs at Central Elementary and Druid High Schools, and people throughout the community expected us children to have big dreams. One of their favorite pieces of advice was, "Make something out of yourself." I thought of Dr. Martin Luther King Jr. as part of my village as well. I remain grateful to him and the other Civil Rights leaders for their contributions to my life as a little Negro girl in Alabama in the 1950s and 1960s.

There were a few stumbles along the way during my teen years. After several interventions—including being selected for the Stillman College Upward Bound Program—I graduated from high school and was accepted at the University of Wisconsin-Madison. I thought social work would be my major so I could be like my high school guidance counselor. But with some redirection, I decided child development and family life might be a better choice, and it was. My career path was set: preschool teacher, parent educator, speaker, trainer, volunteer, and child advocate.

Through a series of miracles I started my business, Purvis Communications, in 1985. I knew little about business, but I knew a lot about the work ethic, building relationships, doing extra, remaining humble, treating people with respect, and being confidential. I didn't have a business plan—I can laugh now in sharing that I didn't know what a business plan was. I could barely answer some of the questions people asked about my business, especially those around quarterly projections. I knew I was starting at the bottom; that was both familiar and fine.

Today, I am blessed to be a corporate consultant and communication coach. Just recently a Fortune 500 company outsourced a function to Purvis Communications, a first for us. The company is located near our office, and I am a part of an awesome team. I also speak my truth by giving speeches to college students, business leaders, and professional associations.

That brings me back to the question about the shotgun house and the business card: "How did I get from there to here?" Thanks to the time spent reflecting and writing, I have some answers. While in The Bottom and beyond I learned some powerful lessons. These lessons have served as a travel guide for my journey. I now call them my "bottom lines."

I think of my #1 bottom line as the preface to my travel guide.

Simply put, God loves me. I was born in a shotgun house in The Bottom and at the bottom. God loves me. What if I had been born in a mansion on the other side of town? God loves me. When I was a child, some adults, through their behaviors, put stumbling blocks in my way. God loves me. I take responsibility for having put stumbling blocks in my own way. God loves me. I've been on top. God loves me. I've been back to the bottom. God loves me. I've been helped back up. God loves me. Yes, God loves me. Period.

My journey has taken me many places—literally and figuratively. No matter where I go or what I do, I am proud to be that little girl from The Bottom. I noticed that after we moved from The Bottom to McKenzie Court, some people treated us differently. I recall being invited to be a part of a group soon after we moved; yet, I had not been invited before. Though others saw us differently, to think of ourselves differently (as in "better") was not an option. Yes, McKenzie Court was a step up in the housing category. It was not a step up in terms of values (check, they were solid and remained so), our sense of family (check, it remained the same), and how we felt about who we were in the world (check, we saw ourselves the same). In that instant when we were given the key to 52-B McKenzie Court, we didn't become better than those who remained in The Bottom, or my friend and his family who didn't qualify to move to the suburbs with us.

With time, I understood the human tendency to relate to people differently based on their station in life. Knowing this, I made a commitment to myself: I would not look down on others because of their position—especially those in the service industry. Not only would that be disrespectful to them, to do so would mean that I'd forgotten that my mother served other people in their homes as a means to make sure my siblings and I had opportunities to pursue our sky-high dreams.

Here's a real-life example: I was attending a business meeting in a conference room. A young woman from a catering company came in with refreshments in hand. Being new to the group and not being the facilitator, I waited for someone to thank her. Nothing. Nada. Suddenly, the business topics were of no interest to me. When the young woman left, I quietly stood up, walked out into the hall, and thanked her. She was visibly shaken when I approached her, thinking she had done something wrong. I assured her otherwise. No judgment about the other professionals in the meeting but, coming from where I'm from (as Anthony Hamilton sings), I didn't see the difference between the young woman who delivered the refreshments and the big shots who developed the agenda. If one of them or another so-called big shot had walked in with goodies, we would have fallen over ourselves thanking them. That young woman deserved the same. Bottom line.

Another thing this lifelong journey has taught me is that — in most situations — I can make a change and I can make things better. Earlier, I mentioned that while living in The Bottom, the inside of our house was well kept. Additionally, when we lived in McKenzie Court, my parents budgeted carefully and purchased two sets of encyclopedias, Golden Book and World Book. Through these and other actions, my parents made a strong statement: We will not allow where we live and how much money we have to define who we are and dictate who we can become. They were passionate about the power of making changes and the promise of better outcomes.

This gift from The Bottom keeps on giving in my life, my coaching, and my business. Sometimes the change I need to make is of encyclopedic proportions. But most of the time, all that's needed is a small change. Just look at the day I arrived at the dentist's office early. That small change produced significant results: From a 10-minute investment, I was given this opportunity to speak my truth.

Some say that *everything* depends on your attitude. But since I'm speaking *my* truth, I'll admit I'm not quite there yet. I've been in some situations where I tried to adjust my attitude and it didn't seem to work. Or, maybe it did and I just didn't know it. My truth is that *a lot* has depended on my point of view. We could have seen living in The Bottom as an embarrassment. Instead we saw it as a starting point with the guarantee that we could only go up from there.

I can look back at some of the stumbling blocks that were put in my way and be angry, or I can be grateful that I am still here, that I have life, liberty, and love. I'm self-employed, and sometimes it's a challenge to keep all the moving parts in place. I can view having a business as a pressure or a privilege. What is my answer when I look at my business card with the photo of my birthplace in the background? From that point of view, there is no question: Having a business of my own is a privilege.

I am very grateful for this privilege and all of my blessings. However, recalling the many lessons I was taught about being respectful and humble, it's easy to understand why the idea of *celebrating my journey* has been a conundrum. Now that I've had the opportunity to look at my life from The Bottom and beyond, I am ready to celebrate. When I start to wonder if that's okay, I remind myself that if a friend's business card had been tucked in the corner of the frame with that house in the background, I would say, "Good for you, let's celebrate." Well, bottom line, that's *my* business card and *my* shotgun house. I thank the Lord, and I go forth from here in celebration of my journey. Amen!

After Charlotte wrote this chapter, tornadoes that are among the most devastating in history struck Tuscaloosa and the surrounding areas. She wishes to thank everyone who offered prayers and support for those affected by the tornadoes. Charlotte enjoys speaking her truth and is proud to be represented by Great Black Speakers (greatblackspeakers. com). To contact Charlotte, please send an email to charlotte@ purviscommunications.com.

LIFE HAPPENS, SUFFERING IS OPTIONAL

Debi Bauer

Since the line "It was the worst of times" has already been used, this story can't start out that way, but it certainly could and be totally accurate. Even so, no pity parties or consolation prizes are needed or requested. I'm pretty sure everyone experiences the same or similar things as those in my story, we just handle them differently. And that makes all the difference in the world.

Ten years seems like a long time when you're a kid, but I swear the years speed up the older you get and they're gone in the blink of an eye. Are you paying attention to the decades as they roll off the calendar? I wasn't, but I learned I really needed to. Ten years can make a huge difference in how the following decades will turn out.

During my decade from hell, I came perilously close to the breaking point, but with the help of good friends and a few good dogs, I'll be a happy, sassy old woman yet (one day, a long time from now!). What started out as a few health issues with my husband turned into what I considered a mass extinction with the fear of "am I next?" To understand the impact, you need context.

I grew up in a "Leave It to Beaver" type of nuclear family. You know, breadwinner Dad, who in my case was a Phi Beta Kappa chemical engineer (that's the long version of brilliant); stay-at-home Mom, who only later started working; and three adorable daughters, one of whom was me. As I look around today, I realize my family was not the norm. We respected our elders, did what we were told, and never, ever talked back. We weren't allowed to use the word "can't," as in "I can't do that" or "I can't figure this out." Instead we were taught to say, "How can I do this?" or "I can do anything I decide to do."

The bar was set very high at an early age. That has been a blessing all my life—although as a teenager, of course, I had a much different viewpoint. But that lesson of striving to achieve and believing in myself has made all the difference through the

187

years. The women of my generation I meet today feel pretty much the same, younger generations not so much, and I wonder what has happened. For all the striving to give children a boat-load of self-esteem, it looks to me like we've achieved the opposite end of the spectrum.

I thought I was fairly strong and somewhat courageous, but what did I know – I was young and untested. Most of my life was easy compared to some I know of today. We had chores and responsibilities but never held a job because going to school was our job. And, school didn't end at 12th grade but continued on until college was completed, no if's, and's or but's, that's just the way it was. I finished college in three years instead of four. I wish I could say it was because I was an overachiever, but the truth is more mundane – I just wanted out and to be finished.

However, I wasn't prepared for the ending of school. Since I had never held a job, I didn't have an idea of what life was supposed to look like without school. The day after my college graduation, in 1973, was the most frightening day of my life. Imagine if you will, a brand new college graduate, sheltered from the cold hard world, with no experience in the work world so no resume, and all of a sudden I was expected to get a job and fend for myself. Looking back on it, the self-reliance and belief that I could accomplish anything given to me by my parents kicked in, but that doesn't mean I didn't wish for a knight in shining armor to ride in to my rescue. I did manage to find a job and the lecherous boss that went with it, but that's a whole other story.

All through school my mother's mantra was for me to make sure and get a teaching certificate, no matter what I majored in, so I'd have something to fall back on in case something happened to my husband. All my ideals went out the window (*I am Woman, hear me roar*). I wondered, *What happened to that self-sufficiency lesson? Why was I supposed to have a husband? Couldn't I make my way in the world on my own?* Following graduation, during the 1970s, the women's movement took hold and I received so many conflicting messages that I felt like the song "Dazed and Confused." Like a lot of my friends, I was uncertain as to who I was supposed to be and what I was supposed to do. I obviously didn't reach any plateau of enlightenment because my first husband decided to leave me after 12 years of marriage.

I found myself once again out on my own and making my

way in the world. This time I had a bit more sense and work experience so even though the pain of failing was ever present, at least for a while, I discovered a deep well of strength and determination that I didn't know was there, fueled by pure terror. I bet you know the kind. It's what shows up when you finally get mad at any given situation and swear it's never going to happen again. I guess it's true that you don't know what you are capable of until you are tested.

I eventually remarried and entered that union a lot differently than the first. Life rocked along, things were good, everyone around me was healthy, and I was progressing in my career, which was good as I was the breadwinner.

As the new millennium started, things began to unravel in a hurry. I discovered what being tested by fire meant. Other than surviving a divorce, I had never experienced the kind of disappointments and trauma I had seen around me on a daily basis – as supplied by the news media and well-meaning friends letting me in on the latest scoop.

That changed in early 2001 when my husband began complaining of neck aches and in general feeling puny. After what seemed like every diagnostic test known to man, the last being an MRI, the doctors discovered a brain tumor. It was an ugly sucker sitting on the left optic nerve, but at least it was not malignant. Nevertheless, it had to come out. Brain surgery was scheduled and my caretaking days started with what I naively thought was the worst thing that could happen. I'd never experienced anything of this magnitude, so at age 49 my education into the real world started. His recuperation was fast and totally without incident, so I was breathing a sigh of relief. Silly me.

The cycle of life is such that we are born, we live a life worth living (at least that's the idea), and we die when it's our time – think *The Lion King*. That looks okay on paper and makes logical sense until something very different happens to your loved ones and you. After my husband's brain tumor, in the space of a few years I lost my mother, my oldest sister to melanoma, my Air Force pilot nephew to a plane crash (he's a hero buried in Arlington National Cemetery), my dad to Alzheimer's and became executor of his estate, nursed my husband through various surgeries including the aforementioned brain surgery and Stage III lung cancer, commuted 700 miles to work for five years while dealing with fibromyalgia, and retired and started a new business. Everything eventually comes to an end and I'm grateful to say most of the items on this list are over, but not all. My husband has been cancer free for more than two years as of this writing – a 10% chance of that happening and a true miracle from God.

But that didn't stop me from having my version of a nervous breakdown – uncontrollable crying where I couldn't catch my breath and shaking so bad the bed began to dance (and not in a nice way). All I could think was, *Well, at least if I pass out from lack of oxygen I'll start breathing again.* A few days of recuperation and getting my act back together stomped it all down into the little box labeled "everyone is counting on me, so get over it." I didn't want to think about it too hard because that would trigger another meltdown. Overachievers don't have meltdowns, or so I thought. Another silly me moment.

Everyone experiences health issues and the loss of loved ones, it's just that mine have come so fast and close together that I haven't had time to grieve or bounce back from them. Two whole years are nothing but a blur. I guess I'm glad for that, except now the price has to be paid. My mantra for the last 10 years was "I have a backbone of steel" – it was the only thing I could say to get me through every day. I stopped asking "what else could happen" because something invariably would. My prayers changed over time to become, "Please make me strong enough." The downside is that I not only became strong, I became hard. Also, empty.

Courage is a funny thing, isn't it? You don't know you have it or even notice it when it shows up. It's just there one day when you need it. In my case, auto pilot turned on and I simply put one foot in front of the other day after day until 10 years had gone by.

I think courage shows up due to our life experiences and the foundation we were given. I learned to lean on those early life experiences and to overcome the ones that didn't help whenever they got in my way of just surviving. Well, most of the time. It required friends to listen, dogs or cats to pet, chocolate in copious quantities as needed, and a strong belief in God. The courage came from God, friends, dogs and cats, and of course the chocolate. But I failed to lean on all those resources as much as I should have. As a result I made my journey a lot harder and more painful than it needed to be.

Things have finally started to settle down to small bumps in the road instead of huge mountains to overcome, but only because there aren't that many of us left in the family. I'm coming through the darkness and finding my way back into the light a very different person than when all this started. Life is precious, it is tenuous, and it is fragile. It is here one second and gone the next.

The big question is "What have I done with mine?" I want to say at the end of my life that I made a difference and lived a life of significance. I may not be known by many people, but the ones who do know me will say that I touched them and made the world we shared a better place. With the help of God, friends, family, and dogs (not so much the chocolate), I'm finding the courage to let the empty space slowly fill back up with what I need to create that better place. I'm through with walking alone and bearing the burden. It only takes a small amount of courage to ask for help, but a huge change of mind to be okay with it.

I'm okay with it, now.

Debi Bauer worked in corporate America for over 20 years and held technical and management positions before moving into performance coaching. Debi received her coaching training via the Coaching Development Program through the Organizational Learning Center, MIT. Debi's area of expertise, besides change management, is helping other people learn what is their true passion and purpose in life. Debi helps people discover "what you want to be when you grow up" as well as offer options to pursue. Her viewpoint on life is "We were not put here to worry, moan, and fret; we were put here to laugh, dance, and sing. If your life isn't like that, let's turn it around!"

FROM DEATH TO LIFE - A JOURNEY OF THE BREATH

Casey Feicht

Floating above the hospital bed, I see a small child lying there and wonder, *What is next for her? Will her next breath come? What will happen to her?*

It felt like the world had ended. There was a sense of limbo as time slowed down and in essence stopped. Nothing mattered expect the breath, and the breath was such a challenge. I felt like I was dealing with the most difficult maze or puzzle I could ever imagine. The energy to take a deep breath in and a deep breath out felt like moving a 10-ton truck.

The disease of asthma is so intense. This life-threatening disease brought me so much pain. I could not really afford to think about the future or the past because the present moment was so gripping, so challenging and so fleeting! The tears were intense, the pain was intense, and the essence of life was unknown. Would there be a tomorrow? Would I stay in the hospital? Would there be that next breath? These were the questions I lived by.

Although not able to articulate it at the time, I had a deep-seated belief of a better life, it was always there and I just didn't know it yet. I was a fighter, I would survive and eventually thrive! I had a desire beyond comprehension of breathing freely, pursuing joy and living fully in the moment. This was a dream that I knew I would fully realize someday.

Mixed feelings arose as I looked down at myself lying in that hospital bed. Two paths were present. Should I move forward into the great beyond, the unknown, the safer and easier place to be? Or go back into the world of pain and struggle and uncertainty, where there must be a way to find peace? I went back into the body of a 10-year-old girl fighting for life, believing that things would get better.

I opened my eyes and there I was again. *Oh my god, it's painful. I can't breathe. Why? Why me?* The fear was so strong that I didn't know what else to do but panic. Gasping for air was frightening.

The cold, sterile environment of the hospital made me wonder if there was good in the world at all.

Having this quandary of time on my hands felt like a curse. Not knowing if I would live to see tomorrow was stressful and agitating. I watched the other kids play, participate in sports, and run around smiling and laughing. I was so far removed from that reality. There were restrictions on my physical activity, there were many pills to take, there were weekly visits to the doctors, boxes of Kleenex used and tons of tears shed. In church they spoke of hell. I understood, because I was living it.

The pain was so intense and the desire to sleep and never wake again consumed every waking moment and thought. I lived in a world full of needles, IVs, breathing machines, unfriendly nurses at 2:00 a.m., and the tremendous loneliness that consumed me as my parents went home for the first time in a few days to shower and see my sister.

Hoping for my favorite Jello flavor for lunch was the highlight of my day, and I wondered how other kids celebrated their birthdays. My parents arrived with presents and my sister was there. That year, 1982, there was no party; I turned 10 in the hospital. Life sucked! Yet a few nurses (the ones who were sweet to me) gave me a few balloons. I prayed, believing that next year I would be "normal" and have a birthday party with friends and fun.

I spent a lot of time just being, being sick, being in the hospital, being at the doctor's office, a being trying to breathe. When I was in the midst of numerous asthma attacks and dozens of weekly hospital stays over the first 10 years of my life, I was very ANGRY! I was in a spiteful and vengeful, angry relationship with the creator, because the pain was so intense. I was even angrier with my parents, as I somehow felt they should have protected me from this, and made it go away. There was no room for happiness or joy in any of my relationships; I was so upset and distraught that I had been given this disease! *Why was I being punished? What had I done wrong? Why me?*

I didn't get answers so I formulated my own which were self-blaming and full of critical and judgmental illusions. I had to make some kind of sense as to why this was all happening to me. Swadhyaya, a Sanskirt word, which means self-study, became ingrained for me. I have been on a personal growth path ever since. My journey began with wanting to feel better, to be free of dis-ease. From there health and fitness became my goal, then over the years I deepened into a desire to experience a deeper sense of health and wellness. I wanted a connection to wholeness, to oneness, in my body, in my mind and in my spirit. This developed exponentially in my yoga practice.

My asthma eventually did improve with the help of natural hormones that arose during puberty. I went boy crazy in high school, and then immersed myself in the world of alcohol and drug addiction in college and beyond, to numb all the pain and suffering from the disease. I also immersed myself in health and fitness. I become a personal fitness trainer and group fitness instructor. This led me to a fun-filled life as a health clubber by day, a partier by night. One day I decided to try a yoga class at my local club and from there I was hooked.

Due to my teaching and training schedule I was not able to attend many yoga classes, but was very interested in practicing yoga at home with a videotape. I started with a commitment to practice one day a week. That was all I could get in. To my amazement, after three months I felt great. The biggest benefit was stress reduction. I began to let go of my anger and resentments at the world.

Over time, my perception would shift; I would know that this experience was a gift. The breath brought me to a place of so much gratitude. I was led to teach others to breathe deeply and to connect with their bodies and breath, through yoga. Yoga is an ancient practice of uniting the mind, body, and spirit. It is the gift of the present moment, the ability to truly BE HERE NOW, as there really is no other place to be; there really are no other options.

After studying yoga for many years, I learned that yoga is so much more than physical exercise as I originally thought it was. I easily mastered the basic poses and had a fair amount of strength and flexibility as I was deeply immersed in physical fitness. What I learned is that yoga is a holistic system. Initially I enjoyed the physical aspects, but what kept bringing me back to my yoga mat each week was the ability to emotionally move through things without flying off the handle all the time.

In the year 2000, I attended my first retreat, a yoga teacher training. Being full of cockiness that I had taught all kinds of fitness classes and I could teach yoga too, comforted my ego, yet there was a soft humbling, and openness that I was there to learn so much more. Walking up to the retreat center, I saw the campus full of light; the grounds were covered with inspirational landscapes, from the Buddha fountain to the flat top hall and the mountaintop view of the beautiful valley below.

Anxiously I waited for the group to gather for the first time. The uncertainty that lay ahead of me took me back to the uneasiness of breath from childhood and held me in an anxious state that I previously numbed. Having to abstain from alcohol and drugs for two weeks was a challenge. (Now I have nine years of recovery, but that's another story.) I realized it would be doable, as I was about to be consumed in my next favorite love—yoga!

We gathered in a circle wearing white for purity. I sat among 18 other women and two men to create a community of teachers to be. It was my first yogic community and one I will never forget. Our teachers opened their hearts and shared their paths. They asked us to hold the talking stick and share what had brought us to this place.

Words of compassion and a desire for serving others, for growth and transformation came out of the beautiful souls around me; they ranged from age 18 to 60 and inspired me deeply. I knew I was in the right place.

Finally it was my turn to share. Coming from a small place, feeling like that scared 10-year-old, I shared that I was there to learn to love myself, and that I didn't know how to do it. I went on to share that I have seen glimpses of it and was willing to be open to grow and learn how to love myself unconditionally. A wave of relief hit me, as the talking stick moved on and I shifted back into listening mode. A deeper transformation had just begun.

Each day began with a challenging uphill walk to the yoga room; it was lessened by the search for a prayer rock to add to the mountain of stones that gathered over the years. Gratitude washed over me as I placed my rock among the others. Daily we practiced shoe removal outside the studio door, and entering mindfully into the room. Living in a full immersion environment of yoga opened my heart. Through moving my body, chanting, and being surrounded by souls who were happy, joyful and fun loving, I began to realize that it was possible to love myself. This belief was slowly coming true.

On the last day, during our physical practice of yoga, I felt myself going through the asanas (poses) as I always did. I was present with my breath, and then something happened. As I moved fully immersed in the present moment, Krishna Das was chanting in the background, I found myself feeling a deep sense of connection to the moment, one far beyond this mortal life. I was guided into the pose Baddha Konasana (Bound Angle Pose/ Butterfly Pose). With feet together and knees wide, I folded forward to go deep into the pose and to my surprise, I found myself deep in tears, emotional, and completely overwhelmed. I breathed and cried, and cried and breathed. I let go and transformed, cracked open to a sense of self-love. A realization came to me: *Love is who I am, have always been, and will always be!* It was the beginning of a healing that continues to this day.

That night we came full circle, literally and figuratively; we met under the softness of candles to share. We gave voice to our processes—our growth, challenges, whatever had arisen during our time at the training. This time I sat upright, full of lightness and joy. I was a new person. I had gained a sense of self-esteem and self-love! I'd healed old wounds and was able to see a world of love.

I continue to practice and teach yoga, and have done so for 13 years. It connects me to the root of life, the breath. I believe I am truly here as a gift from the divine. I believe that my life is meant to be an inspiration to others, that what you believe, you can achieve. I believe I have powerfully manifested a magnificent and full life. Everything I have ever dreamed would happen to me has happened and so much more. I know that my life is a gift and I am so grateful for being given the chance to find self-love and be love and give love!

Each time I step onto the yoga mat, I am reminded of how precious life is. Many times I still feel like I'm that sweet innocent child, believing that there has got to be more than this. It's humbling to know that without breath, there is no life, which is obvious yet so many of us take it for granted. My inner child sometimes still struggles with living through so much tragedy. Gratefully I take a deep breath in and out! The loving adult that I have become reminds my inner child that I have turned into an amazing woman who gives her heart to life and loves all there is. It is my joy to be of service and give to others what I have graciously been given. Namaste and Play!

Casey Feicht has over 20 years of experience in the health and wellness industry as a personal trainer, life coach, and yoga teacher to kids and adults. Casey has been consciously manifesting her dreams ever since. With her background of being able to understand difficult personal experiences, addiction issues, and the power of overcoming these obstacles with a positive and healthy lifestyle, Casey created her business, Fun and Healthy Lifestyles LLC. Casey facilitates an expansion of consciousness that empowers you to take positive action. Her passion is to transform the world, by sharing yoga with babies, toddlers and kids of all ages. To learn more about Casey, visit her websites, http://kidsyogaguide.com. and http://caseyfeicht.com.

THE MIRACLE
OF A SECOND CHANCE

Amy Stark

November 29, 2010 was a cold winter morning. Two and a half years of giving up many things in my life to finish my master's degree all came down to this week. I had seven days to finish the comprehensive exam. If I passed, I graduated. If I did not, well, you know, no master's. This day changed my life. Life as I knew it would never be the same.

A few months earlier, the light in my life was so bright. I was looking forward to the next stage of life post-graduation with sheer excitement. I met a man who felt like "the one," was looking forward to having weekends once again, and was excited about the possibility of moving to D.C. to start a career I was passionate about.

But then slowly I became more and more depressed and could not stop crying. Turns out, life had caught up with me and all the running I had done from the pain of my childhood for the past 30 years had brought me to my knees. The word "burnout" comes to mind. When you can no longer make decisions, no longer care what happens, and become someone even you do not recognize, the moment hits you like a freight train.

I had started the comprehensive exam but ended up so sick with severe dehydration and the flu that the ER became my second home throughout the week. By the grace of God, the wonderful chair of my Industrial Organizational Psychology program granted an extension of a few extra days to finish the exam. Once that was finished, the tears came flooding out and did not stop for over a month. My doctor and therapist pulled me out of work on short-term disability because I literally could not function.

The morning after finishing my exam, I woke to snow and absolutely nothing to do but sit still with my thoughts and the pain. No work, no writing, no boyfriend. I was at rock bottom. The lack of love and complete exhaustion that had overtaken my mind, body, and spirit over the years led to tears for the entire month of December. My parents stood by my side through every moment of it. This made me love them so much more, if that was even possible.

The darkness and despair was devastating. It felt like there would never be light at the end of any tunnel. Suicidal thoughts were front and center, and I could barely get through the day. Right before my breakdown, I had been demoted at work even though numbers showed that I was one of the best at my job in the country. I was dealing with a tyrant of a new boss, the man who was supposed to be "the one" had disappeared, and my health was so bad I was taking what seemed like every medication in the pharmacy, well not literally, but close. I realized that for the 34 years that I'd been on this earth, I never truly thought that I deserved to be happy; only other people deserved that.

Then life took an interesting turn. Barnes and Noble became my sanctuary (even though I swore I would not read or write for a year after school was over). Walking into the store and pulling books that called to my soul became so important. I read books all day and all night, journaling every morning and started to put all my thoughts on paper. It was a painful awakening, almost like experiencing a tornado, and I was at the center trying to claw my way out.

One day, with tears streaming down my face in the self-help section of Barnes and Noble, the book *Fried* by Joan Borysenko, Ph.D., leaped into my hands. One paragraph stuck with me from the moment I read it:

"In a culture wedded to positive thinking, burnout and its first cousin, depression, are thought of as disorders to be fixed. But what if they are necessary losses? Perhaps they are losses of naiveté, false identities, and faulty assumptions that make way for a more authentic life."

That was it! Those words helped change my life. They helped me realize I was putting on the strong face that everything was okay, I was tough, and I could handle anything— all the while missing one thing: Who was I and where in the world was my authentic self?

My life had veered severely off course, and as one of Joan Borysenko's Facebook friends put it, "Hell is a bad place to pitch a tent." Yup, that is where my tent was pitched and it was hell. Where were my passions, my dreams, and my authentic self?

They had completely disappeared. It was then that I realized that I truly never had a voice and I could not really speak the truth to let go of all the pain and silence I had been living with since I was a child.

Thirty years of trying to protect my parents from my meth addict and alcoholic brother took its toll on me. The shame of my brother led to my parents never wanting to talk about it to anyone, even in our family, and left me holding everything in. I never had a confidant to trust with my pain and express what was happening when I was young, which ultimately led to constant overachieving and burnout.

Meeting the most amazing therapist, who made me laugh because he was not afraid to call things "shitty" and that I had a messed up childhood, was awesome. He allowed me to find my voice and helped me work through the pain, which led to a new healthier Amy. This allowed me to not be afraid to truly take care of myself. It always seems that women are afraid to open up and speak their truth. The thing is, when I finally spoke the truth and was not scared to be the true me, I vibrated at a higher level that ended up bringing in blessings that were not even imaginable two months earlier. The individuals who came back into my life, the ones who have come into my life and the love that has found me is overwhelming.

The journey of truly looking at who I was and putting me first is the best gift I have ever given to myself. Speaking the truth and opening my heart has brought joy and creativity to my life. I soon began to realize everyone has a story; everyone has gifts of wisdom to share if I just listen. Could it be? Did I actually deserve to be happy?

Never did I think there was a creative bone in my body, because I never let myself find it. By letting my authentic self shine through, I was able to create a beautiful painting in my art class, which was liberating and gave me a wonderfully healthy outlet. It has so much meaning to me, and I realized that I might be an artist with special talents that have been hidden until now.

The beginning of February 2011 was the coldest on record here, and I had bronchitis and an inner ear infection. But it might have been my best week in recent history. I received devastating news that my short-term disability was running out in a week, and I had declined long-term disability. When I first took my job three and a half years ago, it never crossed my mind that I would ever need long-term disability. I had serious decisions to make NOW.

Two minutes after hearing the news, I was in tears and completely stressed at the thought of having to go back to my job in a toxic environment. After all my healing work, I did not want to have to go back there. I knew I could not do it. Well, here is the fantastic news! Miraculously, I received an email from a wonderful company in Washington, D.C., that I had been dying to work for. They asked if I would be interested in a paid internship with them. I was elated! Finally, validation that the last two and a half years of working towards my master's degree might pay off. The next thing I knew, I was filling out an application and the HR manager, who had gone to bat for me, was creating a job description with the president for me.

While I was in D.C., I was able to interview for my dream job. I had also realized I was stronger and if this did not work out, I would still be ok. After looking at a million places to live, I finally found a place that felt like home with a girl I connected with instantly. She has a dog, which my dog, Keeva, will be able to hang out with. Best of all, I can be me in the living space. The local community is within walking distance to every store I could possibly need, and Keeva can come in the stores with me. Walgreens even gives treats to the dogs that come in! This is the perfect location for the both of us.

I moved to Washington, D.C., secured a waitressing job, a great opportunity with the company of my dreams is in the near future and found a wonderful place to live four blocks from the water. I realized after my trip to find housing and a new job that the high paying job in Denver was not worth it anymore. It was more important for me to be in a healthy situation and find a career I was passionate about. I truly believe that if I heal, love, and believe in myself, my greatest dreams and intentions will manifest. I am along for the adventure to see what other wonderful things I can manifest now, in my new, authentic self.

Incorporating yoga, painting, and writing for my soul centered me. Attending a prayer group every Wednesday made me hopeful. I built a new, healthier relationship with my parents that did not have the hurt of my brother involved. The work I have done helped release my authentic life. Two months ago, the despair, the pain, and the willingness to take my own life to stop the pain all feel like a blessing now. I had a big wake-up call. I will never be afraid to ask for help or speak my truth ever again. I love myself too much to do that.

Is that not what life is all about? By being gentle, loving, and compassionate to myself first, I could allow my authentic self to shine. How cool! I learned that it is never too late to love myself and live the life I have always wanted. I allow myself the freedom to change my life direction, if it feels right, LISTEN to my intuition, and to take risks. Who knows what amazing things will happen. Learning to love myself did not happen overnight, but it is a most wonderful process. It is the journey I am enjoying as I learn to live in the present moment.

The greatest lesson I have taken out of the darkness, the therapy, the painting, the writing, and just being still, is that if I do not keep my balance, or recognize the signs that I am out of balance and correct it, I will end up where I was. I will take the beautiful painting I created with me to D.C. where I can look at it every day to help keep me centered and put me first. This is my gift to myself and I am damn worth it! As my beautiful and amazing friend Jess always says to me, "Embrace your greatness and honor yourself." Everyone has greatness, I just had to dig through the pain and find it!

Lastly, the blessing that started the healing and realizing I needed help was when my mom and I were taking Keeva for a walk on the beautiful trail I live on. We ran into my friend, Jess and her boyfriend, when I was barely able to function in public. She asked if we would be willing to do something with them. She asked if we would scream, "I LOVE MY LIFE!" aloud on the trail. We looked at each other, thought she might be a little crazy, and said, "Why not?"

After screaming those liberating words, I realized life could be good again, and amazing people will step up to carry you through tough times. To this day, I giggle and find myself driving along in my car listening to my favorite song and all of the sudden screaming "I LOVE MY LIFE." It is silly, fun, and liberating all at the same time. To my friend Jess, whom I met that day on the trail, you helped save my life, and now I do love my life! You were one of my gifts and that is so cool.

So try it somewhere where you feel comfortable, in the shower, in the car, the pillow or even outside. You will feel the freedom and you deserve it. Once I started believing in my life, I believed that I might be the light for someone else and touch him or her so profoundly that it could change the course of his or her life. That is living an authentic life. Slow down, take care and listen. Do you hear it? It is you speaking your truth and asking you to listen. I LOVE MY LIFE!

A native of Colorado, Amy Stark loves her home state, her friends, her family, and her adorable dog, Keeva. She recently finished her Master's in Industrial Organizational Psychology and is ready for her new adventure in Washington, D.C. This was the perfect timing for a breakdown to face her demons and learn how to speak her truth through the journey. She discovered she loves painting, writing, yoga, meditation, and does not mind being still now. She believes in practicing random kindness and senseless acts of beauty, because even if you are having bad day you can make a difference for someone else.

TURNING FEAR INTO LOVE

Emily Burgos-Rivera

It was October when I arrived for the first time in Atlanta, Georgia. I was among a thousand students heading to the city during a cold, windy and cloudy autumn. The Olympic Summer Games that had taken place in the city were over, and the Georgia Institute of Technology, in which I was about to begin a master's degree, was ready to start its delayed fall quarter. Eager for new experiences, I left my hometown in Puerto Rico ready to take charge of my life and my decisions.

Being the youngest of three siblings and the only female, I wanted to live my life differently. I grew up in a male chauvinist family, and ever since I was a child the "role of the woman" seemed completely wrong to me. My chores were not a man's responsibility, and I didn't have certain privileges because I was a girl. I always argued about and fought against all I thought was unfair. The happy and fun memories of my childhood were many times clouded by a strict upbringing and a lack of affection.

During my adolescence, all those ideas were strengthened in my mind as I started to reject the stereotype of a traditional woman. I knew in the future I didn't want to be just a housewife taking care of the kids, the house, and the husband. Fortunately, my parents were very supportive and encouraged me to study for a higher education degree. For me, learning became the key to my life's knowledge, and Atlanta represented the beginning of my growing experiences.

At first I saw myself as an independent student getting ready to be a successful professional. But soon after I started my first quarter, reality took over. I didn't like my master's degree program and I started to miss my family as well. Everything became unclear to me and the mature, intelligent, and responsible woman that for many years I tried to portray, wasn't enough to cover my unease. Unfortunately, there were moments of regret. But it was too late to step back on my career's choice. Maybe it wasn't what I wanted, but it was the chance I was looking for to prove myself as a woman. I decided to move on and finished my master's degree. What I proved with that decision was a reflection of my fears and insecurities, the ones that grew up with me since I was a girl.

Over the next couple of years the fears and insecurities took over, as I made decisions to please others rather than myself. As hours, days, and years passed by, I became an unhappy woman betrayed by herself. I lost sense of who I was and what I wanted to be. Even so, life went on; I got married to a loving husband and years later we had a beautiful child. I covered the present with highlights of happiness, but nothing could fill the emptiness within me. My husband became a silent witness to my misery and despair. Despite my feelings, I worked in a career I didn't like until I eventually quit my job to become the housewife I didn't want to be.

I became clever in the use of my words, always trying to convince others and myself that the present situation was temporary. As I struggled with my ideals of how to become a successful woman, I began to sink into depression. I had many headaches, neck pain, and unexplained crying; I was feeling anxious, lonely, and left behind with my thoughts. It took me five years since coming to Atlanta to admit I needed help to heal, forgive, and love. It was difficult to accept what other people saw in a negative light—many think that the person who suffers from depression has serious problems or is mentally ill. In everyone's eyes I was living a normal life and nobody could tell I was suffering. In reality, these symptoms require attention and are commonly associated with stress; I couldn't ignore them because they were real to me. But I had hope and would frequently tell my husband, "There must be a better way to live. Something beautiful must be awaiting me."

After six years of living in Atlanta, we moved to my husband's hometown, Monterrey, México. I had mixed feelings but thought maybe this was the change I was looking for. Maybe I needed to run from my reality as far as I could. I learned the hard way it doesn't work like that, because no matter how far I ran, my fears remained with me. My depression signs returned and intensified. Many women in México reminded me of who I didn't want to be, as male chauvinism was part of their daily life. I became impulsive and contradictory trying to make decisions to balance my personal and professional life. Decisions, I thought, would change the course of my life; however, I kept hurting myself in every possible way.

After multiple therapies and anti-depressant pills, I was finally able to go on with my life thanks to Neuro-Linguistic Programming therapy, which became part of my life for four years. I made big steps forward while reprogramming a new state of mind. Thinking positive thoughts and changing my life perspective helped me to say goodbye to my depressive symptoms. As I became more conscious of my childhood traumas and unaccomplished goals, I started unloading my heavy burden. But I still felt emptiness within me. Something was missing! At some point in the process, I questioned whether all my efforts were worth it or not, thinking that maybe I wouldn't find the success and happiness I was looking for.

Unconsciously, my life became a relentless search for what I have named today my "sense of meaning." Through a path that required time to go down into myself through my own experiences, a path that sometimes threw me down to the ground, I was able to stand up facing life with more strength than ever. Only God knows how I undertook the long journey to self-discovery. On this journey, I found other healing channels through yoga, painting, and even boxing-fitness classes. Everything was helpful as my journey continued. In more control of my life and emotions, I learned to believe everything happens for a reason.

Then, on a warm August night, a series of events turned my life around. I was reading in bed, enjoying one of those moments that appeased my mind when, suddenly, my older son interrupted my reading saying, "Mom, I can't fall asleep." This had been his behavior for the past couple of weeks: going back and forth into my room to let me know he felt worried. An hour would pass by, then two, three, and even four before his tiredness put him down to sleep.

That night, I confirmed one more time my hunch that something was definitely going on with him. I felt his anguish and anxiety, so I tried to comfort him. Even though I tried to find the reason for his lack of sleep, as on previous nights, I had no answers. My son is a very secure, intelligent, and outgoing child who started to show fear and anguish when bedtime came. I knew it was time to look for professional help. The next morning,

I decided I would call my son's pediatrician for guidance, as my concern got bigger.

That night he went back to his room trying to give sleep another chance, but within 20 minutes he came back and said, "Mom, I can remember now why I can't fall asleep. I can remember something that happened to me when I was younger." I didn't know how to react to his words, as he continued, "Mom, I do want to tell you, but I can't. You are going to get upset."

I became concerned and tried to convince him that maybe it wasn't that bad, but his body language was telling me something different. He was anxious and distressed, moving around my bed and touching his head with both hands. "I want to, but I can't," he kept repeating. Uncertainty put a lot of strain on us, until he broke out of silence and said, "Mom, the babysitter."

"What happened with the babysitter?" I responded quickly.

"She wanted me to touch her there." He pointed at my chest. "It happened when I was six years old." There was a pause in my life, as I found out my son suffered an abuse when he was only six years old.

There is no way to express how badly I felt. Alone with my thoughts, I cried as I had never cried in my entire life. My heart was broken into a million pieces. This time I cried for a different reason, I cried for my loving son, an extension of myself. I was angry and full of regret. I had many questions and no answers. All I had in my mind were pictures of my son's memories, and resentment toward the woman I trusted who had harmed my son. My head exploded with ideas of why bad things kept happening to me. I couldn't sleep the entire night, for I was in deep pain.

The next morning, somehow I felt strong enough to handle the situation. I guess it was the courage of a mother. My son needed his family's support and, somehow, I knew we would all move forward. I went to my yoga class looking for peace and light, for I needed to make important decisions for his life. Later on that day, I found the right support and guidance for my son's well-being: a spiritual energetic therapy called SAGRAV as well as a psychiatric therapist.

At first, I tried to contact the psychiatrist but he was, coincidentally, out of town. Time was passing by and I needed to help my son. His sleeping problems persisted the following days, so the spiritual therapy became my first option.

These types of spiritual therapies were not new to me, as I chose alternatives like this in the past, although I didn't see any change in me at all. With a feeling of skepticism, I took my son to SAGRAV therapy a week later. We entered the room and I could sense a peaceful atmosphere. The therapist began a simple procedure, even abstract. Essences were used and beautiful prayers were made for my son's well-being; I was part of it. I could see immediately how the expression on my son's face changed; his anxiety diminished and his happiness surfaced. I felt better, too, as I saw him release the pain. We talked about the events and the therapist explained the lessons to learn. To my surprise the lesson was not only for my son, I had much more to learn, as he said, "Emily, you know your son is all right, but this message comes to you through your son's life."

I wasn't sure what he implied, but I guess it had something to do with what I told my husband that night, "I have been trying to deny the spirituality in me. If our son sleeps through the night, I have to believe." That night, just as the therapist had assured me, my son fell asleep with no problem in less than five minutes and has been sleeping through the night ever since.

Still doubtful about the previous experience, we took our son to one of the best psychiatrists in town. After only two therapy sessions, he substantiated that our son was totally recovered and discharged him. In other words, he confirmed what the spiritual therapist had said. Fortunately, in less than three weeks the calm returned to our lives. I finally understood there was only one explanation for this: GOD's MIRACLE.

It wasn't until I experienced the spiritual therapy myself that my life began to brighten. During the therapy, I felt the presence of God within me, His energy and love. On the following days I started to see life from a new perspective. It was like my mind had been unblocked. I felt released from a false sense of isolation, deprivation, and disaffection. I shed my fears. These new feelings that surfaced in me made it possible for me to forgive myself and to forgive others, while I learned to love myself. Now, I am a new woman full of light, with a flowing creativity and a lot of love in my heart to give to others and to life itself.

Today, I believe this is what God was preparing me for. SAGRAV opened up endless opportunities for me to live in love, peace, and tranquility. The past doesn't matter anymore, since each step I walk along the way helps me to enter a state of consciousness by following my instincts and inner voice. It was finally God's enlightenment that made me learn and understand the most important principle of life: *We have to remove fear from our head and let love enter our heart.* What I experienced with my son was a call to attention for me, because to go on with my life I needed to have *absolute faith in God's existence.* HE showed himself as a miracle in my son's well-being.

This is definitely what I had been looking for, my sense of meaning, my happiness and success. Everything else that I am able to accomplish from now on is for the benefit of us all, as I have a message to share: "Love yourself, so you are able to recognize the Love of God in your heart. Believe in yourself; do not let fear cloud your sight. Have absolute faith in God. HE will show you the way and the real meaning of life." Be blessed!

Emily Burgos-Rivera was born in San Juan, Puerto Rico. She is the mother of two boys and is married to a loving husband. She lives with her family in Monterrey, México, where she works freelance in her healing and creativity studio, DaLú Art, teaching meditative drawing and creative painting classes as motivational tools for her students. Currently studying a Certification in Capability Art Therapy, Emily's skills and education complement her path. She also practices yoga, and is a SAGRAV certified therapist. SAGRAV is a spiritual energetic therapy that enables people to achieve what they want in life by the Law of Attraction. Visit www.daluart.com for more information.

Family Matters

CHILD OF MY HEART

Donna Mazzitelli

There she was—a tiny child—a stranger in the arms of another stranger. Ringlet pigtails, big round saucer eyes, beautiful olive skin—these were the features I noticed in those first seconds when I spotted her in the crowd. A bottle hung from her mouth. As she bit down on its nipple, the bottle swayed from side to side whenever she moved her head.

This chubby cherub was the reason for my early morning visit to a school parking lot. She was the little girl I'd been told about, the toddler whose mother could no longer care for her. I was so focused on this round-faced angel that I never even saw the woman who held her. To this day, I have no idea what the woman looked like.

I got out of my car and moved towards the two of them and the orchestrator of our impromptu meeting, Mary, my parents' neighbor. I'd learned about the child from my parents. Her name was Amanda. Mary had taken care of her over the weekend, attempting to place Amanda with a family. Neither prospect had worked out. One couple admitted they were on the verge of splitting up. The other family thought Amanda's deep olive complexion and dark brown hair and eyes were too "brunette" for their Northern European roots. After hearing what happened that weekend, my heart cried out to this little girl—a victim in a story where her mother was as much a victim as Amanda was. It made no sense to anyone, not even to me, but I had to meet her and see her with my own eyes.

I stood there for a moment in that parking lot, about to meet Amanda and have both our lives changed forever. Once I saw her, there was no going back. My heart made its way to Amanda long before my body got there. As I approached her, Amanda looked up at me. I reached out my fingers to her, thinking about how her mother cried the night before when she learned that no family would take her daughter.

213

I'd spoken to Mary the previous night and learned more about Amanda's plight. I also discovered that her mother was only three months younger than I—not quite 21 years old. Mary was deeply concerned about having to return Amanda to her. Although there was no evidence that anything had happened previously, Mary believed Amanda's mother, Barbara, was at a desperate point in her life and feared for Amanda's safety. As I listened to Mary's concerns, something welled up in me, an inner urging that said I had to do something. I and my husband needed to help!

Although we'd just married in May, we had a three-bedroom home. We had the space in our home and, I believed, in our hearts to care for the child. We could step in for a couple of weeks while Barbara got assistance to place her with a new family. This is the story I told myself and my husband—it would just be for a couple of weeks while things calmed down and got sorted out. To protect Amanda, we could step in.

The decision to meet Amanda turned out to be my act of "sealing the deal." In that moment when my heart first arrived, Amanda was forever imprinted on my soul.

I headed to work, immediately called my husband, and announced that we would be taking care of her, at least for the next couple of weeks. He'd already agreed the night before, with some reservations, that if this seemed to be the only way to keep the child safe, we would take her in. I reconfirmed what we'd discussed the previous night: I would take time off work to find daycare for Amanda and care for her over the two weeks while a permanent home was found. What I couldn't admit to myself or any other human being, including my husband, was that I wanted my home—our home—to become her permanent one.

Arrangements were made for me to pick up Amanda at Mary's office after work. Barbara was to provide her belongings—clothing and toys—so that Amanda would have what she needed during her stay with us. I would not meet Barbara. Mary and Amanda would wait alone.

I arrived at Mary's office shortly after 5:00 p.m. It was still daylight when I drove into the parking lot. There they stood. As Mary handed Amanda's meager belongings to me, I found out that Amanda had just turned two years old on September 16, 1976, four days prior. I transferred her few things, some stuffed animals and a little suitcase containing summertime clothing, into my car. I buckled Amanda into the front seat.

I brought her to our home—the fourth home Amanda had been in since the weekend. I fed her dinner, leftover veal parmesan and rice I'd made the night before. Amanda gobbled it up, calling me "Mama" in between bites. I learned within a day that every female Amanda met was "Mama."

I unpacked her belongings and discovered Amanda didn't have a pair of shoes or diapers. I waited for my husband to get home so I could go to the grocery store for the supplies we needed. I explained to her that I had to get diapers and something to put on her feet. I told her I'd be right back. At the grocery store, all I could find were socks, so I bought them to keep her feet warm until I could take her to get shoes.

By the time I arrived home from the store, my husband was panicked. Amanda cried the entire time I was gone and was so scared of him that he didn't know what to do. She wouldn't let him come near. We learned in the days ahead that Amanda was terrified of men. In time, she would grow to love my husband and call him "Daddy," but on this first night, alone with him in our home, Amanda cried hysterically.

That night I put her to bed with her bottle—they were inseparable—and Amanda went to sleep quickly. I was surprised that, except for the time with my husband, she seemed to go along with everything. "Adaptable" was the word that came to mind.

In the following week, everything came together quickly and easily. I was able to take the time off work with the blessings of my boss, who instantly became one of our biggest supporters. I found a daycare provider with the right qualities—she was willing to take a toddler still in diapers, cooked homemade meals for her daycare children, and believed in child enrichment, allowing them to paint, draw, and explore their creativity in a myriad of ways. This wonderful provider even documented every milestone for working parents who missed those "firsts."

As I made these arrangements, I considered myself lucky that everything fell into place within a week. Years later, I realized that much more than luck had been at play.

The two weeks with Amanda flew by. I'd taken the first week off to find daycare and help Amanda adjust. Since daycare was arranged within two days, we had the rest of the week to get to know each other. We played, visited the daycare provider, and shopped for much-needed clothes and shoes. I knew Amanda would need these items no matter where she ultimately lived.

At the end of the two weeks I hesitantly called Mary, who was also Barbara's boss. Mary told me that Barbara hadn't done anything to find placement or connect with Social Services during the two weeks Amanda had been with us. In fact, Barbara considered everything resolved: Amanda had a home. In her desperation to find a way to cope with her life, Barbara considered Amanda safely placed in a loving home with parents who would take good care of her. Barbara didn't look for other options or other support because she wanted us to be Amanda's parents. She just wanted everything to be over.

Now my husband and I were faced with a dilemma. What were we going to do? Secretly, I was relieved—this was what I'd wanted all along, to be Amanda's parents. But I knew my husband wasn't on the same page. He pointed out how young our marriage was and that we'd planned on having children much later. He was right. Having a child at this point in our marriage was not what we had planned.

Although I knew what he said was true, I just couldn't bear to let Amanda go. What would happen to her? Would she survive? Would she be safe? Amanda was beginning to be more comfortable around my husband, but how would she react to other men? Had Amanda been hurt or frightened by a man or men in the past? What had her living situation been like with Barbara? What would her living situation be like in the future? Mary had been afraid for Amanda's safety before she came to stay with us. What would happen if Amanda was placed with Barbara again? If Barbara didn't feel capable of caring for her anymore, where would Amanda go? I couldn't stop wondering and worrying about how Amanda would ever survive.

Here we were at a crossroads. In our young marriage we had a dilemma to resolve. This was the first time in our married life that we had divergent needs, opinions, and perspectives. The common ground was that we both wanted to protect Amanda. Both of us feared for her safety and what would become of her. The way to assure Amanda's safety, however, was where our paths parted.

My husband wasn't ready to commit to being a father. But I, simply put, had fallen in love. I loved holding her in my arms. I loved rocking her. I loved her smell. I loved singing to her. And I loved how she held onto me, too—how she needed me. I'd become attached and connected to her, and I couldn't imagine letting her go.

By this time, Amanda had warmed up to my husband; he was feeling more connected to her as well. Although they were beginning to bond, the idea to have her live with us permanently and adopt her was only my dream. I told him how, as a young child, hearing about the suffering in the world, I'd announced to my parents that someday I'd adopt one child and give birth to another. I pondered out loud to him: had this situation presented itself in order that I could do just that?

At 24 and 21 years old, we really weren't equipped to make such a life-altering decision without outside guidance. In 1976, no one suggested that we seek professional help to come to a decision. We talked to our friends; they thought this step was premature in our married life. We talked to family members; they fell into both camps. Some believed Amanda was truly a blessing in our lives while others thought we weren't ready for such an awesome responsibility.

Ultimately, my husband couldn't say no. To make me happy—to not disappoint me—he agreed to go forward with Amanda's adoption. At that time, I didn't know for certain those were his reasons nor would I allow myself to entertain such thoughts. Years later, I uncovered the truth and realized this was the beginning of the end of our marriage. It's impossible to build a marriage on a shaky foundation of non-disclosure and fear.

When the social worker came for the first home visit after we filed for Amanda's adoption, she told us that had we tried to adopt a child through the system, we would have been rejected. This state representative itemized all the reasons why: we were newly married, I worked full time (at that time, the woman had to be a stay-at-home mom), and we would not be able to support her on one income. However, because Amanda had been placed in multiple homes over such a short period of time, the state would not move her again. We had other factors in our favor, too. My husband had worked for the same company for a number of years, we owned our home, and we had enough bedrooms so that Amanda would have her own.

You might wonder why a woman just 21 years old, married

for only four months, and working full time, would decide to take in a two-year-old child. You might think it was because this woman needed to be needed, to be loved unconditionally, to feel important. You'd be right. All of these were true, although I couldn't acknowledge my motivations at that time.

But there was something else at work that went beyond the psychology of the situation. That something was Divine Intervention. I believe Amanda and I were brought together on September 20, 1976, for a bigger reason—one that cannot be explained or understood in any easy, simple way. We were meant to walk hand-in-hand together through life. She needed to learn what I had to teach and, equally important, I needed to be taught many of life's lessons through the experiences we've shared together. I am the woman I've become in part because I've been Amanda's mother.

Looking back years later, I believe this Divine Intervention is the reason everything came together so easily in the beginning. It was also the reason the social worker did not reject our petition and remove her from our home, even though she knew this had been handled in an unorthodox manner. Despite the unconventional— and maybe even illegal—method that ultimately landed Amanda in our home, the state allowed her to stay with us. I know today that all of this happened because Amanda was intended to be my daughter and I her mother.

Yes, I did become Amanda's mother. My husband and I officially adopted her on May 20, 1977. We kept her birth name, Amanda Danette, because that was her given name. It was beautiful, and it was who she was. When we stood before the judge as a family of three, all dressed in our finest clothing, my heart overflowed with joy. This little girl was my daughter, and I felt so proud to be her mother. The judge asked Amanda to show him her daddy and mommy. She pointed to each of us and, at two-and-a-half years old, spoke those words that still make tears well up: "Mama. Daddy."

Today, Amanda is 36 years old with a family of her own. I was at the birth of her first-born, Bethany. Amanda and her husband Wayne asked me to cut Bethany's umbilical cord, a gesture I'd not expected nor anticipated. With tears, I cut the cord knowing that now the circle was complete. We were forever connected by blood as well as by heart.

Donna Mazzitelli is a writer, author, editor, and coach. Donna was one of the contributing authors to Volume I of Speaking Your Truth. *She has joined the "Self-Publishing Experts" team, working with Andrea, Lisa and Jan Haas to provide full-service expertise to those who want to self-publish a book. Donna is also the founder of Bellisima Living, LLC, www.bellisimaliving.com, a place to find your voice and connect to a more beautiful life and world. Donna offers writing and editing services to assist others in expressing their written voice in various forms. She also offers guidance and coaching to inspire others to connect within. She enjoys writing articles for magazines, online publications, and her own blog, www.bellisimagoddess.com. Donna continues to listen to her Inner Voice, speak her truth, and strives to live an authentic life.*

A SIMPLE DIAGNOSIS
OVERLOOKED FOR YEARS

Jody Morgan

I knew before I received the test results what they were going to say. My gut had been telling me for months that the doctors were treating her symptoms and not trying to find out the cause of her constipation, stunted growth, mystery fevers, nausea, cyclic vomiting, and, most recently, fainting. My precious nine-year-old daughter, Leah, had been sick since the day she was born.

When she was born eight weeks premature, she was the healthier of the twins for a few days. Lizzie was the one who was born with immediate health concerns. Lizzie's health improved and she was cleared to come home after 3.5 weeks in the hospital. Leah was the classic two steps forward, three steps back scenario. She developed reflux after liquids were introduced to her for the first time. We were told she had preemie reflux because her little belly was underdeveloped. She had to grow to catch up with what her body was trying to digest. She came home after almost seven weeks in the hospital. Included with her in home arrival were lots of medications and an apnea monitor which would alert us if she stopped breathing.

I look back now and I can't imagine how we got through those first six months. Every time the apnea monitor went off, we had to determine if it was a false alarm. When she burped from acid reflux, she couldn't clear the gas bubbles on her own and she would quit breathing. The problem eventually corrected itself as she grew and got stronger. My husband Jim and I took infant CPR to prepare ourselves for handling our situation.

In nine years we have seen over 40 doctors, had countless tests performed, and spent thousands of dollars trying to find the answers. We have gotten used to treating Leah's individual symptoms to give her temporary relief to a much bigger problem. Benefiber for chronic constipation, antibiotics for fevers, Zofran to stop the cyclic vomiting, Prevacid for acid reflux, and no explanation on the fainting.

She has been such a trooper through it all. She is the most graceful vomitter. Why is she vomiting? It couldn't be what she eats. She is a picky eater and loves only the blandest of foods. Milk, rice, pasta, bananas, yogurt, and pretzels make up her diet. She takes her meds without being reminded. She lets the doctors poke and prod and "listen." Tests, tests, and more tests that would come back normal causing the doctor to want to order more.

I had had enough. I wanted answers! I *needed* answers! Leah's symptoms were getting progressively worse and the doctors kept increasing the meds. She was becoming pale and had little energy. I wanted to scream, "STOP treating her symptoms and find out what is causing them!" One doctor even suggested Leah see a psychiatrist. She could be bringing it on herself and need to "talk" to someone.

Last October, I was dropping off meds at Leah's elementary school. My friend Shannon overheard me telling the health room aide about the dosage Zofran as needed for vomiting. "What is going on?" she asked. "Why is she taking medications for VOMITING?"

We stepped outside the school on this gorgeous October morning and continued our conversation outside. Little did I know that the next two hours talking with Shannon were going to be the turning point to getting Leah properly diagnosed.

Shannon told me about her own personal journey to finding out answers to her son's health problems. She asked me if I had ever had Leah tested for Celiac Disease. I rolled my eyes and said, "No. The doctors have never mentioned that as a possible diagnosis." I had heard of Celiac Disease and gluten intolerance. "Gluten free" is everywhere! Isn't that the new "rage"? And if it were something as simple as Celiac Disease, why hadn't any of her doctors ever recommended getting her tested?

I decided to listen to what Shannon had to say. She told me of a great doctor she had found, one who was board certified but also used integrative medicine in her practice. "It takes a while to get an appointment so call now! Check out these websites…" Shannon was talking so fast, I found it hard to process it all. My head was spinning. I typed all of the information she was giving me into my phone. I couldn't wait to get home and research what she was telling me.

I spent the rest of that Monday in October on my computer

soaking up as much information as I could about Celiac Disease. "Celiac Disease is a multisystem disease in which the gastrointestinal tract is the major site of injury," I read in *Celiac Disease: A Hidden Epidemic* by Dr. Peter Green. I read on. Celiac Disease "is one of the most underdiagnosed hereditary autoimmune disorders." I couldn't believe what I was reading. There in front of me in black and white were Leah's symptoms. Every single one of them. The symptoms she had had for years. The symptoms that were getting worse.

There are so many symptoms to this awful disease and no two people are the same. Leah's symptoms might be different from someone else's but they could both have the same disease. I cried as I read. I cried from relief because I knew these were the answers we were looking for. I cried out of frustration and anger. Honestly, this was a simple answer. Why has it been so difficult to find? Why hadn't one doctor, nurse, or physician's assistant in nine years explored this as a possibility?

After I stopped crying, I got excited. I made an appointment for Leah with her regular doctor. I made an appointment with the new doctor. I called Jim, relatives, friends with the news. "I KNOW THIS IS WHAT SHE HAS!" I told them.

I felt it in my gut and I couldn't wait to have the proof of a diagnosis and get her on the road to recovery.

My excitement was diminished as we met with her regular doctor later that week. "Well, she could have Celiac Disease, but I don't think that is what it is, but we will do a quick little blood test to rule it out," said the doctor. "I want you to see a pediatric GI doctor also to do more tests."

In my research, both online and with people I had come in contact with who had either gluten intolerance or Celiac Disease, I had learned that very rarely was anyone diagnosed the first time with a blood test. Many times they come back with a negative result only to find out months or years later that they were indeed positive. I was no longer going to let the doctors tell me what we HAD to do. There is a fecal test that can be done that has 100% accuracy and it would test for the celiac gene as well. It was also less invasive. This test wasn't covered by insurance, but I was sure this is the way I wanted to go.

I decided not to tell Leah's doctor about the stool test and would wait until we had the appointment with the pediatric GI physician. She would listen to me, I thought. She was the expert. It took six weeks to get an appointment with the "specialty" doctor. Leah had only one vomiting episode in that six weeks but missed a week of school because of a fever. I was growing impatient with the wait but was still trusting that the pediatric specialist was going to listen and help us get Leah on the road to recovery.

We were familiar with the routine of tests and questions. Height, weight, date of birth, symptoms? How long has this been going on? What was your pregnancy like? Has she had any surgeries? Any allergies to medications? What is she on now and why? Leah sat patiently as I answered then she was examined. I told the doctor everything she wanted to know. Then I told her about my conversation with my friend and how I knew that Leah had Celiac Disease but she had never been tested for it.

The pediatric physician's solution was to order up a laundry list of invasive tests...an upper GI, a lower GI, blood work, a possible endoscope—"Let's not leave any stone unturned," she said. "We will test for Celiac Disease when we draw her blood." She didn't believe in the fecal genetic testing.

I said NO! I wanted to start with the test for Celiac Disease before we do ANYTHING else AND once we either rule it out or confirm it then we will discuss further testing. The doctor didn't want to hear this and insisted we schedule the other testing. Instead of arguing with her, I said okay and we left. I didn't schedule the tests. Instead, I ordered the fecal genetic test on my own.

By the time we received the test, followed the instructions, sent it back to the lab and received results, another five weeks had passed. Leah continued to get worse but we still kept treating symptoms. She started to look pale and have even less energy. Thanksgiving passed and Christmas was approaching. Her appointment with the doctor Shannon had told me about was scheduled on December 22. My gut was still telling me the test results would have the answers we were looking for, but I started to doubt myself. What if I was wrong? What if we should have done that other testing because it might be something else that she could already be receiving treatment for? Jim reassured me that if the tests were negative for Celiac Disease, we would be that much closer to finding out what WAS wrong with her.

The weekend before Christmas we had a quick little getaway to the mountains. It snowed the entire time and the kids had a blast playing in the snow, skiing, building snowmen. The tests results were going to be in any day. They would be available online and I checked daily. Leah seemed to be doing okay and it was a nice break getting away and not constantly thinking about what was going on in my daughter's body.

That changed suddenly on Monday morning, December 20. The kids were lounging in front of the television as I prepared breakfast. I let everyone know breakfast was ready. They got up and started serving themselves when I heard a loud *THUD*. I looked over to see Leah lying flat on her back.

At first I thought she had slipped and was going to jump up saying "OW!" but instead she lay there motionless. I ran over to her. Her eyes were open and dilated but she wasn't looking at me. She was looking into space. For a good 20 seconds, she lay there. Then she looked at me and said, "What just happened?" My heart was beating out of my chest. I was shaking! We were all shaking! Lizzie started to cry and said she was shaking! I tried not to cry because I didn't want to freak her out anymore than we were all already freaked out. Was it a seizure? No signs of a seizure. She had fainted!

This was a new symptom. Was it the altitude? It couldn't be. We had been there for days. I asked Leah what happened and she said she didn't know. She had seen blue stars when she stood up then next thing she knew she was on the ground with me standing over her. I talked to her some more about the blue stars. She said she sees them every day. Every day? "Yes, every day, but this is the first time I fainted because of them," she said.

We called the front desk. Was there a doctor in the hotel? No, but there was an Urgent Care nearby. We got her to the Urgent Care and her vitals were perfect. Everything was good. The doctor ruled it a "benign fainting episode." I was happy that her vitals were fine, but I was terrified about what her body was trying to tell us. I had never seen a child faint and it wasn't a good sight. I was so emotional inside, but—mind over matter—I wasn't going to let her see how frightened I was.

Leah was perfectly fine the rest of the trip. I told her she had to tell me when she saw the blue stars again.

Later that afternoon, I receive the email I had been waiting so impatiently to receive. Leah's results were in. She had Celiac Disease! She also had a positive immune reaction to cow's milk which meant she couldn't digest the protein casein in dairy. That is what has caused the constipation for years. We didn't expect that one, and I wasn't quite sure how Leah was going to handle having to give up her much loved bread, pasta, AND milk. Her appointment with her new doctor was in two days. We had found hope in her diagnosis. We couldn't wait to get her on the road to healing and being healthy for the first time in her life.

Meeting with her new doctor was refreshing. She spent two hours with us getting Leah's complete medical history, starting with my pregnancy and working our way forward to today. It was the first time a physician nodded her head and agreed with me about her symptoms, the treatment of her symptoms, and she confirmed the diagnosis of Celiac Disease. She also said that she was going to be okay. "It is treatable. Leah is going to feel so good once we rid her body of gluten and milk," the doctor said. The damage that was caused to her body after all of these years would heal over time. It would take discipline and education on our part but we were so ready for it.

The feeling of gratitude that filled my heart as the doctor spoke was incredible. I was grateful for my friend Shannon for having the courage to talk to me that beautiful day in October. I was grateful for family and friends who were sending constant emails and text messages and calling to check on us. I was grateful for positive test results and to be moving forward with a treatment plan. I was grateful that my daughter would finally start feeling better.

As I write this it's January 2011 and Leah is doing incredibly well. She is off of all of the prescribed meds. She doesn't see blue stars anymore. Her energy level is at an all time high. The color is back in her cheeks. She walks around the house singing and dancing. People are commenting on her changes. She has embraced her new gluten free, milk free lifestyle with strength and grace. She is learning to read labels because she doesn't want to "poison" her body.

As the endless mail from the insurance company and the various doctor's offices piles up on my desk waiting for payment or my attention, I smile because we have found the answers and I know everything is going to be okay.

Jody Morgan left the Gulf beaches of Florida for her new home in Colorado in 2007. Married to her best friend Jim, they have twin daughters, Leah and Lizzie. Jody is on a mission to spread the word about Celiac Disease. With the help of her daughter Leah, she is working on her first children's book on the subject. She recently left a successful career in the direct sales industry to pursue her writing and speaking. She is also passionate about helping others transform their homes into non-toxic environments through eco-friendly products powered by nature. Jody would like to thank her incredible support system. Her husband, family and friends have lifted her up when she needed it the most. A special thanks to Shannon Weston; without her courage to speak up and educate Jody on Celiac Disease, Leah might not be living the healthy life she is currently enjoying. For more information about Celiac Disease, visit www.celiac.org. For fecal genetic testing, visit enterolab.com. Jody can be reached at jodysgonegreen@comcast.net.

GARLIC PEPPER AND FAMILY TIES

Andrea Costantine

The road leading to my grandparents' house is lined with beautiful homes sitting on half-acre lots or larger. The street is a strict 25 miles per hour zone, with curvy roads, towering shade trees, and a neighborhood security officer who sits in his favorite spot on a blind curve under a large shadowing oak. The slow drive down the mile-long entryway gives us plenty of time to admire the Tudor, Colonial, and ranch styles of the old houses in the neighborhood. I always dreamed I would live here when I grew up. Today, my grandmother's cooking is leading me home, a place my heart knows well because I have visited a hundred times.

The turnoff to my grandparents' home is just to the right of the community park, with lake access, tennis courts, and a playground that my siblings and I frequented through the years. As we pull into the drive, the walls in the front of the house are the first thing you see. The house is no beauty from the outside, a Spanish-style home with a front courtyard surrounded by 12-foot-tall towering walls. I'm sure at one point it was stylish, but through the years the neighboring houses began to outshine this one. Built in the 1960s, the exterior lacks in style and charm, but we all know it's not what's on the outside of the house that matters.

We pull around the long driveway to arrive at the back door, the primary door used by friends and family. You only park in the front circle drive if you have never been to the house before, or if you need to leave at a decent hour. If you pull around back, on any given night you can easily get blocked in five or six cars deep. We all know this like a secret handshake: pull around back—staying into the night, park in front—you have to get out of the house before midnight. Although the front walls of the house portray tight boundaries, the backyard is an unfenced grassy wonderland. Now littered with a plastic deer and a satellite dish from the '80s, the backyard is rarely used except for the grandkids, and now great-grandkids who occasionally come out to play and enjoy the humid Florida heat.

Walking through the back door, my sister and I know our grandmother awaits our arrival. "Andrea...Kim," she calls out to us. As sisters we are practically one when it comes to visiting our grandparents. You rarely get one without the other. She, Mommom as we lovingly call her, sits in her chair, unable to make quick movements but stretching out her hands to scoop us in for a long hug and a kiss on the cheek. The smells in the house are familiar. Floating in the air is cigarette smoke and the enticing aroma of tomato sauce simmering on the stove. You can never leave the house without smelling of cigarettes, food, and perhaps coffee too.

In the years before my grandfather passed away, this would be the time my grandmother would yell out to get his attention. "Dick, the girls are here!" He would slowly putz out from wherever he was looming, from either watching his big screen TV on the leopard print couch, or counting and polishing his coins in the bedroom.

"Are you hungry?" Mommom would ask. It was always one of the first questions out of her mouth. When she was more mobile, she would get up quickly and hurry herself into the kitchen. If it wasn't close to a meal time, she'd start pulling out the leftovers in the refrigerator. "What do you want? I have spaghetti, a ham sandwich, leftover green peas and eggs—oh, these are so good. You should have these." I've had them many times before, and they are good, better than one would imagine. I would comply. You eat in this house, even when you are not hungry. You eat because it's a family tradition.

"Who else is coming over?" we ask. And just like that the names roll off her tongue. We get an update on where everyone is, what everyone is doing, and whether or not they'll be stopping by. We love hearing who is coming. Aunts, uncles, and cousins will all make their way over.

My grandmother is the glue to the Costantine family. She knows the old family secret that yummy Italian food keeps people coming to the house. In her best days, it was quite common for Mommom to fix meals for up to 20 people on a regular basis, but now that she is 81, the meals and family gatherings are fewer and farther between.

I can hardly remember a time when family wasn't coming in and out the back door. We would even joke how friends of the family always just "happened" to arrive right around dinner time. But they were always welcome, the more the merrier. After all, family isn't just about blood. Life at the Costantine household was different than others. My grandparents weren't the kind of old-fogey type people who ate dinner at 5:00 p.m., went to bed at 8:00, and rose before dawn. In fact, they were just the opposite. They were cigarette smoking, coffee drinking, up-to-the-crack-of-dawn type of people. When I'd stay at their house as a teenager I'd come home exhausted. We stayed up later there than we ever did at home. As kids we'd fight to keep our eyes open until midnight, besides we knew if we fell asleep we were sure to miss something, like my uncle performing magic, or my second cousin getting into a heated religious discussion. As I grew older I graduated from watching TV with my grandfather to those late night talks gathered around the dining room table.

Those talks would go on until the wee hours of the morning. Back in the days when I was a pack-a-day Marlboro Lights smoker, I'd sit there for hours drinking coffee, smoking cigarettes. When I finally left, my throat would be killing me, but I wouldn't change that time for anything. To this day, that house makes me want to light a cigarette, although the last time I tried I immediately had to spit the taste out of my mouth after a single puff. Despite how tempting it feels with my after-dinner Maxwell House coffee, I pass.

"What can we help with?" That's what the women do in Mommom's house, they help in the kitchen. It's rare for a woman to come over and not offer to help. Sometimes it's all done, but lately there's always a need for a helping hand. "Well, you can start the water for the spaghetti," Mommom would say. The sauce is already cooking, simmering a blend of spices, including garlic pepper, to perfection. We fill the gigantic pot of water to cook enough spaghetti to feed a small army. It's no wonder she can hardly cook anymore, these pots weigh a ton, and with food they become dishes of steel. "Lots of salt," she reminds us. Her lots of salt and my lots of salt greatly differ. She watches me out of the corner of her eye. Hobbling over to the pot, she takes the salt from me. "That's not enough." She throws handfuls into the water. It's no wonder my spaghetti doesn't taste the same.

I open the lid to check the sauce and give it a whirl. It smells incredible. My mouth waters. All that's left is to finish the salad and warm the bread, both staples to every meal. Kim and I set the table as we anticipate the arrival of other family members. As we get everything ready we linger around the galley kitchen, recently updated with granite counters, a tile backsplash, and a new refrigerator. After over 20 years, there is finally an icemaker that works.

"Andrea, can you grab the parmesan cheese out of the closet?"

"Sure, Mommom." I head out of the kitchen and through the dining room where we will soon gather, past the antique room, and down the long narrow hallway. The hallway as a child used to scare the living daylights out of me. It was so dark and long that I'd run through it praying that I'd make it to the other side alive. This time I walk, but I can remember the fear I felt as a child, and even as a young adult when I lived here for a few years. I open the hall closet. Some things never change. Despite less family coming around, the closet is stocked for a natural disaster. The hall closet, originally for linens, became the food den before I was even born. A four-foot-by-four-foot closet lined with shelves and stocked with food. There isn't just one of anything, there's plenty of everything. *Parmesan*...I scan the shelves from top to bottom.

I can't help but notice what else is in there. As always, I look for the chocolate. Chocolate covered peanuts, peanut butter chews, and candy bars were always around when my grandfather was alive. He was addicted to candy. He'd hide it from us when we were little, but we always found his secret stash. I think he got a kick out of us scouring the house looking for it. *Ah, found it.* I grab the cheese and close the door behind me. As a young girl, I was proud to bring my friends over and show them the food pantry. Even then I felt the bond of food and family. The two outside freezers are also stocked full with food. If you mention you've got to hit the grocery store on your way home, Mommom will ask what you need, and it's likely she'll find it in the house and send you home with it. No need for the grocery store now.

Family begins to pour in. Hugs and kisses abound. The energy level in the home starts to rise as people begin filtering through. The men typically come into the kitchen and say their greetings, and then wander off into the living room to follow where my grandfather used to spend his time. Sports, movies, or most recently concerts on television seem to dominate the screen. The women gather, talking, chatting, catching up, helping in the kitchen.

When dinner is ready, someone is sent out to gather the men. "Dinner is ready" echoes through the 4,000-square-foot home, calling relatives to the dining room as they emerge from the antique room, the safari room, the porch, and the garage.

There's no grace, and no waiting for everyone to arrive. When the food is ready, you eat. It's practically a sin in this house to wait and let your meal get cold. "*Munge,*" Mommom would say, one of the few Italian words ever spoken in our family—meaning "eat." When your plate was empty or as you neared your last bite, you better believe she's looking your way encouraging you to eat more. "But you hardly ate anything," she'd say, often frustrated. To her, there's nothing worse than too *skinny*. The taste is incredible, so you almost always eat a second helping, even if it is just a little. Not eating is an insult.

"My sauce just doesn't taste the same," I tell her.

"Are you doing what I told you? Are you using garlic pepper?" It's her secret ingredient to everything she cooks. I assure her I am. But I know now that's not what the difference is. The difference is in her love of cooking, her love of feeding, her love of family. All of which I carry, but she comes with years of experience.

As dinner winds down, the women clean the dishes. Sometimes the men hang around to help, especially if they are in the mood to talk around the table. Other times they disappear into the other parts of the house. Even though we are full, we make room for homemade lemon pound cake. Once again, with coffee and dessert in hand, we return to the table, this time for talking. It is around this table that our family history has been shared. It's here I've had the kind of conversations that will forever be etched in my memory. My grandfather bragging about being the most handsome man around town. And my grandmother chasing after him. Stories of their childhood. Of my father when he was alive. Of my aunts and uncles when they were young. Of money, of love, and of loss. It's here at the dining room table where the family ties are sealed. It's the table of truth and tales.

Living 2,000 miles away it's rare that I get to enjoy more than two or three of these family dinners a year, but how treasured they are. I see now that it is in my blood to carry on that tradition, in my own way. Sometimes it will be through food and Italian dishes, but I know I can feed people in other ways too, through my wisdom and the dreams that dance around in my head. I know it won't matter how I choose to do it, as long as I am sure to add garlic pepper.

Andrea Costantine always dreamed of being a writer, is a lover of books, and an avid reader. She is the co-creator of Speaking Your Truth: Courageous Stories from Inspiring Women *and* How to Bring Your Book to Life This Year: An Exploratory Guidebook on Writing and Self-Publishing. *Born with an entrepreneurial spirit, Andrea is passionate about service, self-expression, and creativity and enjoys unleashing that spirit in others. Andrea is a professional freelance writer, author, speaker, and artist. www.andreacostantine.com.*

TAKING A STAND

Lee Weisbard

Rarely leaving the confines of her small, well-appointed apartment, she finds both comfort and loneliness in the things she has accumulated in her 75 years. She enjoys the beauty and diversity in the paintings that cover all exposed walls, until the thoughts racing through her mind take complete control of her being.

Mom can no longer keep all those thoughts to herself, and she lifts the phone.

On the receiving end, I answer politely, totally unprepared for what is about to come. After 52 years, I should be used to the routine. She begins with the usual "Can I ask you a question?" The question is never the real issue, but the way it makes me feel takes me back 40 years. The volume and intensity of the conversation rises, as does the defensiveness in my tone, as my body tightens and my face transforms into a person from another time.

Blindsided again, I become a child, explaining my whereabouts or actions as I have on hundreds of other occasions. The cyclical behavior of my mother has always followed a regular schedule, coinciding with unhappy events in her life. Nevertheless I am always caught off-guard, hoping to have real conversation with the person I so wish to have a normal relationship with.

Her depression is hard for me to understand, but in reality it has been with me most of my life. For most of my childhood, I remember spending time with my dad and my brother, while my mother, who was barely functional, stayed in bed.

I can still smell the aroma of the bacon and eggs from my childhood, sometimes sizzling on the grill in our kitchen, other times from the diner down the street. Our dad had his own booth there, where he ate often, and the ladies knew his order. Most weekends, we were out with dad. He was adventurous and exciting, more like a big brother than a father, often taking us out on the small boat he kept docked near our fifth-floor apartment in

Far Rockaway, New York. We'd fish or water ski for hours, never wearing the proper safety gear or adhering to any conventional rules. My dad was a risk taker and included my brother and I every chance he had. My mother rarely joined us, preferring the quiet solitude of the four rooms we called our home.

Over time, my mother seemed to become less functional emotionally, while my father spent more and more time at the beach handball courts, smoking marijuana, until the summer I came home from camp, at age 15, and he was gone.

I left home at 16, and my mother never really got over it. I'd already graduated high school, worked at the local neighborhood convenience store, and was ready to move on. I knew I needed to leave if I were to change the patterns developing in my family and fulfill my dream of becoming a dentist.

By this time, my dad had moved to Colorado with his girlfriend and her children. My mother never understood why I moved to Colorado, she saw it as though I was abandoning her and my brother. After living with my father for nine months in a trailer home in Basalt, Colorado, I moved to Boulder to attend the University of Colorado. Neither of my parents were college educated, but I knew they valued education and the professions.

The relationship between my mother and I seemed to change, even if temporarily, once my first daughter was born. We spent a lot time together, as my mother and her husband had moved to Colorado to be closer to our family. They sold everything— their apartment in New York City, the home they built in the mountains, and the liquor store and building they owned in Brooklyn. Over time, we settled into a nice routine of having Shabbat, Friday night dinners, together as extended family. Her proximity increased my feelings of affliction towards her, and I began to feel a sense of anxiety and loss of control over my life and my family.

Within a number of years, my parents found themselves out of money from poor financial planning and hazardous spending. My mother's lack of self-control extended beyond her voice; it became a lifestyle. My relationship with my husband deteriorated after my parents moved into our unfinished basement. Between her depression and her loss of independence in her own life, she began controlling mine.

It was a time in my life when my husband was unemployed,

the nanny cared for my youngest daughter and her own child, and a housekeeper came once a week while I worked long hours, cooked dinner for my family, and still needed to hire babysitters if I wanted to go out with my husband. My mother would not help with the children or the house and regularly told me what I needed to do. Rarely feeling valued or appreciated, I felt inadequate in the face of her judgmental and negative attitudes about me. It was never about what I did, but what I didn't do for her that she seemed obsessed with. I felt every move I made was being watched and scrutinized. I was trapped in my own life, in my own home.

Eventually my parents moved into an apartment they hated, but it was their own and they were out of my house. By this time, my mother's behavior had become cyclical in nature, with regular and unpredictable attacks on my family and myself.

Her lack of compassion and selfishness was most apparent the day I signed my divorce papers. My parents were watching the children as I sat in the attorney's office, working out the final details of the dissolution of a 20-year marriage. It was a difficult time emotionally as I was sad my family was being dismantled. I called my parents to let them know we were running late, and I'd be on my way soon. I called again from the car to ask if I should bring dinner home. When I arrived home, instead of finding the love and compassion I needed at that time, my mother harassed me about keeping her waiting and having her dinner late. She made an extremely emotional and painful event in my life trite. This was normal behavior for my mother as everything was about her and how it affected her life.

I remarried a few years later and began to rebuild my life with my new husband, which required time and attention. My mother couldn't understand our need for privacy and time to form trust and bonds. It was important that my children had time to develop a relationship with their new stepfather. She took it as a personal affront when we stopped our old traditions and tried to make new ones. She acted as though my husband, David, had taken me away from her, and she wasn't willing to share me with him. She became increasingly angry with him and his relationship with me and my girls, which subsequently fueled many of her unpredictable outbursts and attacks.

The real problem was that she had allowed herself to become

isolated and lacked the social skills necessary to build relationships with her own peers. Having no friends or passions to pursue, her life had revolved around my girls and me for so long that she couldn't find personal meaning for herself. Once again, I became the awful daughter who didn't care about her needs. As she aged, she seemed to know no boundaries or have any understanding of social norms. She would often say whatever came into her mind, often embarrassing my children or myself. We found ourselves avoiding her more each year.

It became increasingly difficult for me to maintain a relationship with my mother, who could turn on me at any moment. We would go for weeks on pleasant terms, but I found myself worrying when the next cycle would start again with me hanging the phone up and not speaking to her for weeks. Never having resolution to any of the issues, this pattern of behavior continued for years, until the day I knew it was over and I was done.

It was a special weekend for me in the mountains at a woman's retreat, hoping for some time to think and rejuvenate, when I noticed I had missed four calls from my mother. Since my parents are in their seventies, I thought this could be a legitimate emergency and stepped outside to return the call. She was upset again. The dogs had broken through the electric fence, and my daughter Rachel had to chase Tucker for blocks. Tucker then decided to bring my other daughter, who was home alone at this time, a present—a dead bunny—and placed it under her bed. Rebecca was frantic, but I had handled the situation a few hours earlier. Everything should have been under control, but in my mother's need to find purpose, she was compelled to get involved. Not that she would or could do anything about either situation, but her complaining and putting me down as a mother seemed to give her purpose. Once again, I found myself explaining how I'd talked Rebecca through the situation, called her dad to help clean up the mess, and calmed my child down. As usual, my mother found a way to reduce me to a childlike state. As I was trying to convince her that I had handled the situation well, I found myself trying to gain her approval and support.

Caught off-guard again, the conversation quickly turned to my husband, where she venomously recounted yet another incident of his rudeness to her and her continued disdain for him. I had already established rules by not allowing her to talk negatively about members of my family, so I said, "Conversation over" and hung up.

This time was different. She called back, pushing me emotionally until the moment I knew I was done. I said the words, "You are a very sick woman and need to be hospitalized." And then I hung up again.

I knew in my heart this was it. I no longer needed to take the emotional abuse I had been going through all my life. I felt empowered, and a weight was lifted. She did not call back.

Not many people in our family speak to my mother as she has already burned many bridges. I suddenly felt in control. I didn't need her approval, nor was I willing to pay the high price for it anymore.

I didn't speak to her for several months, although her husband, Poppi, as he is affectionately called, continued to spend every afternoon with my girls as he had done for the last eight years. They had developed a very loving, special relationship. I, too, valued his time spent with my girls and our family.

Most recently, my mother's internal turmoil and lack of control pushed her to cross the line from which there is no return, when she impulsively threatened my husband's life, vowing to make him as miserable as she was. I am sorry she struggles so much with depression and loneliness, and I do know that much of her behavior is beyond her control. I also know her mother suffered from depression as well.

It took me many years to really understand what was happening in my life and my family. I had questioned her intentions and behaviors, but I had never been able to make any sense out of it. Today, I'm still not sure why I am her target and why those hard feelings are taken out on me. I have moved to a place where I can begin my own journey of healing and forgiveness, seeing her for what and who she is, and also honoring my own life and desires.

I feel fortunate that I have been able to take control of my life and stop the cycle. The anger that had built inside has dissipated over the last six months. I now feel I am able to be the matriarch of my family with a new freedom to raise my children as I see fit. I am sad that I no longer have a relationship with my mother, but I know it is better than struggling with the unhealthy behaviors we have lived with for so many years. I want to be the mom I never had to my children, and I want the cycle to end with me. Finally, at 52 years old, I am stronger, happier, and empowered to be the mother, wife, and doctor I was meant to be.

Dr. Lee Weisbard received her Doctor of Dental Surgery degree from the University of Colorado School of Dentistry in 1984. After working for six years in Public Health Dentistry at Westside Neighborhood Health Center, she opened her unique practice in the Denver Technological Center, where her business continues today. Her areas of expertise include implant and cosmetic dentistry along with general practice. Dr. Weisbard is married to David Rosenthal and has three daughters and three adult stepsons. She enjoys the arts, skiing, and cheering her children on in their sports and activities.

FORTUNATE LIFE

Sharlene Douthit

One summer day when I was six years old, I came home sobbing. My mother jumped up when I burst through the door. "What happened? What's wrong?" she asked, alarm rising in her voice.

Through my heavy breathing and a stream of tears, I was finally able to get out that my friend Lisa said, "You must have been a bad baby if she didn't want to keep you."

Even with the shock and horror of hearing what Lisa told me, I thought she must be right. After all, she was older and seemed to be the authority on everything. I honestly had never considered that being adopted wasn't normal, because it was normal for me. All I knew was that I was born in Quincy, Florida, and my parents got the phone call to pick me up and bring me back to their home to Olney, the small Southern Illinois town where they still live. I remember seeing old family films of my parents carrying me out of the hospital, beaming and proud. This new revelation, that I was a "bad baby" who had "not been wanted" and was "thrown away," devastated me and, in turn, really upset my mother.

My mom, Dorothy, spent the majority of her adult life as the secretary at our church on Elm Street Christian. She is quiet, humble, and sometimes shy. She has a calm maturity and a level head. When it comes to drama, she just never engages in it.

However, this time was different. I saw my mother get angry and defensive. She gave me ammunition to go back with guns blazing. This was a new side of her I'd never seen before!

My mom knelt down in front of me, wiped a couple of tears away, and then put her hands on my knees to ensure she had my full attention. "That is absolutely NOT TRUE!" she said. "Your mother loved you very much. Giving you up was the hardest thing she had to go through, and she did it because she wanted you to have a better life than what she was capable of at the time. Plus your Dad and I had to wait 10 years for you! We had to pay

$10,000 to get you, out of all the kids in the world that were up for adoption, we picked you! So you are very, very special. Don't ever let anyone tell you different."

She proceeded to add, "If Lisa or anyone else ever says that to you again, you tell them that their mother only had to wait nine months for them, and she was stuck with them, whether she liked it or not!" Not the typical church lady response I was used to! I guess no one had triggered her motherly instinct to protect her child like that before. But it surely kicked in that day.

Done. My tears were dry, I felt all better, and really, really special, like I was the luckiest kid on the block. It was from that moment on that I felt so grateful for my life. I was adopted. I was chosen. I was special. I was cared for. I never had to be in a foster home, tossed from family to family like so many kids have to go through before they find a permanent home. My parents are good people. They loved me. I always had a roof over my head, hot food on the table, and clothes on my back.

Certainly there were times I wondered about my birth family, but the curiosity was never enough to rock the boat. I never dreamed of bringing it up because I didn't want to hurt my parents' feelings. I thought if I asked questions they would think I wasn't happy or didn't appreciate all they had done for me. Plus, I assumed it had been a state adoption and it would be a lot of effort to contact the state of Florida and do the actual search. I didn't have any money to do that on my own, so I kept my curiosity at bay.

Many years later when my mom retired from her job as secretary, the church gave her a vacation as a retirement gift. She chose a week's cruise to Nassau, deporting out of Florida, and asked me to go with her. Perhaps she felt sorry for me as I had just finished going through an awful divorce and had been near a nervous breakdown. We would have over a week together, the longest Mom and I had ever spent together, just the two of us. I was happy to get away, see and do something different, and enjoy a few fruity cocktails with my mom. (Which she actually tried and I liked!)

We were catching up and I was telling her about my company reorganization and that my new territory would now include the Florida panhandle, where I was born. My mom tried to make a little joke, saying "Well, when you start dating again, just make sure you don't date your brother down there!"

I about stopped the car. "What?" I said. "What brother?"

She said, "You have a half-brother that was four or five years older than you, so make sure you're not dating him by accident!" My heart started to race. I never imagined having siblings.

"How do you know this?" I asked.

She then told me the whole story. She said that the minister who was instrumental in my adoption was her old boss and that the church in Tallahassee where he pastored had been founded by my biological grandparents. My birth mother's parents told her that the only way she could give up the baby for adoption was if it went to a good Christian family. In stepped the minister, who knew my parents badly wanted a family and had been trying for 10 years to get a pregnant. They hired an attorney, drew up the papers, and made all the arrangements. When my birth mother went into labor, the minister called my parents to come down to Florida and get me. It was as easy as that!

My heart was pounding now and my mind was racing. *What if I had a whole huge family out there with tons of brothers and sisters! What else did I not know?*

My mother laughed and assured me that that was all. She did let me know that for several years the minister and his wife would stop by for a visit when they would travel back to Illinois to visit family. They'd check in on me and maybe report back to my biological grandparents that I was doing fine and was happy. She said she still keeps in contact with the minister and his wife through Christmas cards and if I ever wanted information all I had to do was ask him.

When I got back home to Atlanta, I was still getting used to being single again. I was going through a huge shift in my life that was completely unexpected and now this— I had a half-brother!

Shortly after returning from vacation with my mom, I had a scare with breast cancer. There were some small lumps under my arms and my gynecologist suggested I have a mammogram. Since I was under 40, insurance would pay for it only if there was a history of breast cancer in the family. My whole life I've been filling out doctor forms with "Adopted" written in the "Family History" area. But now I had a legitimate reason to find out more about where I came from.

I got the courage on a Sunday after church to call my mom

to tell her about the lumps and ask about my birth family. Tentatively I asked if she thought I could call the minister and ask some questions about the health of my family. She said, "Sure! Hold on, let me get my address book." It was that simple. She gave me his name and I said "thanks!" and that was it.

Before I lost my courage I called the minister and left a message saying who I was and how I got his information. I left my number and hung up, figuring I had taken the first step.

I let it go and went back to painting the kitchen. I was in total redecoration mode after my husband moved out. I was all about changing things up and making the house my own.

A few hours later, the phone rang. It was the minister. He was excited to hear from me and in great spirits. He said he'd wondered when this day would come. I explained to him that I didn't want to upset anyone's life. I was just looking for some family health history and wanted to pass my number to them if they were interested in sharing some information with me.

He said, "Sure, your mother Nancy is a nice lady."

Nancy? I thought to myself. My mother's name is Nancy! I grabbed a pen and scribbled it on a piece of paper. The minister told me that he and my biological grandparents were great friends. My grandfather had already passed away, but my grandmother was still living and lived near Nancy.

He said, "Let me give them a call and I'll call you back." Not 10 minutes later the phone rang. The minister said he'd spoken to my grandmother and she was excited to hear from me and was expecting my call. He said that Nancy was a nurse and gets up early, so it was too late to call, "but go ahead and call Cletis."

So here I was, just a few hours after I called my mom for the minister's number, now calling my biological grandmother. She answered right away with a big, happy "Well, hello! How are you?"

She sounds really nice, I thought. "I'm fine," I said. "How are you?" We proceeded to go through the question and answers like long lost friends. *Where are you living? Where are you working? Are you married?* All the questions you would ask an old classmate or friend you hadn't seen or talked to in years. I guess it would be 30 years to be exact.

She said, "Nancy is going to be so surprised to hear from you! Here is her number so you can call her tomorrow." Then she said,

"Greg is here. Do you want to talk to him?"

"Who is Greg?" I asked.

"Greg is your older brother!"

Turns out Greg had just found out about me when the minister phoned Cletis less than an hour before. He was five when his mother was pregnant and didn't remember any of it. They never made a big deal out of it with him, so he was just as shocked as I was to learn he had a sibling.

He and I spoke for a short time and agreed to talk again in a day or so when we'd both had some time to absorb the news.

That night I went to bed smiling and feeling happy that I made the move to call the minister. Tomorrow I would get to talk to my birth mom!

The next day after work, I dialed her number. She answered quickly.

"Nancy?" I asked.

"Yes," she said.

"Do you know who this is?" I said.

"No," she said.

"This is Sharlene, and I think you are my birth mother," I said. She giggled a little and I could tell she was surprised. She switched to another phone line, and then it felt like long lost friends catching up on each other's lives for the next half hour. We exchanged emails and agreed to make a plan to meet the next time I was in Florida for work.

When that day arrived we planned to meet in the hotel lobby where I was staying. When I pulled up and rolled my bags into the lobby, the three of them stood up—my grandmother, mother, and half-brother Greg. I was shocked that it was happy and no one cried. We were all a bit nervous and it went like this: Nancy gave me a tight, long hug. She grabbed my upper arms and then pulled back to stare at my face for a moment. She was smiling and I noticed right away that I have the same shaped eyes as hers. Later I noticed we have the same dimples as well. Then Cletis gave me a big hug for a long time, then also wanted to check me out up close for a moment. I also look like her. Then Greg and I hugged and exchanged welcomes. After I checked in to drop off my bags, we all went to dinner.

I remember showing them the photos of me when I was a baby. I brought a couple of photos along for Nancy to keep as well. We had a nice evening getting to know one another. The next day after work, Greg picked me up and took me over to Nancy's office so I could see the clinic where she works. All the ladies she worked with stopped what they were doing to come in and say hello to me. They all gave me big hugs and I saw that Nancy had placed one of the photos I gave her on her computer monitor. It was really cute.

I have a couple of photos from that visit. One of favorites is of my grandmother sitting on the swing out back playing with a litter of stray kittens Nancy had taken in.

It turns out, besides looks, my birth mother and I have so much in common. She is a huge animal lover like me, has dogs (and the stray kittens), is a big shopper, and loves to decorate her house. In addition, we both played the flute in band when we were younger. The thing that is the strangest coincidence is that we went to the same Christian Bible Camp in Flora, Illinois. It was just one of those coincidences that I don't think is really a coincidence. I'm certain God has had his hand in my life this entire way and is still showing me how great things can be here on Earth.

I am grateful to have met my grandmother before she passed away in 2001 at the age of 85 from a stroke. She was a sweet, dear woman who I am happy I take after. I am certain I will see her again in Heaven and get to catch up with her some more. I feel good knowing both she and God are looking out for me from above, the way they did before I was even born.

After a 20 year career in corporate sales and marketing roles for Fortune 500 consumer packaged goods companies, Sharlene Douthit took the leap of faith and became a serial entrepreneur, launching five companies in two years. Following her passions for photography, real estate investing, and interior design, she created businesses that specialize in making things more beautiful, whether people or properties. She also sits on the Board of Directors for Fashion Group International of Denver. Sharlene enjoys traveling, cooking, hosting parties, and soaking up the Colorado sunshine by running, skiing, and hiking with her beloved dogs, Chauncey and Foster. Sharlene's pride and joy is Financially Fit Females, an education based women's financial support group she founded in 2008. Learn more at www.FinanciallyFitFemales.com.

TALES OF GREEN CHILE

Gina Autobee

No matter how old you get there are some smells you will never forget, smells that remain not only in your nose but in your heart, smells that will live forever in your soul. It is a scent so strong that it becomes substance, substance that defines who you are and sometimes who you become.

As for me, I am a middle-class woman working diligently every day to support this life that I have built, and this home that I am proud of. I wake up every morning and look in the mirror, and I am not perfect. As matter of fact I am far from perfect, but I work hard at maintaining my beauty, not only with makeup and hairspray but with actions. I am a woman who attempts in all aspects of my life to be a good person, to exude politeness and positivity, but this is not always an easy feat.

Especially when you have faced rejection and discrimination as many times as I have. You see, I am a Chicana (a chunky Chicana, at that). This means that I am of Mexican descent, mixed with French, Navajo, and Filipino all rolled into one beautiful, lovable woman. I am proud of who I am, and of where I come from.

Like my mother, I am the heart of my family. As tough as it may be, I keep our life rolling like a well-oiled machine. As women we are all the nucleus of our families. We come from different backgrounds, have different looks, and have mothers and fathers of different races and circumstances. We all have our own family histories, irreplaceable stories, and unique traditions.

Sometimes, the traditions we are raised with and continue to impose on our families, don't make much sense. They can feel outdated, pointless, and sometimes all-out silly. However, these crazy little things that we continue to do are done out of love and habit. They give us the ability to create memories, as well as something to teach our children and loved ones. I like to say, "Traditions are an ode to the past and a toast to the present."

It almost seems as though you can rewind time and remember the days of old. I can still see Gramita in her apron singing and dancing around the kitchen, saying *"vienen aqui mi jita baila conmigo"* (come here baby, come dance with me).

Traditions strengthen the days of now, too. I see my son fumbling through making dough from a family recipe for the first time, and then later watch him be ever so nervous and excited to bring his girlfriend over and have her participate in the tradition. I see him make eye contact with her, as his aunt tells her she is doing it all wrong. Watch with disbelieving eyes as he gently grabs the dough and shows her how to knead it, the way he was taught many moons ago, not in a condescending way, but lovingly.

As the bread rises and browns, the smell begins to build and peak. The butter and freshly canned jelly are already on the counter ready to be spread upon a warm, soft layer of goodness. The excitement is growing, mouths are watering, and bellies are yearning, though the taste is familiar; it is comforting and heavenly. As the fragrant aroma fills the room, I glance at my son and can still catch a glimpse of that same fervent boyish look on his face, and I can't help but swell with love and pride.

When I get just a tiny whiff of this evocative smell, I get a smile on my face and a hunger deep in my belly. I can feel just a slight warm breeze in the air. I look up at a beautiful-hued, cloud-speckled sky, and I see the leaves that are beginning to cover the ground, gold, red, and slightly brown. I become childlike with a free heart.

The sounds that I hear as the smell is brewing are beautiful. It is Little Joe y La Familia, singing in the background "Hey Baby Que Paso." It is the sound of *bolios* hitting the table with every roll and flip. It is the sound of my Tias and Great Gramita all speaking in Spanish (which sounds like jibberish to me) at the same time trying to get my mother's attention. The best sound of all is the sound of my mother's laughter illuminating an already sunny room.

The stove has taken on a new role. It is not only a piece of metal encompassing four burners and an oven, it is our hearth. It is also a worker bee, blending, simmering, and frying the best home-cooked Chicano meal anyone can imagine.

It is fall, harvest time, and the women have worked hard,

picking, chopping, and bagging. They are getting ready for a winter that is not as harsh as the ones they knew growing up. The winter will not bring wood gathering and foraging, nor should it bring struggle. After all, these are modern times. Safeway is down the block, we live in the times of super foods and, with global warming, winters have lost their tenacity. However, stocking up for winter has become part of who they are, and who I am already becoming.

Every fall growing up, I watched them working so hard, all in their aprons roasting, peeling, and bagging for hours. It was like, now is the time, and if we don't get it done, we will not make it through the winter. As a little girl, I thought this was totally normal and that every family had to do this, for survival, throughout the cold harsh days ahead.

However, now that I am older, I giggle when I think of the fact that if we run out of chile, or anything else for that matter, we have the ability to get in our car, drive down a few paved streets, and go into the grocery store, where they have just about anything you could possibly need to put a meal together.

I guess the funniest and greatest part of the whole ordeal is that the tradition didn't stop, it didn't die! In fact, every fall the women in our family still get together, take a trip to the farms, gather chile and produce, and yes, we roast, peel, chop, and bag, like the next few months depend on the groundwork that we lay today.

Sadly, many of the Tias and Great Gramita have passed on. It is not their voices all speaking in Spanish at the same time, like we once heard. It is now a younger generation. My mother still plays beautiful New Mexico music and tells stories of the old days, as we all laugh and sing along, even though some of the words we do not understand. The men all sit in the family room watching football anxiously waiting, every now and then coming in to get a peek of the beauty and magic being performed, as well as to steal a fresh tortilla with butter.

As the tortillas brown, the potatoes fry, the frijoles thicken, the just-picked green chiles roast, I begin to smell it. Oh my goodness, what a smell! Beautiful, panging smell, it is green chile. Cooking in a big stock pot with pork, onion, and garlic...mmmm. It is the smell that I grew up with, a taste that I crave, a part of who I am, and a history that I will gladly pass on to my children. It is our culture! *La Cultura.* It is a tradition that we want to last. In a world where so many things have lost their value, our culture remains rich in our hearts!

Gina Autobee is not a writer by profession, but a writer by heart. She has been interested in writing ever since she can remember, and loves reading as much. She is a married woman who has two children, and holds her family and friends dear to her heart. She is proud to say that she is a product of her environment, because it has shaped her into the strong woman she is today.

Finding Your Path

GOING FOR GOLD

Barbara Robins

I sat there, glued to the television screen, watching the Winter Olympics. "My athlete" was just about to take her second and final run. Being in last place meant she had to go first. This was it—her final opportunity to move up and take a medal. I used every minute between her first run and this moment—and every bit of myself—to help her. As she waited in between runs, I went through each millisecond of her routine to look for energy blockages and remove them. Now, sitting on the edge of my seat, I watched as she began her performance. It was incredible—beyond amazing—but would it be enough for her to medal? I, and everyone else, now had to wait as her competitors took their turns. As we watched their performances and the changing results, the minutes felt like an eternity. I found myself holding my breath—and mentally blank.

The years leading up to this moment in time had been filled with many difficulties—my health problems, being a single mom with children who suffered from physical and emotional conditions, endless doctors' appointments, being unable to work, and having a "wasband" (ex) who berated me for each step I took to help our children. How did I get from those events to where I sat now? How did I go from being a victim to becoming the energy healer I am today?

Lao Tzu, a Chinese philosopher, said in about 500 B.C., "A journey of a thousand miles begins with one step." Although my entire life experience brought me to where I am today, my journey to healing began with an illness that developed when I was seven months pregnant. I thought back to that time and all that transpired since then.

During the pregnancy with my second child, I developed a severely painful inflammation around my eye. Within three days I was so sick I could barely walk or take a bite of food. I became so weak that all I could do was lie in bed and sleep. I was taken to several doctors before I received a diagnosis and treatment plan. For one year I battled this painful inflammation. I gained about 80 pounds because the medicine made me continually hungry.

My illness took a toll on my new baby as well. Three years prior I'd been able to lovingly nurse my first child until she was almost two years old. Now, because the medication could adversely affect her, I was forced to stop nursing my new baby girl after just a few months.

I grieved for a long time over the loss of closeness with my second child and my vision of how her early life would be. It was through this experience, however, that I first began to realize the significance of the name my husband and I had given her. The meaning of my baby's first and middle name together is "Praise God, this is His will." Her name became my prayer and my plea. Through her name, I asked daily for the strength, courage, and perseverance to accept the circumstances of my life.

After three years I fully recovered. By then, my baby had developed health problems of her own that overwhelmed our entire family. She had reoccurring ear and respiratory infections and needed tubes in her ears before she was two years old. Her tonsils had to be removed before she was three. Through all these events and experiences, "Praise God, this is His will" became my mantra. When she had anxiety and panic attacks and we couldn't find any way to help calm her, I said, "Praise God, this is His will." When she developed ADHD symptoms, I called out, "Praise God, this is His will." And when nothing worked that regular and alternative medical professionals suggested or prescribed, I cried, "Praise God, this is His will." This phrase— her name—became my life line. With each problem, I clung to the meaning of her name to get us through.

Her name helped me through other stressful events as well. IHer name helped me through other stressful events as well. It seemed my older daughter and my husband also had signs of ADD. Additionally, my husband had anger management issues. In fact, his outbursts grew more frequent with the passage of time. The criticism wore me down so much that one day I found myself sitting on the couch, unable to do anything—even go to the grocery store—because with everything I thought to do, I could hear him yelling at me that I did it wrong. Ultimately, my husband and I divorced. Through all of these hardships, I clung to my daughter's name to get me through. "Praise God, this is His will" continued to be my life raft in a sea of chaos.

Although divorcing was best for me and my daughters, I was now faced with finding help for my youngest daughter on my own. I was also confronted with the question of how to support us financially. Every time I asked for guidance on how to do that, the answer I heard was, "Take care of your children." Every time I called out, "What is my job? What should I be doing?" the answer I received was, "Take care of your children." Looking back, I see that taking care of my children was the most important work I could have been doing at the time. I also realize we were provided for along the way. Whenever I needed money, there was a solution, including help from my parents. Truly, the answer to my mantra, "Praise God, this is His will" was for me to be there for my children.

Along with my daughter's name, certain principles guided me through the most difficult moments of my lifetime—perseverance, quality, intuition, and health. First, I had to accept our situation and my daughter's continuing mental and physical challenges. I also had to accept my wasband's critical opposition. While I continued to deal with a hyperactive child who frequently suffered anxiety and panic attacks, I was reminded that it was up to me to see us through. I plummeted deeper and deeper into feelings of weakness. Simultaneously, however, something kept pushing me forward. There must be a solution. I needed to persevere, to grab onto inner strength, to trust "All That Is" to lead me to the right people and answers. My inner desire for quality—to find the best help—continued to propel me forward.

I started testing the waters in the alternative health community with vitamins, herbs, and homeopathy. One evening, after a rare dinner out with the kids, they asked me if we could go to the bookstore next to the restaurant. I agreed. As we walked in they went to the children's section and I headed to the self-help section. Standing there I felt "someone" move my head down and then move my eyes to focus on one book, Dr. Richard Gerber's *Vibrational Medicine for the 21st Century*. I picked it up and glanced through it. Although I'd recently begun my journey of helping my daughter with alternative healing modalities, I still knew very little about them. This was an encyclopedia of various energy healing modalities. I bought the book and began to play with one of the modalities mentioned in the book.

Ultimately, that book led me on a path of exploration into the world of energy healing. I kept reading and learning. And I continued to take my daughter from one doctor to another based on recommendations from others. I was certain that one day I'd find "the one" who would truly help her. The latest referral came from a woman I recently met. Trusting her advice that "he'll take care of everything," yet knowing nothing about this man's work, I booked an appointment.

After meeting with him and as we prepared to leave, my daughter and I both felt disappointed that nothing eventful had happened. Upon shaking hands to thank him for seeing us, I could feel him reading my life as he looked into my eyes. On our way home, at exactly 8:00 p.m., I felt tingling and heat on my back. I knew that sensation was a sign of a healing. Could that have just corrected my scoliosis? The next day I learned that at that precise moment he was in a session with someone who had the same problem I had—she also needed to wear a lift in one shoe.

When I got home, I took off my shoes and hurried to my mirror. I couldn't believe my eyes—I was standing straight and my shoulders were squared without the aid of my shoe lift! Every five minutes for the next hour and a half, I returned to the mirror to recheck my body. It was still straight! The next day I ran to my chiropractor to confirm that this healing had really happened. After taking a look at me she asked, "Who is this man?" I told her I didn't know, but I was going to find out.

A few days later I was able to attend a lecture/demonstration he gave. He asked people who had physical pain to come up on the stage. In just a few minutes, without touching them, their pain vanished. Excitement and so many other emotions welled up inside me. I needed to learn this! He presented a basic workshop the following weekend, and I was there.

The technique was very easy for me to learn, and from that weekend forward, I was healing people. One of the first healings I did was to take away a headache my mom had been experiencing for two weeks.

Learning this healing modality changed everything. It was as if I had been slowly climbing a very steep roller coaster all my life and didn't even know I'd made it to the top until everything sped up with ease. Within three months, people were paying me to provide them with distant energy healing. Within one year, I had helped more than 800 people with a 97% success rate at reducing or eliminating their symptoms. I was coaching student healers, developing enhancements to the process, and writing stories and articles.

When I look back, I am in awe of what transpired. It was a miracle—what a gift I was given. I see that each step I took early on was to survive—to keep breathing, to keep eating, and to continue taking care of my children. Once I found energy healing, my life began to improve on many different levels. And finally I knew with certainty that my life was going to be okay. I was going to be able to support myself and my children.

There were days when I hid under my covers and cried and slept all day. There have been some days like that even recently, but now I know it's okay to hide and cry for a moment or a few hours and release those emotions. It's part of the process. When I allow myself to feel my feelings, to simply be with them without making them my whole life, they detach and disappear after a while. In their place comes clarity—the blue sky of hope and revelation and direction.

Eventually, I took some time off and started to wonder if this truly was my life's purpose. Yes, I did miraculous healings and taught others how to do it too, but so what? I had automated a lot of my training and had created a number of healing CDs so people could be helped without me having to be there. I decided to attend a workshop that helps people clarify their life's purpose. I had no clue how significantly my life was about to change.

Two days before I was to leave, I received an email requesting a session for a world-class athlete who had become so injured, she and her family feared she might become incapacitated. With the Winter Olympics just a month away, the situation was urgent. I knew the only free time I had would be as I traveled to my workshop. They agreed to allow me to do a remote session from the plane.

At the workshop I discovered a renewed purpose and responsibility to continue with my work. My mission statement became "to brighten and amplify people's self delight so they can rock their life." I was once again excited about my rockin' life and my purpose to help people love their lives.

When I returned home, I heard back from "my athlete" who reported great improvement. By the time the Olympics began she was able to participate. I was commissioned to continue sessions, which I did partially while watching her performances live on television. I continued to do energy optimizations up to the very last second of her live televised final performance.

We were now into the final moments of her event. The last competitor was finishing her routine. We had waited for nearly 30 minutes to see if someone could beat "my athlete." Within seconds of the last competitor's performance, the pronouncement came. "My athlete" had won her first Olympic gold medal. I jumped up from my chair and continued to jump up and down and cheer as I've never done before. She was the winner—a gold medalist!

In those moments of exhilaration and triumph, I realized I was a winner as well. My journey to excel in my own life, my quest for quality help on behalf of my children, my perseverance in times of deep despair, my undying hope when all looked hopeless, and my unstoppable belief in the potential for health and healing had taken me on a journey to the top of the roller coaster, to the peak of the mountain. Now, looking out from this vantage point, I could see that I was a gold medalist as well. Just as "my athlete" came from last place to take the ultimate prize, I too had journeyed from the deepest, darkest places and come to the pinnacle of my life's calling.

I know, just as with any ride, there will be twists and turns, ups and downs, and even loops back. What will carry me through—just as it did all those years ago—is the deep knowing that I am never alone. My daughter's name is as relevant in my life today as it was in the past. I now stand in my purpose. I commit to serving to my peak potential. What a ride this is. "Praise God, this is His will!"

Barbara Robins has been at the top of her field in offering innovative healing services and training since 2001. She has worked successfully with world-class athletes, artists/performers, healthcare professionals, international speakers/trainers, and welcomes new clients who are exploring their potential... To receive a free copy of 5 Simple Actions to Unblock Your Energy Flow go to www.healingisfun.com/action. For more information about Barbara and ways she can assist you in reaching your goals visit her online at www.healingisfun.com.

EMBRACING THE CHANGE

Karen McKy

Monday morning, December 17, 2007, I found myself standing in the tiny bathroom of my home, my forehead pressed to the locked door with tears streaming down my cheeks. My heart was pounding. I felt like I was ready to crawl out of my skin. I wanted to get away from me, who I was and everything about my life. I was miserable even though I had a beautiful home in a highly desirable area of town, two great kids, and a business I was building with my second husband. I had material abundance around me. *I should be happy*, I thought, but I was not. It was a turning point in my life. I knew it, because I had been at this place before. Every cell of my body was screaming. If I didn't step out of my current marriage, it would destroy me. I had to get out, but how?

Two months earlier the most important person in my life, my beloved grandmother, died at the age of 96. The one person in my life who was always my strength, my mentor, my encourager was gone forever. How I missed her. She was the one person who could perk me up when the chips were down. She would help me see hope in the darkest of times. Just hearing her voice would coat my heart with warmth and tenderness. Grandmother was the Pollyanna who believed with every challenge there was a reason, with every cloud there was a silver lining. I had learned to believe her outlook on life was best. Better to be the optimist rather than the pessimist, but when I found myself in the dumps it was hard for me to find that silver lining or the reason for the challenge. No longer could I count on her insights or guidance to soothe me and light my path. Somehow, I would have to find all her well-nurtured strength within me and pull myself through this hardship alone. My world felt empty. I felt alone and I was.

In spite of the beautiful home, the material goods, and the business, I was miserable. My second husband was a determined, tough, emotionally demanding man. I felt trapped by this man

259

who continuously challenged me. At first, I had appreciated that he was unyielding. He was the brick wall I could run at, smash into, and he wouldn't give way. He stood his ground, knew who and what he was. He was the total opposite of my first husband, who would bend easily and could be pushed to accommodate whatever direction I wanted to go. When I met my second husband, I liked his strength. It felt decisive and sure. What I had not seen in him was his dark side. He was tough on my children and pushed his agenda about how to parent them.

I found myself in a war zone, tiptoeing between husband #1, the father of my children, and husband #2, who thought his way was the way it needed to be. To keep peace in our house, I was always negotiating between the two men, the kids, and trying to squeeze in what I wanted for the children, too. The longer I was with my second husband, the more he found ways to diminish me personally, to undermine my self-worth.

We started a home-based business before our marriage which demanded every ounce of my energy. After five years of living with my second husband's anger and tirades, my two wonderful kids became so frustrated they left our home to live with their dad a few miles away. Tensions were so high in our house they wanted out.

They had a way to get out, but I did not. I was stuck. I had no personal income. Everything we earned was rolled back into building the business. We were still living pretty much month to month with no true disposable income. I was juggling credit card debt as well and hated it. There was no financial safety net to catch me if I bailed out. I was anxious, restless, and in a deep state of panic and despair.

Ideas of suicide began to creep back into my thoughts. I had been to this dark place before, spending the first year of my first marriage in a hellhole of despair. Fear of botching the attempt and living as a vegetable prevented me from exercising that option. How had I gotten to this point again? I knew. It was the darkest of my secrets. The one I did not want to look at because then I had to face my own personal fear, the one that scared me so much it took away my life force.

The fear? I believed I could not take care of myself. Specifically, I thought I could not provide for myself financially. Therefore, I became dependent on men in my life, first my father, then my first husband, now my second husband. Even my beloved grandmother had unknowingly helped build the trap I was caught in. Even though she was my greatest supporter, she taught me women were to be dependent upon their husbands. It was the old standard, the old model, now outdated in our current "modern woman" thinking in the U.S.

Hiding in the bathroom my body started to tremble. It felt as if there were a vibration coming from the core of my body expanding all the way to the furthest fingertip. In a moment of amazement, feeling this very strange quaking and looking at my arms, hands, and fingers, I puzzled over what could be taking place within me. There was no visible evidence they were moving, yet the feeling of the vibration intensified. My body was fully involved in this experience. It was real, not my imagination! Surely the feeling would pass in a few minutes, I thought. I sat down on the toilet seat and felt my tears subsiding as now my focus shifted to this weird sensation pulsing through me. It was not scary, rather almost pleasurable. A good half hour must have passed as I waited for the sensation to go away, but it did not. Then an urging came to my awareness to visit a friend whom I had not seen in many, many months.

I gathered my things, left the house, and jumped in the car. After dialing his phone and hearing my friend's familiar voice, I raced toward the highway exit. "Doug, I was wondering if you and Debra were available for a visit. Something very weird is happening and I am unable to understand it. Would you have some time to chat?" I asked. After being soothed by his warm voice, we decided we would meet in a few hours. Time passed; however, the strange trembling within me remained, strong and sure.

Doug and Debra met me with open arms. A sunny room greeted me along with hot tea and engaging conversation. Hours passed and the sun began to set over the Colorado mountains; all the while my body was shaking from the core. Then the question came from Doug: "So, what have you been reading?"

My response tumbled out with passion and intensity as if uncorking a bottle of shaken champagne. After my grandmother's passing I had voraciously been re-reading books about hypnosis, specifically regression work, as though I was being pulled back to them by some strong force. I could not put those books down once I started reading them.

This area of study was always a deep desire of mine. Never had I allowed myself the opportunity to pursue it. It was in the category of "someday." It seems we all have that category—that miserable place where we stuff our dreams, our aspirations, the real gift we are here to share with the world. We hide these thoughts and ideas away because there are sabotaging beliefs deep inside us that say, *I am too small and insignificant to make a difference. I am incapable of attaining my goals. I am not good enough. It's not the right time.* Each of us has our own sabotaging beliefs, but we all have them.

Now I was face to face with the monstrous, seething dragon hiding within me. The dragon's message: "You can't do it. You can't make it on your own." Damn, I did not want to see this adversary I'd been running and hiding from for so many years. Yet to ignore this challenge would mean certain death. Several years prior I'd been diagnosed with pre-cancerous breast tissue. And earlier in the summer of 2007 I'd had a complete hysterectomy because uterine polyps were causing bleeding. With a family history of cancer I felt this was the safest move at the time. All it would take for cancer to get a footing somewhere within me was to continue ignoring my Divine calling, the purpose I was here to live.

To stretch outside my confining world would mean leaving my business behind as well as my second marriage. No matter which way I turned I felt trapped. Escape would come only from confronting the dragon and defeating it, once and for all. I could not keep living the life I had been living, always running away. Yet it was so terrifying to consider being on my own, making my own way doing what I felt called to do. I had always been in service to the men in my life, building their lives, growing their dreams. I had been successful with them. It stood to reason I could be successful building my own career for me. A leap off a tall cliff was what was being called for now. If I jumped I would either perish or find the wings to fly.

More voices from the dragon: "What will everyone think of you leaving another marriage? What will they think of you in such an odd profession as hypnosis?" This certainly was not a "mainstream" career choice and seemingly would continue my classification as an "oddball." My fears were intense.

Doug brought me back to the moment and hit me with another statement. "Promise me as soon as you get home you will go online and sign up for a hypnosis class." Oh my God. Could I really do that? The challenge had been made.

I quickly told him, "Okay, I will." I had made a promise, if not for me, for Doug and Debra.

Driving home the trembling continued. Why was this happening? The 30-minute drive gave me plenty of sabotaging thoughts to wrestle with. I had made a promise, outwardly to my friends and inwardly to myself. I would follow through even though there were plenty of valid reasons not to.

It was getting late and my husband would be expecting dinner, but it was forgotten the moment the door swung open to my home. I sat down and started my search online. Several programs looked interesting. All of them started in the New Year with the earliest class beginning January 23, 2008, in North Carolina. How would I tell my husband what I was going to do? Ugh! I filled out the online registration and paid the deposit for the class. *Shit! What will my husband say about spending money for this class?* I worried.

But I felt an inner urging that said *Keep going. What's next?* Another search showed a quaint-looking motel named after the Wright Brothers with a boardwalk to the beach in Kitty Hawk, North Carolina. I love the ocean! This place just felt right so I selected it. With flight scheduled and a hotel chosen, the next decision was a rental car to drive from Norfolk, Virginia, to North Carolina. This trip was going to cost a lot of money. The quaking within me was as strong as ever. *Oh, to hell with it. It's now or never!* I entered the credit card number and hit "purchase."

I sat back in my chair and…the vibration STOPPED. As weird as it was, somehow it all felt strangely "right." A profound sense of calm came over my being. Suddenly it didn't matter what my husband would think or say about my decision. I knew this was the right thing for me to do and it would all work out.

Fast forward to today. So much has happened in these past three years. My second husband and I divorced after I took the hypnosis classes and started my new career. He bought me out of the business we started together, which gave me seed money to get my life going. I met and married my soul mate, who is 23 years my senior. Most of all, my life is being lived by me, for me!

That fierce and terrifying Dragon occasionally reminds me of the original message. However, his voice is calm and I see it for what it really has been all along: a shadow of myself encouraging me to remember who I really am and why I am really here in this world.

Certainly, there were times I felt fearful and had doubts starting my new life. The small rewards, insights, and growth in my personal accomplishments kept me going. The inner knowing I would find my way and make the right decisions made it possible to push through the fears. If I had not taken the chance, I would have resigned my life to mediocrity and lack of personal and spiritual fulfillment. I would forever be subservient and never able to speak my truth.

Now, at the close of my 49th year in this body, I embrace the opportunity to finally live my life and be of service to more people than I ever dreamed possible. Doors are opening I never expected or thought possible. A whole new world of friends is finding me, rather than me seeking them. I have the most incredible love relationship and marriage with my best friend. Life is more than hopeful now. It is fantabulistic! My spiritual life is deeper and richer than it has ever been. My work with people allows them to confront and embrace their deepest and darkest fears and move through them.

Thinking back to how lost and terrified I felt all my life, I stand in amazement of how paralyzed I was only three years ago. Poor self-esteem imprisoned me since childhood and kept me from seeing or fulfilling my potential. Now I fully embrace my courage and live my potential each day. Being able to transform my past and live in the present moment was the magic that changed my life, and it all began with an unceasing quaking within my soul.

Karen McKy, MHt is a speaker and author who teaches internationally as a Certified PSYCH-K® Instructor trained by Rob Williams, M.A., Dr. Bruce Lipton, and Larry Valmore. She is also a clinical hypnotherapist specializing in regression and spiritual work. Karen loves assisting people in removing fears and blockages to their full potential by identifying and changing self-limiting beliefs in the subconscious mind. Her greatest joy is witnessing the awakening of one's soul and the embracing of its true calling in life. She can be reached at Karen@AwakeningKnowledge.com or Karen@SubconsciousChange.com or 303-952-0596. Visit her websites www.SubconsciousChange.com and www.AwakeningKnowledge.com.

FINDING MY GIFT

Carol Calkins, PhD

The day was filled with the joyful celebration that surrounds the miracle of a new born child. I was told I was quite the birthday gift as I was born at home on the 31st of May, my mother's 31st birthday. I was delivered into the gentle hands of my loving father who was a successful doctor. From that dawning moment I was told I was born under a lucky star and that sense of luck and good fortune would be something I would carry with me throughout my life.

My parents were extraordinary people. From a very early age they instilled in us four kids that we could be and do anything we dreamed of. Despite being painfully shy when I was growing up and experiencing a variety of trying events and losses, I've always maintained a positive outlook and optimistic view of life. That's not to say that life didn't challenge me with difficult times. I lost my father when I was just 22, divorced in my thirties while I watched my young daughter struggle with her own hurt and sadness, and I felt helpless as my mother faced a recurrence of breast cancer after 31 years in remission, a dreadful disease that ultimately exhausted her strength to fight it any longer. Nevertheless, I have always been able to see the silver lining, the good in everything, and value the lessons learned from each experience.

I began my life as a gift and always knew I had something wonderful inside me to share with others. However, recognizing exactly what it was seemed to elude me. I was good at everything I tried as a child. I was the best ballet dancer, the best at fencing, the best swimmer and diver, and the best in many of my school classes. However, all of these activities were short lived; I never pursued anything for very long. I would try a variety of things and always wonder, *Is this it? Is this my gift?* But each time for various reasons I found myself moving on.

Many times the practicalities of life seemed to get in the way and my focus was needed elsewhere. I lost my father just prior to becoming an adult and realized quickly that I no longer had that personal and financial support. The thought of fending for myself was once a distant idea that had suddenly become a reality. My mother was going through her own loss and pain and I knew I had to take care of myself and be independent. I married a few years later and instantly became mother to three stepchildren. Over the course of 12 years this marriage went through many ups and downs. As the years passed the relationship affected me in some negative ways where I felt as though I was losing my true identity and self esteem. Despite this, it was extremely painful when the marriage ended because not only did I lose a husband, I lost the love and contact with the three stepchildren, who felt they had to stick by their father.

In spite of all the heartache there was a blessing. I still had my wonderful daughter, who at eight years old was having lots of confusion, anger, and sadness about why her whole family and life was being pulled apart. What's more, I had lost myself during the marriage, which had been a constant frustration for me, as I still longed to find out who I truly was. Throughout these years I had many roles, a wife, mother and caretaker, all these things I aspired to be but who was I? Although finding my gift was not in the forefront of my mind, finding myself certainly was.

I began the healing process and the search for myself. Through books, seminars, and classes, I began asking questions: *Who am I? What do I like? What makes me happy?* Not too long after, while my daughter was visiting my sister in California, I did the first spontaneous thing I'd done in years: I took a quick trip to Albuquerque to visit my best friend.

It was there I met the love of my life. I found that when I was with him not only could I totally be myself, he was supportive of me in all ways, including finding myself and ultimately finding my gift. However, there were definitely challenges in bringing a new family together. My daughter, who was still struggling with the divorce, was now dealing with a new stepfather. Nuturing and strengthening my family became the most important focus in my life.

Fast forward to my forties. I found my career as an administrator in healthcare and higher education. Simultaneously, I took courses at Mile Hi Church and became a licensed Religious Science practitioner. Although I didn't formalize my path as a professional practitioner, I incorporated much of what I learned into my everyday life. There was a time that I thought maybe providing spiritual counsel to others was my gift.

It was during this time my mother lost her battle with breast cancer. She was my best friend, my confidante, the person who always made me feel better no matter how bad or difficult things seemed. I felt as though a part of me had been ripped away and there was nothing I could do. However, at the same time, I couldn't help but feel blessed to have had such an extraordinary woman in my life; how fortunate I was to have had her as my mother. Getting used to her being gone was a long and difficult process.

In my early fifties I received my PhD. Between my graduate program and my position in higher education it became apparent that I was a good writer. I always knew from the time I was relatively young that someday I'd write a book. I realized I was a wordsmith and not only could I write well, but I was outstanding at editing others' writing. So I asked myself, *Is writing my gift?* I explored writing a book with a primary focus on self-help for supervisors in a business setting. Although I even put together a writing schedule and for several months followed it, something wasn't right. I didn't feel like what I was expressing was my true gift. My heart was telling me something just did not click.

Things seemed to accelerate right after my sixtieth birthday. I took a four-day course created by Cathy and Gary Hawk of Clarity International called "Get Clarity for Life & Work." The experience was life changing. During this long weekend you have an opportunity to deeply focus on what turns your "lights on" and what doesn't. It became clear to me that writing a book was high on my "lights on" meter. This is an oversimplification of what actually occurred within me because of the Clarity experience. I had finally put together the intricate pieces of my inner happiness as to what turns my "lights on." At the end of the four days I felt more clarity on my direction/path and what lights me up. I still wasn't completely sure how to get there, but I knew I was closer than I'd ever been before.

Around the same time that I was reaching milestones in finding myself, a dear friend of mine had overcome breast cancer—or so it seemed. Ironically, around Halloween she went in for her annual follow-up exam and was given some of the most horrible news she could possibly hear. The cancer had returned in another place in her body, except this time it was inoperable. Her doctor wanted her to get treatment as soon as possible and would continue to monitor the size of this new tumor. My friend got so sick from the chemotherapy she had to be hospitalized. She wanted so badly to be home for Christmas that they let her go home to be with her family.

Everything now seems like a blur after Christmas. She found out from the doctor soon after the first of the year that the tumor was growing very quickly; she had only two options. Option number one was to have chemo again in the hospital, but it could possibly kill her. Option number two was to go home to hospice care with maybe three to four months left to live. I will never forget my friend confiding in me how she truly wished she had another option.

We spoke on the phone regularly. On my way home from work I went by to see her every week or two throughout this period and during her entire illness. My friend had a wonderful talent and gift: she made the most beautiful greeting cards. She had a garden and would take photos of the colorful flowers and place them on the front of each card. Each one was unique and sending these greeting cards to people always felt very special. I remember feeling that I wanted her to pass this gift on to me, so we spoke about her teaching me. That never came to pass because my dear friend lost her battle with cancer two and half weeks after she was told she had two options. I felt more determined than ever to figure out how to take photos and make these beautiful greeting cards.

Sometimes what you think is the gift someone is sharing with you isn't really the gift at all. Two days after my dear friend passed away I was meditating. During my meditation I felt her presence; it was an overwhelming, yet peaceful feeling. What I sensed is that I needed to help others, those who were close to her, heal from their loss, especially those who felt like they never got a chance to say goodbye. Then the words "We Said Goodbye a Thousand Times" came to me. When I came out of my meditation, I went to my computer and began typing. It was automatic writing; when I was done, I read the most amazing poem.

I didn't completely realize at that moment that she had given me a gift, but it became clear about a month later when poetry began flowing from me. I started to think in poetry. When people would speak, I would pick out words or phrases that later became lines in a poem. Situations or conversations would become inspiration for a poem or poems. Since that day more than a year ago, I've written over 600 poems, published my first book, *Bring Poetry to Life*, recently published my second book, *Bring Poetry into Your Life*, and am working on three others books including a 10th Anniversary Tribute to 9-11.

Poetry has given me so much. Now when I'm around people, I listen to everything they say not only to hear the words, but also to sense the feelings they are experiencing. I pause before I move on and truly focus on them. I've found this true in almost everything I do. I can honestly say that I am spending more time smelling the roses, seeing the beauty in people, nature, and life. It's as though I now perceive other dimensions that I never saw before. My perspective has made a shift, and I now feel more satisfied and have more confidence than ever before. I also find that more and more people are coming to me for advice and support.

As I look back at my life thus far, I know that I always wanted to live a full and happy life and also to leave behind a legacy once I'm gone. My daughter, son-in-law, and new granddaughter are certainly a huge part of my legacy. But now I feel exhilarated that my gift of poetry is also a part of my legacy. I feel passionate about poetry and how it can change the way a person feels, bring them comfort and peace, and lift their spirits. It's as though I've found a new language that with few words paints a picture, tells a story, expresses emotions, and hopefully heals the hearts of those who read it.

I know now that all of my life's experiences and at times what seemed to be distractions have culminated together to guide me to finding my life's path and true gift, the gift of poetry. One thing I'm absolutely sure of is that my future is expanding into new and exciting realms. I will continue creating poetry and sharing not only my poetry, but all my gifts with every person I meet and with the world.

We Said Goodbye a Thousand Times

Don't be sad about my parting
Don't feel like you never said goodbye
For you and I both know deep in our hearts
That we said goodbye a thousand times
And shared so much love and joy every day

Be happy that I am now at peace
Be joyful that I have lived a wonderful life
Be happy that we have shared so much together

And remember I am always with you in a thought and a sigh
Every day when you see the beauty in nature think of me
Every day when you see the colorful flowers think of me
Every day when you see a frisky animal prancing
around think of me
Every day when you look into the eyes of someone you love
think of me

And know beyond a doubt that
I am with you in everything you do
And know beyond a doubt that
I am with you in everything you say
And know beyond a doubt that
I am with you in every quiet moment of your life

Don't be sad about my parting
Don't feel like you never said goodbye
For you and I both know deep in our hearts
That we said goodbye a thousand times
And shared so much love and joy every day

Carol Calkins, PhD, is a poet and the published author of Bring Poetry to Life *and* Bring Poetry into Your Life. *Carol has devoted over 30 years toward her management career in the healthcare and higher education professions. Carol loves being around her friends and family, including her new granddaughter, Alexxa. She creates personally inspired poetry for those around her which expresses feelings about life's circumstances as well as significant milestones. Carol continues to expand her series of poetry books and has created an inspiring workshop, Five Hearts to Writing Poetry. She is thrilled that she finally found that her gift to the world is poetry. Find out more about Carol and her poetry at www. carolcalkins.com. She can be reached at carol@carolcalkins.com.*

WHAT IS IT TO BE FEARLESS?

Donna Sigmond

For me it was jumping off the edge of a platform with only a cord secured to my ankles as my safety net. I screamed all the way down. I don't know if the loud shrill I heard echoing from the canyon walls burst from my lungs because the fear that had held me back for so many years instantly shattered, or because I was so petrified my voice gave way in acknowledgement to my Soul.

Growing up with little stability I spent my life working for others, never even considering I might have the resourcefulness or moxie to create a business and become self-employed. My sister was self-employed and it always seemed she had one worry after another. Many times it seemed she might not be able to pay her bills and the mounting pressure was more than I thought I ever could or would want to bear. Being self-employed was not an option for me. I liked the security of a paycheck and knowing I had insurance in case I ever needed it.

I worked for a number of years in the telecommunications industry. I was good at what I did, but I was just going to work every day, not creating a career for myself. It was a job, a means to an end so that I could pay my bills. I did not hate it, but I never woke up excited to face my workday.

After a decade of living the daily grind, I was engaged to be married and we made a decision to relocate. I didn't realize leaving the security of my job and planning to move to a new state would present the opportunity to consider what I had a passion for. It was my fiancé that nudged me to open my mind to new possibilities for myself. He was a successful attorney who had always known he had a love for law; he pursued his career with lust. He lovingly wanted to see me expand my human experience by living what I loved. And because he had the financial means to provide me with the security to feel safe to explore my true heart's desire, he asked me, "Donna, what is it you want to do?"

I naturally answered with "get a business degree." I thought that was what I wanted to do. After all, I had been working in the business world for 15 years. To my fearful, rational mind it made logical sense to go back to school and study business.

My fiancé patiently asked the question a few more times. I couldn't figure out why he kept asking me the same question. I didn't understand he wanted me to tell him what my heart wanted to do, not what I thought I *should* do.

I remember getting frustrated with him. I thought he was not listening to me when I would say I wanted "to do" business. Finally I said, in a tone slightly raised with agitation, "Fine, you want to know what I want to do? I'll tell you what I want to do. I want to study nutrition and Oriental Medicine and help people!"

There was a long silent pause. I was in shock at what had just come out of my mouth.

Finally he responded with, "Okay. Then that is what you should do."

I was still in shock. I had never thought I could change gears and do something I had for years secretly desired. I was dumbfounded. I had just voiced my dream, the musings of the fearless part of me. Not to mention, my fiancé was giving me the opportunity to follow my passion. He knew there was a deeper dream living inside of me. I realized he was not gliding past what I was saying and not hearing me, it was *me* not listening to the voice inside speaking my truth when he asked, "What do you want to do?"

After we married we decided not to relocate after all so that I could attend the University of Texas at Austin. My husband faithfully committed to my transition from working to going back to school; he supported me as I worked through a fast-tracked nutritional program designed to graduate students in three years versus five.

After finishing my degree, we decided to move to Boulder, Colorado. My husband found a job that we hoped would be much less stressful and I began to pursue my master's degree in Oriental Medicine. I was so happy. I was living in a beautiful city, was enrolled in my master's program, was happily married, and had started working at the University of Colorado as a research bionutritionist. It was a busy, happy time. I was working and maintaining 21 credit hours every semester.

One day I got a break from my hectic schedule, so I quickly

headed out to the Marshal Mesa trail with my dog Casey. As we reached the apex of the trail, I found myself standing on the mesa looking out at the university. *I am achieving everything I can imagine*, I thought. It was then I had a vision of myself in private practice helping people. I knew deep within I could do it! I felt no fear.

Interestingly, as I was moving out of fear that I could live my dream of helping people, my marriage began to have problems. Unfortunately we did not successfully negotiate those problems, and I found myself starting a private practice without the security of my well-providing husband.

For the next five years I lived in fear. With the sale of our house, I at least had a little money in the bank. I started living in the world of "What Ifs?" What if I can't pay the rent? What if I can't afford this or that? It was a horrible state of being. I was again in denial and not believing in myself. I had been living this way too long.

In fact, it was four years into this distraught state when my beloved dog and companion was diagnosed with cancer. Casey had stuck by me through all my fear and strife, and I was dead set to do the same for her. I was quickly going through my "What If" fund as the cost of her treatments topped out at $30,000. I was unable to work a full schedule so my income went down as well, and the two-year fellowship program in Functional Medicine I was finishing equaled the cost of Casey's treatments. I lived in fear and worry every day. I was exhausted, depressed, and unhappy, but those last 11 months with Casey I will forever cherish and never regret.

After Casey passed, although I grieved her loss I must admit I was relieved to be able to sleep again and begin the process of letting go. I realized I had to let go of holding onto attachments to my ex-husband, my sweet Casey, the home I had, the life I thought we had, my expectations, my perceptions, and my fears.

I decided I best elicit the help of my girlfriends to get me out of my funk. I needed to start living again. I needed to find ways to be carefree and playful again. I needed to build a social life. All the stress and worry had turned me into a boring, fearful person. Over the next year and a half, I decided my goal was to laugh and live lighthearted, much like a child does.

And that is what I did. I went to concerts, rode my bike, and began hiking more challenging trails. I hiked a fourteener. I lost 50 pounds over four months. During one of my fun evenings out, girlfriends in tow, I met a vivacious young man. We quickly found common interests and our companionship grew. The next thing I knew we were planning dive trips together. I was overjoyed. I had not been diving, a sport I love, for over 20 years. I was enjoying life and laughing on a daily basis. I felt alive again after what seemed like an eternity.

Just when I thought things could not get any better, in August of 2010 at the urging of my new friend, I went to Peru. When I was 15 years old I had pictured myself going to Machu Picchu to trek the Inca trails. I felt spiritually called to go. So I booked a five-day Salcantay trek across the mountains and through the rain forest into Machu Picchu. Not one "What If" entered my mind. I was compelled to go. It was me and my friend trekking with a guide, a cook, and a horseman. It was magical.

Three days before the trek, my friend asked me if I would like to go bungee jumping. In my mind I was thinking *Uh, NO,* but my inner voice said, "Let me think about it." I didn't think about it for even a second! Bungee jumping was not on my bucket list, and I was not eager to add it either.

The day before the trek we slept in. When we got up we headed out for brunch. As luck would have it, we passed a bungee jumping office. My wonderful friend takes pleasure in encouraging me to try new things. Persuaded by his "Oh, c'mon, we'll just check it out," we went in.

After seeing their video, we asked when the next tour was. They said, "Right now!"

I looked at my friend and said, "Well, the good news is we haven't eaten yet."

We laughed, and before I could think about it we were in the car on the road for the jump. I was in total denial that I was going to take a 400-foot free fall. Then the thought came to me that symbolically it was the perfect representation of letting go of all my fears, my "What Ifs." Of course, that thought did not make the fear go away. But I saw it as an exercise to release the fear I had held onto for so many years. I yearned, once and for all, to be free from the restraints in which the fear had imprisoned me. I wanted the carefree feeling I had been experiencing lately to be permanent. I am still not clear how I did it; I just know I called on my inner guides that led me to this spiritual and magical place to be with me.

The trek signified my letting go and living again fully. It was a call to those deeper parts of me to connect with all the possibilities for my life. What better way to signify letting go than jumping off a 413-foot crane with only a cord secured to your ankles as a safety net? I let go and never looked back. Truly, I never looked at anything—I think my eyes were closed most of the way down!

I can honestly say that the last two years of my life have been pure joy. I am not without fear from time to time, but I no longer own the fear. I found that I was the only one standing in my way to living, loving, and experiencing joy and the opportunities this energy extends. I just needed to step aside, let go, and get out of the way.

Donna Sigmond, MS, RD, LAc, LCh, Dipl OM, CLT, FAAFM, ABAAHP, holds a master's degree in Traditional Chinese Medicine and a bachelor's degree in Nutrition. She is a registered dietitian and board certified by the National Certification Commission for Acupuncture and Oriental Medicine (NCCAOM). Donna is an Advanced Fellow and board certified in Anti-Aging, Regenerative and Functional Medicine. Her rich educational background is solidified by her experience as a Research Bionutritionist with the University of Colorado, Boulder; interning with North Austin Medical Center in the oncology, cardiology, and renal wards; and studying traditional healthcare in Beijing, China in 2002 and 2004. Donna is the sole practitioner of East West Wellness in Louisville, Colorado.

LIVE DELICIOUSLY!

Teri Karjala

What are you passionate about? I thought I knew the answer to this question until I became aware of the predictability of my life. I was living daily with feelings I thought were deemed "normal" by society. The truth is, I was just existing in what seemed to be a mundane world. Although I was employed with an agency as a psychotherapist and loved my clinical work, I felt there was something missing. Routine had become comfortable for me and ultimately left me stagnant in my life. My passion and zest for life had been lost. I started challenging this state and became curious, asking myself, *What else is out there?*

Since early childhood I consistently faced the challenge of proving myself. My biological father carelessly planted seeds of discouragement with his words of disdain. His messages shadowed my life for many years, statements like "You're never going to be anything" and "You'll never be good enough."I question how anyone can hold so much hate within their heart and speak it to their own child. Words have power. As a therapist, I have empathy for my clients and the traumas they have faced. Yet, looking back, I can appreciate the gift my biological father gave me: a profound sense of drive and motivation that still fuels me today.

While working at the agency, I also maintained a part-time private practice for over five years. There was something about my private practice that made me feel so alive. I went in early and stayed late, leaving energized at the end of the day. After acknowledging this newfound energy in my life, I knew what my next step had to be: leave the safety of the agency to start my own full-time private practice.

My dreams were wonderful and ambitious, yet there was one big problem—I was terrified at the idea of leaving my comfort zone. After all, my agency job was safe, predictable, and seemed to fit me just fine. Like many, I was paralyzed by the unknown.

My mind was filled with unanswered questions. *What will happen if I take this leap?* I felt lost in the world. It felt like life was turning me down at every corner, telling me I could not do more than what my current life situation gave me.

Somewhere along the way I lost being my authentic self. I found myself in a place that felt so disempowering. It took everything in me to get out of bed in the morning and drag myself to work. I blamed my unhappiness on others and unconsciously expected them to change for me. I found myself drowning in my own anxiety and fear. I was becoming defined by my reactions to the circumstances surrounding me and consequently felt even more powerless.

One day I began listening to various books on CD that inspired me to start looking at myself and to create a life that I was in love with. It wasn't until I started doing my own self-development that I was reminded that *I am responsible for my own happiness*. I was tired of waiting for circumstances to change around me. If they were going to change, I was going to be the one to make that happen.

Back at the agency where I was employed, I felt most people were overworked, underpaid, underappreciated, and trapped inside a box. The day I realized that I was the only one responsible for my own happiness, shifts started happening. The biggest shift came knowing within my heart that I could do this. Confidence began to take over as I developed a plan to grow my practice in a structured manner. My feelings vacillated from fear to excitement...and back to fear again. But change had begun.

People began showing up to help lead me on this unknown path. I befriended a beautiful person named Jana who, though at first a stranger to me, became my biggest supporter. I appreciated her gift of faith in me. She supported me by helping to open doors I was afraid to open on my own. Although I had a lot of support from my amazing husband, friends, and family, I was still reluctant to take the "leap" due to fear.

While maintaining employment at the agency, circumstances occurred that made me reevaluate my situation. I was left with no other option but to jump—building my wings on the way down. It was at that moment I realized that I was going to leave and go into full-time private practice.

My husband, fully supportive of me, asked me one evening,

"What is the worst that can happen? If you fail you just go find another job."

I responded with "Oh, that's it? That's the worst that can happen?" It was like a light bulb had gone off, lighting up the darkness of fear and unknown that had been looming in my heart. My internal struggles and uncertainty had limited my vision, blinding me to my unlimited options.

Filled with excitement and relief, I knew at that moment my life would never be the same. That day I went home and wrote my resignation letter. It was the hardest decision I had ever made, but deep down I knew it had to be done.

I chose to leave a salaried job, a consistent paycheck, benefits, and vacation time—yet it seemed so right. For the first time in my life I was taking a huge "leap" without having it all planned out, not knowing what was going to happen, and not being certain of my actions. I had to believe in my own capabilities; I would build the wings I needed to help me soar. Although it was a terrifying time, it was also exhilarating. I finally had gained the faith in myself to take on my life with confidence.

My first day in private practice I was filled with excitement… then reality set in. I asked myself, *What am I doing? Can I do this?* I wondered if the words of my biological father would be my truth. Despite this test, I allowed myself time, understanding that my practice would not grow overnight and that I had to be patient. Patience was never a virtue I possessed and I must say, I had to learn quickly how to just trust in and be patient with the process. The contradicting truth was that I wanted everything NOW. But the more I allowed patience into my life, the more the universe provided me with what I wanted. For the first time in my life I became absolutely clear of my goals and started setting my intentions to make it happen.

I have been so grateful for this journey. My practice is growing beautifully and this journey has allowed us to serve more and more children, adolescents, and adults to help them create their own life of hope, harmony, and happiness.

Our experiences in life impact us all in different ways. As kids the sky was the limit. You ask kids what they want to do when they grow up, and they know with such certainty and excitement. What happens to that passion? As we get older we have people tell us "no" or shoot down our dreams. The sad part is that we allow these people the power to impact our lives. Why do we do that? We forget our dreams, we forget to believe in ourselves. Most importantly we take these comments as complete truth. As a result we live our lives with all the "headtrash" we have collected over the years. I too received these disempowering messages from different people, including my parents, family, friends, teachers, and significant others.

My life seemed to transform overnight but in reality it took about a year. When I took my leap into private practice, the universe opened up its doors to me. It seemed to say, "Welcome to your life! Are you ready to play?"

I was launched into action. There was so much no one had told me about owning your own business. I put myself on the fast track to learning it all. The first few months I felt like a kid in a candy store. My senses were tantalized by all the new deliciousness in my life. I enthusiastically grabbed all the opportunity and excitement that jumped out at me. However, I quickly learned that I could easily be distracted by all the new flavors in my life. Starting at the ground level I started putting the pieces together to create my foundation. My strong foundation was built with the help of an absolutely amazing mentor and coach, and the beginnings of my self-taught education on owning my own business. Along the way, I discovered another passion: the business aspects of my practice.

Within eight months of starting my private practice, I began preparing myself for another "leap" — hiring a part-time therapist. I found that the more leaps you take, the easier they get. Since that second leap, I have taken plenty. Currently I have two therapists working for me, with a third on the way, and an amazing office manager to share in my vision.

My practice is thriving and has continued to grow. The journey continues each day, as my dreams get bigger and my celebrations more numbered. Had I not taken the leap that I feared so much, I would not find myself on days just bursting with sunshine inside. Life is so delicious!

As a therapist, my role is to help my clients heal from their previous wounds and empower them to live the life of their dreams. I take pride in walking the walk along with them and demonstrating that playing outside the comfort zone can be a lot of fun.

Here's what I've learned:

Take risks. I never knew what was on other side of my comfort zone until I took the leap of faith to find out. The more steps I've taken to get out of my comfort zone, the bigger the circumference has spread. My mentor recently told me about a research study done at Harvard that interviewed 80-year-olds to determine what they would do if they could live their life over again. The top two answers were: 1) spend more time with friends and family and 2) take more risks. I'm choosing to take more risks!

Have a support team. I realized that it's okay to ask for help. I have been blessed with wonderful mentors and a fantastic business coach. I have found out many things, two of which are: 1) I can't possibly know everything and 2) there are many people out there who will offer help and support. All I had to do was ask.

Eliminate the "headtrash." In the beginning, my thoughts trapped me from seeing my true potential. Many of us have allowed life's situations to dominant our thoughts and limit our ability to see things for what they truly are. Our internal state has a direct correlation to our external state. By challenging the paradigm in which we live, we can be anything, do anything, and have anything we want. I choose to live in abundance.

Be grateful. Even the most challenging difficulties come into our life for a purpose. Finding the gratitude in the moments that appear to be crisis situations has allowed me to strengthen this skill. This has allowed me to: 1) relax in "crisis" circumstances and 2) show up with a profound sense of purpose.

Own your own happiness. As human beings we all have one entitlement: to be HAPPY. Taking inventory of what I perceived to be holding me back was enormously beneficial during this process. For me, that also meant setting boundaries with people who did not share my passion for my vision. This included placing limits on other people's requests for my time and energy.

Celebrate often. I use to think people thought I was crazy for celebrating the day, the weather, my milestones, or anything I decided to be happy for at that moment. Celebrating has so many benefits but for me; it is the fuel that recharges and revives my inspiration. This means celebrating not only our huge successes but also the tiny ones as well. A quote from Oprah Winfrey summarizes this concept beautifully: "The more you praise and celebrate life, the more there is in life to celebrate!"

My story begins anew each day with a new look at life, one in which I get to choose. Words are powerful, so I am deciding what messages serve to take me to the life I want to live. I believe that each one of us has so much to offer this wonderful world, and it is up to us to make it happen. Each of us is unique and is on a path to greatness—as long as we get out of our own way! I'm making a promise to myself to live deliciously and not settle for life inside my comfort zone.

Teri Karjala, owner of Creative Counseling Center, LLC, maintains a private practice providing counseling services and offering trainings in the community. Teri has worked in the field for the past 10 years specializing in working with children, adolescents, and adults who have experienced trauma. Teri's passion is to inspire and empower clients to live a life of hope, harmony, and happiness. Teri loves spending time with her family, being outdoors in the beautiful Colorado weather, taking part in new adventures, listening to books on CD, and celebrating life. To find more about Teri, visit www.creativecounselingcenter.com.

SIGNED PERMISSION SLIPS
ARE DUE TODAY

Heather Dossey

"You are a writer. You are a teacher. You are a healer. And you ARE an artist. None of that is familiar to you now. You've pushed all that aside because you do not see the value in it yet, but you will. Your passion will be your family, interestingly enough. That feels foreign to you now as well. You're still stuck in the battle, battle, battle. You are like Attila the Hun, a warrior with boobs! But in the future, when you are decorating your house, growing your garden, and writing your books, you are going to be one happy lady. You are going to be really happy… reeeally happy."

This statement came during a reading with my first spiritual teacher, Sonia Choquette, what feels like a lifetime ago. She was absolutely right. I remember thinking *Artist? No way. I just finished my master's degree in logistics. Attila the Hun…not so cute in a skirt, but a warrior with boobs I like! I'm climbing the corporate ladder and plan on going places, lady! I'm a competitive swimmer. I achieve. I'm no artist. That's my brother Alex, he's the only one who draws and plays an instrument in my family.*

It was a bookstore and workshop space in Chicago where I found my heart. I did not even realize it was missing. It was pumping blood but not love. I did not understand emotions or what they were trying to communicate. I did everything in my power to keep them quiet; I stuffed them away in a closet so they did not get in the way of my blue ribbon goals. Yet I connected with everything about Sonia's work. Much of it was foreign to me (to my intellect, that is), but I love it and couldn't get enough. So began the decade-long journey of coming home to myself.

At 35, I can absolutely say I am an artist. I can also see now from my "youthful wisdom" that I come from a long lineage of women who are artists. Two grandmothers, one mother, and six aunts, all with their own art. I do not mean to leave out the males in my family tree; they are all extremely artistic also. However, I want to draw particular attention to the elder generation of females in my family as we take an artistic queue.

My grandmother, Mildred Dossey, was a high school teacher. Every visit started with homemade snickerdoodle cookies and a pot of fresh vegetable soup, most of which came from her beloved garden. She loved jewelry and fashion. She was an artist but I know she never would have considered herself one. She and I have a special bond. I have a pillow she made. It is blue with a hand-stitched daisy and the initials MD, wrapped in an old brown pillowcase that has to be older than I am. It still smells of her. I love to hold it and breathe her in.

My other grandmother, Oleta Bennett, was a tailor and worked at a furniture store. She was an interior designer, helping people decorate their homes long before it was considered a career. We put on the most incredible plays in her living room; she was always the director. I wear her five gold bangle bracelets all the time. Golden bangles…I love picturing her wearing them, adorning herself as a goddess would. She was an artist, but again I don't think it is a descriptor she would have used for herself.

My mother wanted to be an actress. Not an easy dream to achieve living in Arkansas, married with three kids under the age of five. She was able to live a small version of that dream when she was cast as an extra in a television mini-series called "The Blue and the Grey." During high school, she was part of a dance company in Oklahoma City that performed "The Nutcracker." I remember looking at the program when I was little, seeing pictures of my mom as a teenager with toe shoes on, thinking Wow! *My mom is a ballerina!* She is a Realtor and a builder now, and has always been a decorator. "Decorating is in our DNA," she told me growing up. She is also a fantastic cook. Her Dutch apple pie won a blue ribbon at the Benton Country Fair.

All of my aunts are artistic—writing, cooking, gardening, showing dogs, teaching, they all create. My aunt Sue knows sign language and at 60, still loves to water ski. My aunt Suzy took clogging lessons and made me an Elvis quilt in support of my high school crush on "The King." Aunt Sherri, Aunt Kathy, Aunt Karyl, Aunt Debbie…I have so many stories for each one that reveal their artistry, talent, and gifts. Hand-painted "Snow White and the Seven Dwarfs" Christmas ornaments, family newsletters, lots of butter…all art forms. However, do any of these women see themselves as artists? I am doubtful, so I decided to come right out and ask.

I called my Aunt Karyl. "This is going to sound a little left field," I began, "but would you call yourself an artist?" She hesitated. "Well, that's a tough one, honey. My initial reaction is 'no' but I'm actually going to say 'yes.' I've always loved to cook; I see the artistry in that. I love recipes and dinner parties. I love creating an environment with good food for fun and friendship. Artist...of course, I'm not like a great master painter."

After talking for a few minutes, she was able to sum it up perfectly. "The world is a smaller place today. There's so much more empowerment in my generation than in my mother's. I hope I have taught my girls that it is fun to let yourself explore things that are meaningful to you, and anything meaningful to you is your art. I hesitated at first; it does take courage to come right out and say, well, yes, I'm an artist."

I replied, "My cousins are lucky. They've had signed permission slips to be creative and search for their art all along. I think you just signed your own permission slip, Aunt Karyl." We both laughed.

"You are right, honey. And I'll take that with me from here. I cannot wait for you to visit. And do my makeup!"

At 25 years of age, why did it feel so foreign to call myself an artist? It is so clearly in my lineage. I realize now my own artistic permission slip had not been signed at that point. On my quest for meaning, I dabbled with all kinds of artistic outlets searching for a "passion." I was desperately trying to find myself. I bought colored pencils and crayons. I took acting lessons. I went to therapy. I found a life coach. I was immersed in self-exploration with teachers, tools, and workshops, educating and uncovering the real me. I discovered aromatherapy and made sugar scrubs for my girlfriends. I bought a few canvases and painted whatever felt good to paint. I made dream boards with pictures, words, and phrases to create a blueprint for my future and what I wanted it to feel like. And I said the F-word a lot...several of them actually:

FEELINGS. FEAR. FAITH. FUN.

I spent the last 10 years searching for meaning, spiritual truth, self-awareness, and self-worth. I became comfortable with my feelings, so much so I went back to school to get my license in counseling. I obtained a certification in life coaching. I did not understand what any of it meant at the time, but I clearly see it now: a woman comes home to her true self through her art. I come from a lineage of artists but I had not given myself permission to be artistic. Where has it all led me? Makeup. My art has always been makeup.

Makeup is something I have loved my whole life. In 3rd grade, my friend Jessica got a birthday present from our babysitter: BLUE eyeliner. I thought it was coolest present ever. In 6th grade I showed our family friend, Rita Debnam, how to use her blush as an eye shadow. I applied makeup for several friends on their wedding day. I about had to hold down my friend Staci for a second coat of mascara on her big day. She still thanks me. I receive compliments on my own makeup and get asked regularly what kind of makeup I buy. On occasion, you will find me applying blush or lipgloss to a friend, even a complete stranger, when I think they could use a little color. Why not live my passion and become a makeup artist?

That brainstorm led to a very fast and very fun display of the Universe at work. Thanks to my life coach, Tambra Harck, supporting my transition to "fun week," I have a beautiful website being built for *Heather Dossey: Professional Makeup Artist, Life Coach, and Writer*. I am having the most fun dreaming about the future, naming my new company, and buying things like a beautiful new mink powder brush. I am so in love with it I want to sleep with it every night. I could tell early on that there was really something to this new endeavor of becoming a professional makeup artist. Things were happening quickly and easily. A signal the Universe is at work behind the scenes!

I found myself making connections in the world of makeup so quickly. I received an invitation to attend a makeup competition celebrating the memory of Kevyn Aucoin. Kevyn was a celebrity makeup artist and author of *Making Faces* and *The Art of Makeup*. He raised the bar for makeup artistry in a big way. I am at the event, talking to his sister, thinking, I don't know how I got here but I LOVE it! I have also started as a freelance artist with M.A.C. Cosmetics. When I am at the M.A.C. counter, I am home; surrounded by other artists that appreciate the art of makeup as much as I do. I can be standing on my feet all day, going non-stop, and loving every single second of it.

I was struggling in the beginning about how makeup fits with the intuitive life coaching and writing I have known for years is my soul's great work. The pieces are all starting to come together now.

I can see the masterpiece forming before me, a work of art by the most masterful artist of them all—our creator. My path has been one of claiming and nourishing my inner beauty and outer beauty. Combining my passions represents the whole of me today. I am so excited to watch the future unfold and to live the evolution. My essence absolutely is professional makeup artist, life coach, writer, and teacher. A combination of my passions will serve others in the future.

Why would I write about all this now? I am living into my truth as an artist and I want more women to join me! The colors of makeup are my paints. I am the most pure version of myself when drawing out and enhancing a woman's natural beauty. I cannot wait to write update articles on how following the "daily fun factor" can turn out for all of us.

It is scary to transition, to redefine who I am. The best thing I can do for my desire to coach other women through this process is to document what this *feels* like right now. I will follow what feels fun and let it guide me in the right direction. I will notice when *fear* creeps up and instead of halting, run directly toward whatever scares me. There is always something delicious on the other side of fear. And I will have absolute *faith* in the divine support God has given me. This is my recipe for fulfillment! It is exactly what I will be walking others through in the future. I am dreaming big right now, knowing the Universe will shock me at how much grandeur there can really be if I stick to the recipe.

I wish I could have one more day with my grandmothers. I wish I could do their makeup. I wish I could touch their faces and mirror the glow I see coming from inside each of them. I would ask what they thought was fun. I would ask them about their fears, their feelings, our divinity and God's love. I miss them so much, but the good news is the generation of lovely goddesses ahead of me is still intact. To my mom and all of my aunts: I want to do your makeup and say all the F-words. I want to hear what you love the most; I want to know your art. And I want to see your signed permission slip! No one has to give you permission to be artistic…you can sign it for yourself.

As I was finishing this chapter, my Aunt Suzy called and said, "Guess what? I'm officially an artist!"

"I can't believe you just said that!" I replied. "I am not kidding, Aunt Suzy, I am wrapping up a chapter for a book called *Speaking Your Truth* that talks about you being an artist! You have been one for a long time though. You made me an Elvis quilt, for goodness sake."

She replied, "I know, I know, but I'm going to be a real one now. I'm taking a painting class!" Bravo, Aunt Suzy. You love color. You are always so creative. You will love playing with paints and a canvas, I just know it. Divine interaction that phone call was.

We have come a long way, but there is room for improvement, ladies. You ARE artists! Real ones, every day. Love, Light, and Lipgloss, my friends.

Heather Dossey is a life coach and professional makeup artist in Destin, Florida. "A woman comes home to her true self through her art. Makeup is my favorite artistic outlet. My heart's desire is to guide and encourage other women on the journey to embracing their art, beauty, and best version of themselves. A woman standing fully in her grace, beauty, and power...my favorite thing to celebrate!" You can connect with Heather on her website www.Entourouge.com, Facebook, or by sending an email to heatherdossey@gmail.com.

IT'S ALL SUCCESS

✣ ✣ ✣

Deborah Tutnauer

The other day my husband told me that I fail, a lot. It was the strangest comment I had ever heard. He then went on to say the wonderful thing is that I don't know it.

Within these words is the nugget of success, and ultimately the power as a woman and as an entrepreneur. I sometimes wish I had one of those rags to riches stories—poor girl, broken family, makes way in world all alone and become huge success story. Instead I'm a nice Jewish girl from New York, raised with all the comforts of an upper-middle-class suburban home. My parents were always supportive, even when I shunned the predominant 1981 Ivy League college graduate expectations and set out in a bright yellow Volkswagen convertible to become a ski bum in the Wild West.

Twenty years later, I had traveled the world and acquired two master's degrees. I was making a nice living as a private practice psychotherapist in another tiny ski town high in the Colorado Rockies. An idealistic life surrounded by mountain beauty, a tight loving community, and the ability to make a difference in people's lives. This is where today's story begins.

"It's All Success" is a phrase developed out of a spiritual surety that all parts of life's journey are meant to be. There is, in fact, no failure. Those experiences that do not work out as expected provide the fodder and wisdom for that which follows. I've never thought in terms of failure. Even in the darkest moments, failure never entered my mind.

No, actually that is not true. There was a time—painful and poignant—when I had felt that I had failed. How telling, that this instance was one of the few that was 100% out of my control.

Just three weeks after our marriage I discovered that I was pregnant. "Wow, that was easy!" was my thought as a 40-year-old first-time pregnant woman. Pregnancy for me was not the lush, earth mother experience I had expected. Constant nausea and dehydration took care of that. At six months, it finally went away. Relief. Just two weeks earlier I had had an amniocentesis. I almost didn't. Right before the needle went in I had a strong feeling that this was bad. We stopped. We talked—my husband, the doctor, and I—we agreed to go forward.

The nausea went away 14 days after the amnio and I discovered that my baby had died inside my womb. "My fault—my failure," was what my mind screamed for weeks following. "It was the amnio," was my thought. I had failed to protect my baby from that intrusive procedure and he had died. My fault. My failure. Needless to say there were many months of sadness and intense grieving.

Two and a half years later we adopted the most precious baby girl—child of my heart. She was the child I had seen in my dreams. She was the spirit who hovered around me for many years prior. When she looked up at me and smiled at just 15 minutes old, we knew. We knew that she was finally home.

"It's All Success." As horrific as it was, the death of my son set us traveling down the path to my daughter. Ancient Talmudic writings say that a child who is conceived and then dies prior to being born is a very special being with special parents. The writings say that the child needed only to finish out part of his spiritual journey and chose a unique set of parents with which to do this. Noah chose us, and in finishing what his soul needed he opened a door to a pathway that culminated with Kaia.

Around the time my daughter was one, I was exposed to a home business related to selling—or as they so clearly told me, sharing—beautiful children's books. The books were the appeal at first, being one who can never walk out of a bookstore without an armload. But what was also intriguing was that I could make money "sharing" these books. "Who could possibly refuse these?" I thought. For only $120 I received my business in a box. In addition to everything else, it contained 25 books, which was a great deal no matter what.

I went to work just as they taught in the training. I called, wrote, emailed everyone I knew or may have known in my life. People did love the books. How could they not? Book shows in people's homes were the way to go I was taught, and so I approached every mom I knew in our small town and expounded upon the benefits of hosting a show in her home. Many did. I probably sold books to at least one hundred people in that first year. At the regional training they introduced us to a women earning $100,000 per year, by building huge teams of moms selling books. Now this was cool! I could do that. Except that in the entire past years, only one customer took that hook and moved into distributor mode.

Then I did my own accounting and was horrified! Once I had subtracted my actual costs—books, stands, postcards, bags, flyers, cute little erasers, my taxes, the hours spent setting up and cleaning up the home shows, delivering the books once they arrived — my hourly income was about $10 per hour. Given that my other work earned me $120 per hour seeing therapy clients in my office, this was not boding well for the book business. It was certainly not on the track to $100,000 per year. I took my new large collection of beautiful children's books and wrote the business off as a learning experience.

Was it failure? Some would say so. I doubt I even broke even financially after all was said and done. But failure? It's all success in my book and my appetite was piqued for this powerful business model, where one could work part time from home and eventually leverage a growing team to create long-term residual income. The lure that I could be working from anywhere in the world given a phone and Internet connection was very appealing and I was hooked. But I did not yet know it.

Following a few years spent building a house from scratch— alternative materials, recycled interior, organic finishes—we moved in and my mind again had a space open for that crazy idea. The structure of the book business was still swirling in my head.

Along came a juice. A marvelous, delicious, antioxidant abundant juice. "Drink this juice and share your testimonial and you'll soon be making more money than you've ever seen," was what they told me. I drank the juice. I watched the video. Easy. Just "share" (there's that word again) this life-changing elixir with your friends and family and they will be so excited by how they feel, that they'll want to drink it and share it too. In just a few short months you'll have your living room packed with 60 people people listening to you tell your story, and share how to build two "legs" in your team and get rich.

Okay. This time I was going for it. No home shows that needed a lot of set up or book displays. Only a taste of juice and a big flip chart ($150 with the stand). Within a few weeks people in my small mountain town (population 1,500), were crossing the street the other way when they saw me coming. I did better than many. I made enough money to drink the magic juice for free every month and put a little cash back in my pocket. Was it failure?

I discovered rather quickly that it was really hard to build a business of this nature without two things: First, a community that was large enough to allow for growth. And second, a mentor/ teacher/ trainer/upline support person to actually be there to teach me how to do this as a professional.

I didn't have either of those things. I lived in a tiny isolated town and had a totally unresponsive sponsor somewhere in Kansas who did not seem to care about my dreams or my fledgling business.

But given that in my personal philosophy each experience is a stepping stone to the next—a stop on the journey—the struggles produced two things: 1) the understanding that the Internet was where I needed to go next; I might live in a 1,500-person town, but I had access to millions using my screen and keyboard; and 2) the knowledge that if I was going to really make this type of business my path, then I needed to approach it no differently than I approached my two master's degrees. This journey required commitment, education and fortitude. I needed to truly understand how money was made, the best compensation structure, the best types of products, and I needed a mentor. In some people's books I just experienced another failure. In mine— Aha! This launched the rest of my life. "It's All Success."

The promise of the Internet loomed large. Beginning with a two-day boot camp, I embarked on becoming a largely self-taught Internet marketer. Two years of 12-hour days on the screen and I became fluent in the language of Cyberspace. Blogs, social media, self-branding, SEO, PPC, PPV, lead generating capture pages, auto-responders, became my language. In the midst of it all another magic juice company appeared and I jumped in.

You are not going to believe this. In fact, maybe this is why my husband thinks I fail a lot. A mere 12 months after beginning with this company, I walked away from it as well, but this time with a mentor and the opportunity to help develop a brand new company from an idea to a thriving entity. With my Internet marketing experience I became the marketing and branding expert of the group. The owners (my mentor and his partners) relied on me for everything Internet and everything PR. Of course the didn't PAY ME, but as the founding distributor of a soon to be LARGE organization, volunteering my time and expertise was expected and worth it—or so I thought.

My time on the Internet was yielding a lovely group of like-minded friends and colleagues. Hundreds of Facebook friends and thousands of Twitter connections. Search for me and I show up for hundreds of pages on a Google search. Between this and my new company I was busy, and creating a small income. My husband and I were so invested in the potential of this new company that we INVESTED in it to the tune of $10,000. I knew that once the company launched I'd easily make that back in just a few months.

Can you grieve over the loss of a dream? The truth became obvious when I woke up dreading the day and went to sleep with tears of frustration every night. Ten thousand dollars and hundreds of hours and it was not happening. On their end, the company was not performing. All my marketing and branding suggestions were being ignored. The website was embarrassing and my entire team had left because they had no tools to work with. I was flabbergasted. The culmination of four years of intense study and effort was—nothing. Have you ever felt like that? I knew I had to make a change. The writing on the wall was big and bold. I was heartsick by all that had gone into this situation, financially, emotionally and time wise. But to throw more time and energy at a something that was not moving in the right direction or changing was far from smart. The owners of the company had failed me and the company. I had to let it go.

By now you've gathered that I don't give up easily. The dream was still there. Dare I approach another different, yet similar situation? How could I gather up all my learning, experience and resources and create success out of this mess?

Ninety percent of success is based on how you think and what you believe. The other ten percent is what you do. Today I am steadily growing a very large organization in a direct sales company. My residual income doubles every month. I am secure enough in my abilities marketing both online and offline that I have closed my psychotherapy practice and only rarely do private coaching by the hour anymore. I fail a lot. But the wonderful thing is that I don't know it. What I know is that it's all success, because everything I have experienced in this life yields lessons that have allowed for deeper meaning and greater understanding. Every choice I made on this journey touched me and caused me to grow closer and closer to my essence and to my goal. I was enthralled with the direct selling business structure before I really knew what it entailed. And then I kept on going through one mistake after another. But because I never saw it as error, only as movement, each event was another step in an expansive process. I embarked on a journey and my power grew. I discovered more of the person I am and the person I was becoming, My wisdom broadened and my skills multiplied. My power as a strong woman solidified.

Powerful women are beautiful. Claiming our power as we negotiate the journey is our birthright. There is no failure on this trip. It's all success. When my husband told me that I fail a lot, I never saw it as such, he really meant it as a compliment. To fail and pick up and continue is power. The power to transcend judgments and labels. The power to continually move forward with grace, growing every step of the way. I fail a lot, but I never quit.

Deborah Tutnauer, MEd, MSW is a network marketer who builds her business predominantly on the internet. She also provides life coaching for women with a focus on business and entrepreneurial success. Deborah splits her time between the mountains of Colorado and San Diego, with her husband and their nine-year-old daughter. She can be reached at www.DeborahTutnauer.com.

I CHOOSE LOVE

Jess Bonasso

My story is one of LOVE. However, before it was possible for me to really know what love was, I had to learn the opposite by feeling unworthiness and rejection.

This began before I was even conceived. My dad, after agreeing that they didn't want to have children, had a vasectomy. It was with great surprise that they learned of my mom's pregnancy after taking such a strong precaution against it! From the very beginning, my existence had the energy of not being "wanted" around it. Unfortunately, my parents' relationship was already in turmoil at that time. Try as they might to make it work, it didn't take long after my birth for them to decide to go their separate ways.

Following the divorce my dad decided to raise me and we moved from the city to a very small rural community. Visits with my mother were few, mostly Christmas and summer vacations. Because we didn't have electricity, there was no telephone for many years. Contact between me and my mom was limited to only once or twice a month when I'd call her collect from the pay phone down the street. Because she played a very small role in my upbringing, there was always a part of me that felt rejected and discarded by her and wondered why she didn't raise me.

In asking my dad, he said it was because she had to take on a night job when they divorced and thought I would be better taken care of if I lived with him. I accepted that in the moment, but this became confusing to me over time because from the time my parents divorced until sometime around the 5th grade, I was painfully aware that we were living in extreme poverty conditions with no running water or electricity. Visits to my mom, on the other hand, showed me a world where plumbing, electricity, and money didn't seem like a problem at all.

As a result, I found myself at a very young age becoming resentful of my life conditions. I didn't understand why I was living in the conditions I was in with my dad when my mom seemed so financially stable or why she never offered to make things better. I made an assumption she didn't want me and underlying feelings of "unworthiness and rejection" were implanted, something that would hold me back in the future.

I suspect my dad felt unworthiness and resentfulness of his own. He drowned out his worries, fears of being a single parent with limited resources, and the pain of his past with alcohol, setting intentions every year or two to quit and then somehow finding his way back to drinking each time. Deeply creative, he also had the angst of not knowing how to financially thrive by fulfilling his lifelong passion as an artist. Instead he took a job he disliked, making ends meet most of the time but just barely. Many times I felt as if he would've been happier if he didn't have to raise me, and guilt over his sacrifices for me became yet another limiting emotion to add to the list of things that caused me pain.

Living in poverty took its toll on my mental and emotional state and in other ways as well. Because we didn't have running water, we had to be "creative" with the way we handled our bathroom activities. So creative, in fact, that it led to my dad accidentally taking a swig of his own urine once because he picked up the wrong gallon jug! With no running water, I was able to take a bath only once or twice a week because the effort to heat water on our wood cook stove to fill the metal wash basin with hot water was tremendous. Feelings of "lack and scarcity" over not having basic plumbing and electricity were implanted, becoming unhealthy beliefs around money that would affect me well into adulthood.

Of course I couldn't invite anyone over for a sleepover or play dates with conditions like this in place so it was difficult to make friends. To make matters worse, on my first day of school I was rejected publicly by a bully classmate without repercussion from the teacher. This made me target practice from then on, and I became one of the most tormented, bullied, and teased children in class all the way up until the beginning of 7th grade. It also made for a very lonely childhood, and with no friends at school and an adult at home drowning out his own sorrows in alcohol, I had very little emotional support.

I then hit puberty and came back that summer before 7th grade transformed, the ugly duckling turning into a beautiful white swan. From that point forward, with no spoken reason why, I became popular and an overnight sensation. This confused me because those who had previously tormented me now wanted to hang out. I had girlfriends for the first time ever, became interested in boys, and joined and excelled in sports, student council, band, National Honor Society, and Future Business Leaders of America. Although I didn't understand my sudden acceptance, I had craved it for so long and so badly that I embraced it (and the relationships that ensued) voraciously.

Fortunately, this burst of acceptance from my peers and the desire to never be poor again gave me tremendous drive and ambition. I left that small rural town motivated to succeed and get away from the pain of my past.

By most standards, I became financially successful by my late twenties. A salary of six figures was something I was very proud of, but it became the object of my demise. Because of my time spent in poverty, I decided that success equated to money. The more money I made, the more "successful" people would think I was. I wanted acceptance that I was "worthy" from some outside source (my parents, my old classmates, my love interests, etc.) so I became obsessed with making as much money as possible.

My need to feel accepted led to several failed relationships and a lot of unresolved bitterness, anger, and resentment over my childhood. This finally came to a head in my late twenties, when I started taking medication for anger management. In my early thirties, it led to increased communication issues with loved ones and chronic back pain that was so bad it brought my physical well-being to a screeching halt. I was 40 pounds overweight, depressed, unhappy, and angry most of the time. My life was crumbling all around me, becoming the catalyst for the transformation to follow.

One day, in search of a solution to my problems I was synchronistically led to participate in a healing process that changed my life. In two short sessions I released much of the anger, bitterness, and resentment from my childhood, which led to the discontinuation of the medication I'd been on in less than a month's time.

I embarked on a profound path of self-discovery, where I began to study myself, my thoughts and patterns, and the Law of Attraction in great depth. I began to realize that my past negative behavior and beliefs about life were contributing to the unhealthy patterns still showing up in my life. I realized that it was ME creating the reality I so despised! I wasn't sure how I was going to overcome these self-imposed obstacles or create a reality that I really wanted, but I was determined to do so.

Finally, I came to a pivotal moment following my divorce that unraveled many of the obstacles I was facing. Reading a book on spiritual divorce, I came across an exercise that asked me to write down all the traits and qualities of my ex-husband that I had bitterness, anger, or resentment over. I was then prompted to ask the following question of myself, for each thing I wrote down about him: "Where in your life are YOU displaying this quality?"

WOW. The mirror had just been revealed and at first, I did NOT like what I saw. I'd never looked at it like this before, but it was glaringly obvious that what I despised in him, I actually despised myself for. Shame and guilt rose again, only this time it was for all the horrible things that I'd done or said, or the ways that I'd somehow contributed to the very thing I despised in him.

Because of all the healing and self-growth I'd engaged in up to that point, and because of my awareness of how I actually create my own reality every single moment, I finally had a visceral understanding that these traits showing up in my ex-husband were actually wounded parts of myself that still needed to be healed within me. And that these wounded parts of myself would keep showing up in future experiences and relationships *until I had healed that part of myself!*

And then a new awareness arose. I understood deep down that the key to feeling the love and acceptance I so desperately wanted all my life and the key to creating a reality that I really LOVED, was to *embrace, love, and forgive myself completely.*

In other words, I had to LOVE myself first before I could be truly capable of receiving love from others.

From that moment on, how I treated myself and how I interacted with others began to change drastically, which leads me to the REAL love story.

The year following my divorce was one of tremendous spiritual growth and evolution. For one, I became firmly committed to BEING the change I wanted to see in the world. This arose out of the spiritual divorce exercise I'd done because I knew that in order for my life to change and for me to stop attracting painful experiences, I had to personally live in alignment with what I wanted most from others. This was particularly challenging because many of the recurring experiences I'd been attracting were ones that I was not very good at handling personally! To overcome this, I needed to release the pain of the past by forgiving myself and others, and I needed to learn new tools for managing future situations that might arise.

The first tool of great value was that I identified the core values that represented the change I wanted to see in the world. As a result, I became committed to standing in alignment with *honor* and *compassionate authenticity*. My desire was so great for these that I became obsessed with being these qualities in every moment, with every single person I came into contact with. I also had to learn how to ask for these values to be met by friends and loved ones and begin the process of setting boundaries when these values were not honored.

And boy, were there opportunities for setting boundaries! I would notice judgments about others that would come up and each time I asked myself what the mirror was, I would realize it was usually related to my core values in some way and/or something that had happened many times before.

When I lived in alignment with my core values, I started to notice amazing opportunities and synchronicities come into my life, like the perfect place to live, new clients that would come as a result of a referral, a coaching program offered by one of my favorite mentors, an unexpected check in the mail, unexpectedly reconnecting with an old friend from college that turned into the most vulnerable, authentic, passionate relationship I've ever been involved in, and mind-blowing client success stories! In addition, I noticed old patterns falling away…the gentle and timely release of friendships no longer in my best interest to maintain, my judgment of others, unhealthy behaviors, limiting beliefs, and my attachments to how things were "supposed" to look.

The second tool that became the most important tool was self-care. Because I'd been operating in such heavy masculine mode all my life (task-minded, driven, action-oriented, hard-working), I'd completely disregarded the feminine aspects of myself like nurturing through self-care, going with the flow, and receiving. I knew that self-care was the key for me to bring balance back into my life so it became an absolute priority for me.

To really understand the importance of self-care, I chose an intense immersion, a "radical sabbatical" from life and my business where I spent five months in a cabin in small spiritual community up in the mountains. Each day was spent doing ONLY what I was divinely inspired to do and taking care of myself completely, something I'd always struggled with before. This helped tremendously in bringing change to ALL areas of my life and taught me how vital a role self-care played in creating the life of my dreams.

Upon coming back to the "real" world, it was time to redefine myself and my business. Because self-care had resulted in such miraculous changes to my physical, emotional, mental, spiritual, and financial health, I became completely passionate about it. It became the basis of my business model; I began marketing and offering packages and services designed to help individuals live the life of their dreams by taking better care of themselves. Most important, by taking better care of myself, I finally started to value and LOVE myself.

It took me 37 years, but I can say with complete honesty that I love myself and that my entire life is perfect. When I look at everything that led me to this moment, I find that all my life experiences combined are just one, giant, synchronistic event that's led me to LOVE and ACCEPTANCE. All the pain I've experienced, the individuals who caused me unhappiness, and the ways in which I was misguided and beat myself up…it's ALL perfect because it led me to the place where I can now have true love and compassion for myself and others.

I'm profoundly grateful for the pain of my past and I look forward to the future now with hope, love, and light. I now know that anything that comes across my path is a tool for transformation…should I choose that to be my experience. After all, I always have a choice on what kind of reality I want to create!

Last but not least, a word about LOVE. In my opinion, it has become the single most important thing for creating the life of my dreams. Because LOVE vibrates at such a high frequency, it shifts my energy, inspires, and delights me. When directed inward, by taking better care of myself, I love myself more and this makes me more compassionate and less critical of others. As I love myself and others more, I attract effortlessly and efficiently the individuals and life experiences that I REALLY want in life. And

LOVE is something I can choose to do in any moment, regardless of what I'm faced with.

When I'm having a down moment, or I need to raise my vibration, one thing I like to do is to stand up, throw my hands up in the air, and yell at the top of my lungs, "I LOVE MY LIFE!" Sometimes I encourage others to join me (including strangers!) and the effect it has on me is then amplified because of how exhilarating it is for everyone involved to get outside of their comfort zone. It always makes me feel better instantly.

So what have I learned about myself? That LOVE really does make the world go around and when it's present, it has the power to create what I REALLY desire.

I choose LOVE. Do you?

Jess Bonasso, otherwise known as "The Self Care Goddess," inspires others to embrace their greatness, be compassionately authentic, and courageously contribute to living the life of their dreams…simply by taking better care of themselves! Her training and expertise allows her to coach, strategize, and train on any area that needs improvement. Whether it be physical, emotional, mental, spiritual, or financial, she will guide YOU in achieving what you truly desire and assist you in eliminating any self-sabotaging behaviors, beliefs, or attachments holding you back…at a cellular level! For more information, you can visit her website at www.RadiantSelfCare.com, subscribe to her blog at www.TheSelfCareGoddess.com, or connect with her online at Twitter, Facebook, LinkedIn, or YouTube.

ABOUT US

Lisa Shultz conceived the idea behind *Speaking Your Truth* in 2009 ten years after an event that transformed her life, which she wrote about in Volume I. She hoped that by sharing her story, others might gain hope and inspiration in their lives if they found themselves in a similar circumstance.

She invited Andrea Costantine to become her business partner to bring Volume I to completion in 2010. Since that first publication, she has also coupled with Andrea to help writers self-publish their books in their joint venture, Self-Publishing Experts, LLC. www.SelfPublishingExperts.com.

Lisa is passionate about connecting and empowering women and finds the *Speaking Your Truth* and Self-Publishing platforms offer the perfect outlet for her mission. She also enjoys speaking, consulting, and loves to hold workshops for aspiring writers.

She resides in Denver, Colorado and you can find out more about her at www.LisaShultz.com.

Andrea Costantine always dreamed of being a writer, is a lover of books, and an avid reader. Born with an entrepreneurial spirit, Andrea is passionate about service, self-expression, and creativity and enjoys unleashing that spirit in others. Andrea is a professional freelance writer, author, speaker, and artist.

In collaboration with Lisa Shultz, Andrea has also co-written and self-published *How to Bring Your Book to Life This Year: An Exploratory Guidebook on Writing and Self-Publishing*, and solely created *Soulful Marketing: Heart Centered Marketing for Conscious Entrepreneurs*. Andrea resides in Denver, Colorado. She can be reached at www.andreacostantine.com.

ABOUT THE ARTIST

Janice Earhart, the illustrator for the book, is delighted to be a part of this wonderful collaboration of women telling their courageous stories.

iZoar is her primary art business and the Village of iZoar is where her whimsical and inspiring characters live. As an artist, writer and the creator of iZoar you will find her witty, profound, funny, insightful and her characters speak volumes. With a succinct writing style she is able to capture big emotions in a simple sentence. This signature style of whimsical characters and simple clear messages makes her work appeal to women in all walks of life. Her prints, cards and gifts are sold all over the world in boutiques, galleries and gift stores.

Her life is her story. iZoar teaches what she has learned. They deliver the messages she uses to make her life remarkable. Her wish is that you receive inspiration from them and her prayer is that you become all that you can be.

When she is not in the world of iZoar, Janice enjoys hiking the mountains of Colorado with her husband and their Golden Retriever. Chronically curious, she finds the world incredibly interesting. Thus, she keeps her life as fascinating as her characters.

Visit her online at www.iZoar.com.

WANT TO SPEAK YOUR TRUTH?

If sharing our stories has inspired, moved, or empowered you, we would love to hear from you. All of the stories you have read in this book were submitted by readers just like you who have a personal story to tell and who wanted to help inspire and empower other women.

We expect to publish future volumes of *Speaking Your Truth* and perhaps your story could help to inspire and empower other women on their journeys. If you would like to become a part of the *Speaking Your Truth* book project we invite you to submit a chapter for consideration to a future volume. There's no need to be concerned with being a professional writer, simply get your story to us and we can help with the editing. The main thing is to speak your truth. You can simply let others know where you've been, what you've achieved, and help lift and inspire others who have or are now experiencing something similar.

You may submit an original piece that describes your experiences, life story, and/or something you have overcome or succeeded in. To obtain a copy of our submission guidelines please visit www.speakingyourtruthbook.com. You will be credited for your submission at the end of your story.

For information about speaking engagements, other books, workshops, and training programs, please contact us directly. If you are writing your own book and are considering self-publishing, please visit www.SelfPublishingExperts.com for more information and book support.

We look forward to hearing from you.
Sincerely,
Lisa Shultz & Andrea Costantine

Visit our blog and share your experiences with our growing Speaking Your Truth community.

Contact us directly:
Lisa Email: info@lisashultz.com
Andrea Email: info@andreacostantine.com
Website/Blog: www.speakingyourtruthbook.com
Facebook: www.facebook.com/speakingyourtruth

Are you interested in buying multiple copies of *Speaking Your Truth* for your business, network, community, or clients? You can receive special discounted pricing, great service, direct shipping, and more. Inquire with us today.

9174215R0

Made in the USA
Charleston, SC
17 August 2011